# Catholic
# Moral Theology
# in Dialogue

*Charles E. Curran*

*University Of Notre Dame Press*
*Norte Dame*          *London*

# Other Books by Charles E. Curran

*New Perspectives in Moral Theology*
*Christian Morality Today*
*A New Look at Christian Morality*
*Contemporary Problems in Moral Theology*
*The Crisis in Priestly Ministry*
*Politics, Medicine and Christian Ethics: A Dialogue with
   Paul Ramsey*
*Dissent In And For The Church* (Charles E. Curran, Robert
   E. Hunt, et. al.)
*The Responsibility of Dissent: The Church and Academic
   Freedom* (John F. Hunt and Terrence R. Connelly with
   Charles E. Curran, et. al.)
*Absolutes in Moral Theology?* (editor)
*Contraception: Authority and Dissent* (editor)

University of Notre Dame Press edition 1976
Copyright © 1972 Charles E. Curran
First edition 1972 by Fides Publishers, Inc.
Reprinted with the permission of the author and the original publisher
Printed in the United States of America

Library of Congress Cataloging in Publication Data

Curran, Charles E
   Catholic moral theology in dialogue.

   Reprint of the ed. published by Fides Publishers, Notre Dame, Ind.
   Includes bibliographical references.
   1. Christian ethics—Catholic authors. I. Title.
BX 1758.2.C817    1976      241'.04'2      76–14906
ISBN 0-268-00716-0
ISBN 0-268-00717-9 pbk.

# Preface

Catholic moral theology has changed greatly in the last few years and is continuing to change at a rapid pace. There are many reasons for such change, but the most basic explanation lies in the fact that Roman Catholic moral theology has seriously begun to dialogue with all those who have something to contribute to moral theology. Until recently Catholic moral theology carried on practically no dialogue even with Scripture, systematic theology, and its own historical development; consequently, moral theology had remained static, practically since the seventeenth century. Moral theology began to change when this type of dialogue was initiated a few years ago. Today the dialogue extends to all the elements that enter into the moral judgment and all the areas of concern calling for such judgments. The best description of the current state of moral theology is precisely —Catholic moral theology in dialogue.

The essays in this volume, although they originally appeared in different journals and books, illustrate the dialogue now taking place in moral theology. A critical dialogue requires an understanding of the Catholic theological tradition as well as an appreciation of the many other aspects which must enter into contemporary Christian ethical theory. Moral theology is experiencing the same problem of identity which characterizes much of life today. In the midst of bewildering complexity and a plethora of data one must find meaning and ultimately arrive at decisions and actions. The essays in this volume show the multi-faceted dialogue now taking place both with regard to methodological and content questions.

I am grateful for all those who in many different ways have encouraged me and my own work in moral theology. In particular, I would like to thank the following publishers and periodicals for permission to use materials which first appeared in their publications.

Fides Publishers, for "Is There a Distinctively Christian Ethic?" in *Metropolis: Christian Presence and Responsibility*, ed. Philip D. Morris; The Catholic Theological Society of America, for "The Role and Function of the Scriptures in Moral Theology" in *Proceedings of the Catholic Theological Society of America*, XXVI (1971); *Recherches de Science Religieuse* and the Saint Thomas Aquinas Newman Center, Boulder, Colorado, for "Scientific Data, Scientific Possibilities, and the Moral Judgment," which will be published in English in a volume of papers originally presented under the auspices of the Newman Center at Boulder and edited by Paul K. K. Tong; Alba House Publishers and the College Theology Society, for "Roman Catholic Social Ethics—Past Present and Future" in *That They May Live: Theological Reflections on the Quality of Life*, ed. George Devine (Staten Island: Alba House, 1972); *The Jurist* and the Canon Law Society of America, for "The Meaning of Coresponsibility" in both *The Jurist* and *Who Decides for the Church?*, ed. James A. Coriden (Hartford: The Canon Law Society of America, 1971); *The Thomist*, for "The Morality of Homosexuality"; The International Lonergan Congress and Notre Dame University Press, for "The Concept of Conversion" in *The Foundations of Theology* (Notre Dame, Indiana: University of Notre Dame Press, 1971); The Catholic Theological Society of America, for "Roman Catholic Theology in the United States Faces the Seventies" in *Proceedings of the Catholic Theological Society of America*, XXV (1970).

# Contents

To
BERNARD HARING, C.SS.R.
teacher, theologian, friend
and priestly minister of the Gospel in theory and practice
on the occasion of his
sixtieth birthday

# 1

# Dialogue with Humanism: Is There a Distinctively Christian Ethic?

Is there a distinctively Christian social ethic?[1] This question has theoretical implications which have posed questions from the very beginning of theological reflection on the Christian life. The same question retains great importance today for anyone assessing the social function and role of Christians and of the Christian Church.

---

[1] A number of recent studies in moral theology have addressed themselves to this problem. For one of the latest considerations with pertinent bibliography, see "L'Éthique chrétienne à la recherche de son identité," *Le Supplément de La Vie Spirituelle*, XXIII (1970), 3-144. This whole issue contains the papers read at the September 1969 meeting of the French professors of moral theology. See also P. Manaranche, *Y a-t-il une éthique sociale chrétienne?* (Paris: Editions du Seuil, 1969); Karl Rahner, "Christianity and the New Earth," *Theology Digest* (sesquicentennial issue, 1968), pp. 70-77; Johannes B. Metz, *Theology of the World* (New York: Herder and Herder, 1969); "Morale humaine, morale chrétienne," *Recherches et Débats*, LV (1966), contains the papers read at the Semaine des Intellectuels Catholiques, 1966.

## I

Contemporary experience calls for critical reflection on the question of a distinctively Christian ethic, for in our own day and especially in our country Christians and non-Christians have found themselves in theoretical agreement on many of the vital moral issues facing our society and have often engaged in joint political action and protest to further their common cause. The desire for racial equality and now the peace movement have united people of different faiths and of no explicit religious faith in working together to achieve their common purpose. Often Christians find greater agreement with non-Christians than with fellow Christians. A momentary reflection on social ethics in contemporary America indicates that Christian ethics does not seem to contribute anything special or distinctive to the content of social ethics.

A glance back at history also seems to show that Christian ethics has not made any distinctive contribution to the content of social ethics. Many of the great strides in social ethics have been accomplished by non-Christians, and at times Christians have even employed Christian principles to stand in the way of truly human progress in social ethics. One cannot here make an exhaustive historical inquiry to determine the balance sheet on the performance of Christian ethics in contributing to social progress and advance, but one can easily call to mind enough instances to indicate the somewhat ambiguous effort of Christian ethics in fostering progress in the social life of man and his world.

Many contemporary Christian ethicists are wary of claiming any superiority for Christian ethics based on the facts of history. Donald Evans realizes the ambiguous historical record of Christian ethics and practice both in general and in the particular area of peace. "My own 'guesstimate' is that the institution [the Christian Church] has done somewhat

more harm than good in this area, although I am very heart-
ened by new trends since World War II. . . ."[2] Evans, however, does not deny in theory the fact that there can be a distinctive aspect about Christian social ethics: "Although it is
quite possible that a distinctively Christian view of international affairs may provide distinctive political insights,
Christians should be realistically and modestly tentative in
making such claims."[3]

James M. Gustafson writes: "If the question is construed
to be one that asks for historical evidences that the morality
of Christians has been demonstrably better, more humane
and in actuality superior to the morality of other men, one's
honest answer is at best ambiguous."[4] Gustafson cites both
Karl Barth and Reinhold Niebuhr as warning against looking
to history to find verification of the moral efficacy of the
Christian faith. Gustafson, however, even more explicitly
than Evans, and despite the danger of expecting an unambiguous historical proof, still admits a "morality that is peculiar to Christians, a morality that has beneficent effects for
the human community."[5] Loyalty to the Christian gospel
and faith evoke certain attitudes, dispositions, intentions,
goals and norms. To believe and trust in Christ is "to have a
new freedom, to be directed towards one's true end, to be
governed by the law of love, to be disposed to do what is
good for the neighbor."[6] The purposes of the last chapter of
Gustafson's study is "to explore a way of interpreting and
explicating Christian moral life, regarding particularly some

---

[2] *Peace, Power and Protest*, ed. Donald Evans (Toronto: Ryerson Press,
1967), p. 5.
[3] *Ibid.*
[4] James M. Gustafson, *Christ and the Moral Life* (New York: Harper and
Row, 1968), p. 238.
[5] *Ibid.*, p. 240.
[6] *Ibid.*

of the differences that faith in Jesus Christ *often does make, can make,* and *ought to make* in the moral lives of members of the Christian community."[7]

Both Evans and Gustafson seem to claim that there is a distinctively Christian ethics even though history and experience do not verify that claim. In general Roman Catholic theology from within its own tradition would argue for a greater historicity and visibility of God's grace than would traditional Protestant theology. Roman Catholic ecclesiology and sacramentology build on the incarnational principle of the historical and external visibility of the loving gift of God. A poorer type of Catholic apologetic before Vatican II attempted to use history as an apologetic argument to prove that the Roman Catholic Church was the one true Church founded by Jesus Christ. Pope Leo seemed to indicate that there was sufficient historical evidence even for governments to make such a decision about the true Church of Jesus Christ.[8] Catholic apologetics developed historical theses to prove that the marks of the Church were verified in the history of the Roman Catholic Church.[9]

Roman Catholic theology has traditionally recognized the close connection between belief in Jesus Christ and man's moral actions. In the development of the consideration on grace, textbooks frequently asserted as a fundamental thesis that man could not for a long time observe even the substance of the natural law without the help of grace.[10] Such a thesis builds on the biblical data that man's relationship with God is known and manifest in his relationship with his fellow man. Thus the First Letter of John (4:20) maintains

---

[7] *Ibid.*

[8] Leo XIII, *Immortale Dei*, n. 7.

[9] P. Ioachim Salaverri, S.I., *Sacrae Theologiae Summa* (Madrid: Biblioteca de Autores Christianos, 1955), I, 933-962.

[10] Carolus Boyer, S.I., *Tractatus de Gratia Divina* (Rome: Pontificia Universitas Gregorians, 1952), pp. 38-63.

that man cannot love the God he does not see if he does not love the neighbor whom he does see. The so-called judgment scene in Matthew views man's relationship to God in terms of his relationship with others—the poor, the hungry, prisoners, the needy (Mt. 25). The Lord's Prayer reminds us that the forgiveness of sin requires our own willingness to forgive our enemies and those who have offended us.

Although Roman Catholic theology from within its own tradition has given importance to the historicity and visibility of grace, there are also indications which point to the fact that the grace event, the loving relationship between God and man, cannot always be historically and experientially verified. A person can enter into a loving relationship with God in the sacrament of penance, for instance, without being able to verify this change by his own reflection.[11] This does not prove that such a change has not occurred in man, but that man cannot always make an object of reflection what is part of his own subjectivity. Thus even Roman Catholic theology could not logically demand that the distinctively Christian aspect in ethics always be historically or experientially verifiable.

## II

Neither experience nor history can thus conclusively solve the problem of the existence of a distinctively Christian social ethics, although the fact that neither history nor contemporary experience can prove the existence of such a distinctively Christian ethics does add some weight to the possibility that there might be no distinctively different Christian ethics. How have theologians come to grips with this problem in the past? This essay will discuss and examine some of the past approaches to this question and after criticizing

---

[11] Boyer, pp. 364-368.

these approaches will propose a tentative solution to the question.

In the tradition of Roman Catholic theology the general thrust came from a natural law approach, but the words "nature" or "natural" conceal a number of different ambiguities that have been the source of misunderstandings in the past. There are basically two major questions raised by a natural law approach in moral theology and Christian ethics. The properly theological question concerns the fact that there exists a source of ethical wisdom and knowledge, apart from the explicit revelation of God in Scripture, which Christians share with all other men; whereas the philosophical question concerns the way in which "human reason unaided by divine grace" comes to ethical wisdom and knowledge. The theological question bears on the concerns of this study.

Roman Catholic theology in general has upheld the goodness of man and the natural and has in a consistent manner developed a natural theology, a natural law and arguments from natural reason to prove the existence of God.[12] Human nature and man's reason are not totally corrupted by sin, but human reason is able to discern the plan of God the creator or the natural law which is the rational creature's participation in the eternal law of God.[13] Natural, understood in the theological perspective, thus is distinguished from the supernatural which is known from revelation and cannot be attained by man's natural powers without the help of God. All men by the very fact they have a human nature and reason share this natural law so that there is a great area of common ground morality which Christians and non-Christians have alike precisely because of their reason and human nature.

---

[12] There is a general coherence linking all these aspects together.

[13] Thomas Aquinas describes the natural law as the participation of the eternal law in the rational creature in *I$^a$II$^{ae}$*, q. 91., a. 3.

The papal and hierarchical magisterium of the Roman Catholic Church, making the natural law common to all men the basis of its approach, has frequently spoken on issues of social justice. Since Leo XIII the papal magisterium has tried to point out a just social order in the light of natural law which is common to all mankind. In the 1960's Pope John XXIII received world wide acclaim for his encyclical *Pacem in Terris* which developed from the theological presupposition that "the Creator of the world has imprinted in man's heart an order which his conscience reveals to him and enjoins him to obey: 'They show the work of the Law written in their hearts. . . .' "[14] The laws governing men are to be found "in the nature of man, where the Father of all things wrote them. By these laws men are most admirably taught, first of all how they should conduct their mutual dealings; then how the relationships between the citizens and the public authorities of each State should be regulated; then how States should deal with one another; and finally how, on the one hand individual men and States, and on the other hand the community of all peoples, should act towards each other, the establishment of such a world community of peoples being urgently demanded today by the requirements of the universal common good."[15]

The very fact that encyclicals such as *Pacem in Terris* were addressed to all men of good will underscores the ethical wisdom which all men share by reason of the natural law. Perhaps the best illustration of the differences between Roman Catholic and Protestant methodological approaches in the past is found in the different approaches to the question of religious liberty. *The Declaration on Religious Liberty* of the Second Vatican Council begins by observing the

---

[14] Pope John XXIII, *Pacem in Terris*, n. 5.
[15] *Ibid.*, n. 7.

contemporary emphasis on the dignity of the human person and asserts that religious liberty (strictly defined in paragraph two as the immunity from external coercion forcing one to act against his conscience or preventing him from acting in accord with his conscience) is founded on the dignity of the human person as this dignity is known through the revealed word of God and by reason itself.[16]

Despite strong conciliar opposition from many bishops, the final text establishes religious liberty as a human and civil right on the basis of human reason and only in the second part or chapter considers "Religious Freedom in the Light of Revelation."[17] But the Declaration clearly states: "Revelation does not indeed affirm in so many words the right of man to immunity from external coercion in matters religious."[18] The right to religious freedom is based on the dignity of the person, the requirements of which have come to be more adequately known to human reason through centuries of experience. "What is more, this doctrine of freedom has roots in divine revelation, and for this reason Christians are bound to respect it all the more conscientiously."[19]

The statements of the World Council of Churches employ a different theological approach by basing their explicit argument primarily and even solely on revelation. The Declaration on Religious Liberty of the First Assembly of the W.C.C., Amsterdam, 1948 (more than 15 years before Vatican II's Declaration), begins by calling religious liberty an implication of the Christian faith. The first paragraph sees this implication in the liberty with which Christ has set us free and in the light of the nature and destiny of man by reason of his creation, redemption and calling. The Declaration

---

[16] *Declaration on Religious Liberty, n.* 2.

[17] Richard J. Regan, S.J., *Conflict and Consensus: Religious Freedom and the Second Vatican Council* (New York: Macmillan, 1967), pp. 117ff.

[18] *Declaration on Religious Liberty,* n. 9.

[19] *Ibid.*

extends this right to all men merely by asserting: "The rights which Christian discipleship demands are such as are good for all men, and no nation has ever suffered by reason of granting such liberties."[20] The Report on Christian Witness, Proselytism and Religious Liberty of the Third Assembly of the W.C.C., New Delhi, 1966, bases the right to religious liberty primarily on the "noncoercive method and spirit of Christ" who constantly calls for a free assent in love.[21] There seems to be a number of different theological strands behind the W.C.C. statements; but the contrast with Vatican II is obvious, since the Declaration of Vatican II proved that religious liberty was a human and civil right in the light of reason and human experience before elaborating the fact that the dignity of the human person which is the basis for such a right also has its roots in revelation.

The natural law approach employed in Catholic theology and in the documents of the papal magisterium in the last century maintains there is no distinctively Christian social ethics at least in terms of the political, social, cultural and economic structures of society. Such an approach also upholds the goodness of man and the human which are not totally corrupted or disfigured by sin. Likewise the natural law approach presents a theoretical platform for a universalism in thought and action because of the fact that all men share the same human nature. Through this approach Catholic theology and also the papal teaching gave an importance and value to the daily life of man which participated in the eternal law of God. The Church and the Christian were thus interested in all facets of human existence, and the natural law theory provided a theoretical basis for involvement in the life of society.

---

[20] The text of the Amsterdam Statement can be conveniently found in A.F. Carrillo de Albornoz, *Religious Liberty* (New York: Sheed and Ward, 1967), p. 189.

[21] *Ibid.*, p. 195.

The natural law approach, from a theological perspective, embodies certain theological presuppositions which argue against its continued use in contemporary moral theology. Catholic theology and Catholic practice were never able to integrate the natural law approach into the total Christian perspective with the result that revelation and reason or the evangelical law and the natural law formed two separate epistemological approaches to ethical wisdom corresponding to the ontological separation of the supernatural and the natural orders. The natural, conceived in this way, became a self-contained area unaffected by the reality of redemption (the supernatural) with disastrous effects both in the theoretical area of moral theology and in the practical area of Christian life. In practice there existed a sharp division between the ordinary Christian who lived in the world in accord with the natural law and the person who sought Christian perfection by following the evanglical counsels of perfection in the religious life. Although Catholic theology did uphold the goodness of the natural and the life of man in the world, the ordinary Christian in the world was considered in many ways a second class citizen not called to the gospel perfection.

In the theoretical sphere the problem of the natural as a separate area only extrinsically joined to the realm of the supernatural had unfortunate repercussions. The natural was unaffected by the supernatural, or in more contemporary language, the order of creation was not taken up by the order of redemption. Natural law social ethics could easily become static and conservative not only because of its philosophical underpinnings but also because the area of the natural was not relativized by the transforming aspect of the eschatological which acts as a negative critique of all existing structures and institutions. Such a natural law theory also fails to give enough importance to the reality of human sinfulness. The natural law approach based on a separation between nature and supernatural, although such a theory calls for a social ethic common to all mankind, can not be admitted in contemporary theology, since it does not adequately solve the nature-grace relationship. This question will be discussed at greater length in Chapter 4.

Protestant theology has embraced a number of different theological approaches to social ethics which in their own way address the question of the existence of a distinctively Christian social ethic. This paper will not attempt to analyze all these approaches but will just examine some of the more important theories. Lutheran theology developed a two kingdom or two realm theory which corresponds to the Lutheran distinctions between creation and redemption, the left hand of God and the right hand of God, and law and gospel. Sin, which was neglected in the Roman Catholic natural law theory, plays a very important role (an exaggerated role) in the Lutheran two realm theory. William Lazareth, who strongly protests against what he would call caricatures of the Lutheran two realm theory, still asserts quite strongly: "For Luther's social ethics, all offices and stations of life— ecclesiastical, domestic, economic, political—embody in institutional form a particular command of God's law. They are all integrated within the earthly kingdom of man as the Creator's divinely ordained bulwarks in his ongoing struggle against Satan. There is no particularly 'Christian' form of these 'orders.' Though corrupted by sin, the 'orders' are still the means by which the Creator graciously preserves his fallen world from even greater chaos, injustice and suffering."[22]

---

[22] William H. Lazareth, "Luther's 'Two Kingdoms' Ethic Reconsidered," *Christian Social Ethics in a Changing World*, ed. John C. Bennett (New York: Association Press, 1966), p. 125. Elsewhere Lazareth himself admits that "the two realms of creation and redemption interpenetrate each other." John Reumann and William Lazareth, *Righteousness and Society* (Philadelphia: Fortress Press, 1967), p. 241.

The Christian's social responsibilities according to the two realm theory do not call for a transformation of the social structures in the light of the gospel. Theologians such as Karl Barth and Reinhold Niebuhr have severely condemned the two kingdom theory as favoring a perverse social morality by restricting the Christian to live somewhat passively within these orders and do nothing to change or transform them with the inevitable consequence that such an approach favors tyranny and oppression.[23] Although Lazareth would object to such conclusions, he still holds to the two realm theory based not only on the distinction but even on the separation between the realms of creation and redemption, the left hand of God's rule and the right, the law and the gospel, all of which differences are greatly influenced by an exaggerated role assigned to sin.

Liberal Protestant theology as illustrated in some theories of the Social Gospel school reacted against the older Lutheran approach to the question of social ethics. Protestant Liberalism thought that the kingdom of God would become more progressively present in this world as people gradually put into practice the evangelical life of Jesus and his Sermon on the Mount. Such an approach too easily identified human progress with the kingdom of God and forgot about the realities of sin and redemption as a continuing aspect of Christian existence. The eschatological tension was collapsed in favor of a one-sided realized eschatology, and worldly progress was too easily baptized without realizing the creaturely and sinful limitations of everything human.[24]

In reaction to Protestant Liberalism and Lutheran dualism, Neo-Orthodoxy under the general leadership of Karl

---

[23] Lazareth himself cites and refutes the opinion proposed by Barth, (Lazareth, pp. 119ff). Reinhold Niebuhr, *The Nature and Destiny of Man* (New York: Charles Scribner's Sons paperback, 1964), II, 187-198.

[24] Lloyd J. Averill, *American Theology in the Liberal Tradition* (Philadelphia: Westminster Press, 1967).

Barth provided another methodological approach to the question of social ethics. Dietrich Bonhoeffer in his *Ethics* and the American theologian Paul Lehmann illustrate the same general approach to Christian ethics.[25] Against liberalism, Barth stressed transcendence and the need to start with God and his revelation and not with man and his action. Against a Lutheran dualism, Barth and his followers emphasized that the world too was under the Lordship of Jesus Christ. There is no total dichotomy between the left and the right hand of God, no total separation between creation and redemption, no real opposition between law and gospel. These theologians thus affirmed the centrality of Christ in the moral life and proclaimed the Lordship of Jesus over human history by overcoming the dichotomies that had been a part of the Lutheran theory.

Three essays by Barth collected in a book entitled *Community, State and Church* well illustrate this approach. In one essay Barth develops his famous thesis on gospel and law which argues against the opposition between the two, inverses the traditional order of the phrase from law and gospel to gospel and law, and sees law as a form of the gospel. The Word of God is both gospel and law.[26] In the question of Church and State Barth applies his famous *analogia fidei* by which he argues to the role and functions of the state from the understanding he has of the kingdom. Thus Barth overcomes the Lutheran dichotomy, and also the Liberalistic tendency to forget transcendence, but appears to erect a Christological monism which creates problems of its own.

The Christological monism found in Barth, Bonhoeffer and Lehmann in varying degrees results in a disparaging of ethics

---

[25] Dietrich Bonhoeffer, *Ethics* (New York: Macmillan, 1955); Paul L. Lehmann, *Ethics in a Christian Context* (New York: Harper and Row, 1963).

[26] Karl Barth, *Community, State and Church,* introduction by Will Herberg (Garden City, New York: Doubleday Anchor Books, 1960).

and philosophy as a way into the ethical problem for the Christian. Christ and the form of Christ become the only way into the ethical question for the Christian so that in Lehmann, for example, philosophical ethics is incompatible with Christian ethics. However, within this general perspective one could still admit that non-Christians can act properly in this world because of the reality of Christ. One cannot look for or even expect historical verification of a distinctively Christian morality, for ethics is concerned with the actions of God and not the actions of man. The empirical aspects of the act may be the same for the Christian and the non-Christian, but the formal character of that morality is quite different, and the attitudes are quite different. The emphasis on the concrete action of God in the world and the disparaging of any rational criterion to judge the particluar action of God leads to a theological actualism in which many of these theologians seem to be able to discern too easily in complex situations what the specific action of God is.[27] In the complex problems of social ethics I do not think that the Christian can so readily know and assert what God is doing in the world to make and keep human life more human, to invoke the phrase employed by Lehmann in referring to the particular and concrete action of God in the world.[28]

### III

None of these approaches in my judgment satisfactorily answers the question: is there a distinctively Christian social ethic? Lurking in the background of this question lies the methodological question of the ways in which the Christian ethicist goes into the moral problem or what has also been called the sources of ethical wisdom and knowledge for the

---

[27] For a fine summary of this aspect, see Gustafson, pp. 55-60.
[28] Lehmann, pp. 75ff.

Christian ethicist. The question of a distinctively Christian social ethic calls into question the presuppositions of Christian theological ethics such as the nature-grace relationship, the creation-redemption relationship, the Chrsitian-human relationship.

This study will first consider the subjective pole of human reality, the individual person and subject. Is there a unique distinction between the Christian and all other non-Christians? The general supposition or at least the commonly accepted supposition holds to a great difference between Christians and non-Christians because through Christ Jesus Christians have been freed from sin and death and brought into the newness of life in the Paschal Mystery. Theology today is rejecting just such a presupposition. Roman Catholic theology has traditionally maintained the universal salvific will by which God offers to all men the loving gift of his redeeming friendship.[29] A problem for Christian theology stems from the fact that today two-thirds of the world does not recognize Jesus as Lord and many have never heard of him. In the course of history there have been many people in this world who have never heard of Christ Jesus, but no theologian would want to exclude all these people from the reign of God. Catholic theology maintains that God gives to every man the opportunity of divine sonship.

There are diverse explanations of how all men are offered the gift of God's love. Karl Rahner has developed his concept of implicit Christians and anonymous Christians as contemporary explanations of the fact that God does offer all men the loving gift of himself. Rahner employs his transcendental philosophy to explain the fact that God does offer himself in love to all mankind and that man can have accepted such a loving relationship with God and not explicitly acknowledge Jesus as Lord and Savior. "Anyone who understands a moral

---

[29] Boyer, pp. 349-361.

demand of his conscience to be absolutely binding for him, and accepts it as binding for him in a free, although perhaps subconscious assent, is affirming, whether he knows it or not, whether he reflects upon it conceptually or not, the absolute being of God as the reason why there can be such a thing as an absolute moral demand at all."[30]

Rahner continues: "Now insofar as all intellectual knowledge and freedom on the side of the subject and his act is a 'transcendental experience,' that is, an experience of the unlimited openness of the spiritual being as such, there is on the subjective side of all knowledge, a knowledge of God that is real although implicit, that is, not necessarily objectified. . . . . What we usually call 'knowledge of God' is not simply the knowledge of God but is the objectified, conceptualized, and propositionalized interpretation about what we already knew about God unreflectively."[31] It is possible that some would have this transcendental experience of God and freely assent to this transcendental openness and yet not have a propositionalized concept of God and even reject existing concepts of God. In this way Rahner explains the possibility of an atheism which is at the same time an implicit Christianity although Rahner recognizes there are other forms of atheism in which one has not freely assented to this transcendental experience of total openness.

Rahner's concept of the anonymous Christian also has its roots in the universal salvific will of God for all men. Rahner explains this reality in the rather traditional language of Catholic theology: "A man may already possess the sanctifying grace, and may therefore be justified and sanctified, a child of God, heir of heaven, and mercifully and positively

---

[30] Karl Rahner, S.J., "Atheism and Implicit Christianity," *Theology Digest*, (sesquicentennial issue, 1968), p. 49.
[31] *Ibid.*, pp. 49-50.

on his way towards his supernatural and eternal salvation even before he has accepted an explicitly Christian confession of faith and has been baptized."[32]

One might disagree with Rahner's terminology of implicit or anonymous Christians, and one might disagree with his explanation of this possibility in terms of the transcendental affirmation of the absolute, but Catholic theology would maintain the reality that somehow God, other than through contact with the historical Jesus, does offer his saving love to all men in the course of their earthly existence. *The Pastoral Constitution on the Church in the Modern World* also accepts this realization that explicit Christians are not the only ones who have received the saving revelation of God's word and work. After affirming that Jesus is the perfect man in whose image the Christian must pattern his life and existence, the Constitution affirms: "All this holds true not only for Christians but for all men of good will in whose heart grace works in an unseen way. For since Christ dies for all men, and since the ultimate vocation of man is in fact one, and divine, we ought to believe that the Holy Spirit in a manner known only to God offers to every man the possibility of being associated with this paschal mystery."[33]

There has also been a pronounced shift in the way contemporary theology views the reality of the world or what might be called the object pole of Christian existence. The world can no longer be viewed as totally disfigured by sin and ruled by the left hand of God nor viewed merely in terms of the natural as totally distinct from the realm of the supernatural. Contemporary theology has been accepting a theology of eschatology and cosmic redemption which over-

---

[32] Karl Rahner, S.J., "Anonymous Christianity," *IDOC*, I (April 4, 1970), 76.

[33] *Pastoral Constitution on the Church in the Modern World*, n. 22.

turns such previously accepted dichotomies. Redemption embraces the entire world so that the world is now being transformed into the new heaven and the new earth.

The relationship between the present life of the individual and his future existence also becomes paradigmatic for the relationship between the present existence of the world and its future existence. The individual person now shares in the redemptive activity of God and in death the final transformation will take place so that there is continuity between this present existence and his future existence as well as an aspect of discontinuity which will be transformed ultimately in the mystery of Christian death. So too the present world already shares in the redemptive activity of God and looks forward for the final revelation of its resurrection destiny. The world is even now being transformed; but this transformation will not be a totally continuous development, for the life of the world just as the life of the individual human person will undergo a death which is not a total break or even the end but rather a final transformation into the new heaven and the new earth. Thus the world is not just the area of the natural but the world embraces all the different aspects of the Christian mystery—creation, sin, incarnation, redemption and resurrection destiny.

There is a danger to which theology in the 60's frequently succumbed of merely accepting everything in the world and its present state as salvific and good. This naive and overly romantic view with its affinities to the liberal theology of an earlier era has been dashed against the harsh realities of war, poverty, violence, distrust. The world does belong to the sphere of the resurrection, but it still does and always will suffer from the limitations of its own finitude and of sinfulness which in a cosmic way incarnates itself in the very structures and fabric of our social existence and our world. The danger of merely accepting and baptizing the present or euphorically believing that the transformation of the world will be accomplished quickly and without true Christian conversion and suffering remains a perennial danger, for experience and history indicate that man too easily is lulled into forgetting his own limitations and his sinfulness.

A third important theological presupposition closely connected with the first two is the relationship between creation and redemption, which can also be viewed from a slightly different angle under the relationship of the human and the Christian. Creation and redemption are neither opposed nor totally separated but rather redemption brings creation to its final fulfillment so that the new heaven and the new creation are one and the same. Likewise the Christian is not opposed to or even totally separated from the human, but the Christian brings the human to its own perfection. *The Pastoral Constitution on the Church in the Modern World* asserts: "He taught us that the new command of love was the basic law of human perfection and hence of the world's transformation."[34] "Jesus Christ, who is 'the image of the invisible God' (Col. 1:15), is Himself the perfect man."[35] Thus the perfectly or truly human is found in Jesus Christ, but one must remember that all that is in the world today is not the perfectly and truly human.

Theological considerations of both the subject pole and the object pole of Christian existence, together with the historical and experiential data considered earlier, argue for the fact that there is not a strict dichotomy between Christian ethics and non-Christian ethics. The salvific self gift of God (grace) exists beyond the perimeter of those who expressly profess Jesus as Lord. Catholic theology, which has rightly emphasized the intrinsic connection between love of God and love of neighbor and the world, in acknowledging God's saving love outside the boundaries of explicit Christianity

---

[34] *Ibid.*, n. 38.
[35] *Ibid.*, n. 22.

must also acknowledge a corresponding ethic (natural and supernatural in the older terminology) outside the perimeter of explicit Christianity.

Obviously a personal acknowledgement of Jesus as Lord affects at least the consciousness of the individual and his thematic reflection on his consciousness, but the Christian and the explicitly non-Christian can and do arrive at the same ethical conclusions and can and do share the same general ethical attitudes, dispositions and goals. Thus, explicit Christians do not have a monopoly on such proximate ethical attitudes, goals and dispositions as self-sacrificing love, freedom, hope, concern for the neighbor in need or even the realization that one finds his life only in losing it. The explicitly Christian consciousness does affect the judgment of the Christian and the way in which he makes his ethical judgments, but non-Christians can and do arrive at the same ethical conclusions and also embrace and treasure even the loftiest of proximate motives, virtues, and goals which Christians in the past have wrongly claimed only for themselves. This is the precise sense in which I deny the existence of a distinctively Christian ethic; namely, non-Christians can and do arrive at the same ethical conclusions and prize the same proximate dispositions, goals and attitudes as Christians.

The Catholic natural law theory and to an extent the Lutheran two realm theory would have maintained that there is no distinctively Christian social ethic regarding the social structures and institutions of society on the basis that these things are common to all men, whereas in the personal realm and especially in the attitudinal realm there are some things that are distinctively Christian. The proposed understanding also differs from the generic approach of the Barthian school because one cannot limit the way into the ethical problem just to a Christological monism which excludes the important role of reason and all human experi-

ence. The Barthian approach would also admit a great difference in the attitude and intention of the Christian even
though the content of his act might be the same as the act of
the non-Christian.

The fact that there is no distinctively Christian ethic in the
sense detailed above does not imply that Christians need be
defensive about their Christianity or that the Christian message itself has nothing to offer in the way of ethical wisdom
and knowledge for the Christian. The Christian must always
begin his ethical reflection in the light of the gospel message
and the meaning of the new life received in Christ Jesus. To
deny a distinctively Christian ethic merely means that others
who have never accepted or even heard of Christ Jesus are
able to arrive not only at the same ethical decisions about
particular matters but are also able to have for all practical
purposes the same general dispositions and attitudes such as
hope, freedom and love for others even to the point of
sacrificing self.

In general I would agree with the statement of ethical
methodology outlined in the beginning of the Second Part
of the *Pastoral Constitution on the Church in the Modern
World* (even though the document itself did not follow such
a methodology in its treatment of all the chapters in Part
Two). "There are a number of particularly urgent needs
characterizing the present age, needs which go to the roots
of the human race. To a consideration of these in the light of
the gospel and of human experience the Council would now
direct the attention of all."[36]

This approach, if properly understood and utilized, would
differ from the older Catholic approach that talked about the
gospel and reason or the evangelical law and the natural law.
Human experience does not just correspond to the sphere of
the natural which all men can arrive at by the use of their

---

[36] *Ibid.*, n. 46.

reason unaided by grace. Such a dichotomy must be avoided. Human experience in the world today includes elements which belong to the order of incarnation, redemption and resurrection destiny as well as elements relating to creation and sinfulness. The term human experience understood in this way avoids the theological problem created by the presupposition of the natural as an area unaffected both by the transforming and redeeming aspects of the resurrection as well as immune from the limitations and disfigurement of sin. Human experience thus can include at least implicitly what the gospel contains by way of ethical conclusions, and proximate attitudes, dispositions and values.

## IV

In the light of this understanding of the solution to the question of the existence of a distinctively Christian ethics, one can point to certain important aspects in contemporary Christian social ethics. Moral theology or Christian ethics must now develop better hermeneutic tools for interpreting reality in the light of the gospel and of human experience. The truly human does include the aspects of redemption and resurrection destiny, but there always remains the danger of forgetting the transcendent or eschatological dimension in the truly human which was a noticeable defect in some of the theological fads of the 1960's.

The fact that there is no distinctively Christian social ethic in the sense explained in this essay does not signal the end of Christian ethics. Christians, graciously accepting the revelation of God's love in the historical person of Jesus and his Paschal Mystery, must reflect on social ethics and all problems of human existence in the light of this gospel and in the light of human experience. However, the Father in his infinite mercy does not limit the loving revelation of himself to man merely to the historical person of Jesus and his Paschal Mystery. The denial of a distinctively Christian ethic in reality is not as radical as it might at first appear, and such a solution to this question also avoids a number of seemingly psuedo-problems often connected with Christian ethics.

# 2

# Dialogue with the Scriptures: The Role and Function of the Scriptures in Moral Theology

The function of the Scriptures in moral theology has been a perennial question for the science of moral theology. Today the question assumes even greater importance and urgency in the light of two tendencies in contemporary theology which may even represent contradictory trends. On the one hand, the biblical renewal has made a great contribution to the development of moral theology in the last decade. The contemporary moral theologian has rejected the moral manuals of the past for many reasons, but the failure to find a basic orientation and grounding in the Scriptures frequently is mentioned as a most important lack in the older textbooks.

On the other hand, there has been another trend which has expanded the concept of revelation to cover much more than just the word of God in the Scriptures. An increasing emphasis, at some times in an exaggerated way, has been given to this world and the wisdom which persons in this world can acquire from one another and from their worldly existence.

Theologians have recently been asking what if anything is distinctive about Christian ethics which has its primary source in the Scriptures. In the midst of a plurality of sources of ethical wisdom what are the role and function of Scripture?

This chapter will discuss the question from three different aspects: the advantages that have accrued to Catholic moral theology in the last decades because of a greater emphasis on the Scripture; the inherent limitations of the use of the Scriptures in moral theology; two fundamental methodological questions governing the use of the Scriptures in moral theology.

## I. CONTRIBUTIONS OF BIBLICAL THEOLOGY

Vatican Council II attests that a greater stress is given to the role of the Scriptures in moral theology than has been given in the past. It would be wrong to ascribe the beginnings of such a movement to Vatican II, for the Council merely made its own and officially sanctioned a movement which had already begun in the Church. *The Dogmatic Constitution on Divine Revelation* emphasized that Sacred Scripture is the soul of all theology.[1] *The Decree on Priestly Formation* reiterated these words and specified that the scientific exposition of moral theology should be more thoroughly nourished by scriptural teaching.[2]

The history of moral reflection in the Catholic tradition from certain Fathers of the Church such as Clement of Alexandria and Augustine down to the present reveals an insistence on the fact that Sacred Scripture is not the only

---

[1] *Dogmatic Constitution on Divine Revelation*, n. 24. English references to Council documents are taken from: *The Documents of Vatican II*, ed. Walter M. Abbott, S.J.; trans. ed. Joseph Gallagher (New York: Guild Press, 1966).

[2] *Decree on Priestly Formation*, n. 16.

source of ethical wisdom and knowledge for the Christian. There is a human wisdom in which all men share and participate because of their common humanity. This gnoseological recognition of a source of ethical wisdom and knowledge (human reason) outside the Scripture corresponds to the more ontological understanding of the relation of the human to the divine or of what was later called the relationship between the natural and the supernatural. The theological understanding of love in the Catholic tradition well illustrates this approach. Catholic theology has understood the revealed *agape* of the Bible in terms of continuity with, and a perfection of, human love. Likewise the knowledge and understanding of human love also contribute to our understanding of Christian love.[3]

The use of the Scriptures in moral theology has varied at different historical periods, and in the period from Trent to Vatican II the role of the Scriptures in moral theology was very limited.[4] Recent historical studies show that in this period moral theology became separated from dogmatic and spiritual theology and acquired the narrow goal of training priests as judges in the sacrament of penance, with an accompanying minimalistic and legalistic approach concerned

---

[3] Contrast the different approaches to *agape* in the Protestant and Catholic traditions in the following: Anders Nygren, *Agape and Eros* (New York: Harper Torchbook, 1969); M. C. D'Arcy, S.J., *The Mind and Heart of Love* (New York: Meridian Books, 1956). For further comment on these discussions about the meaning of love within the Roman Catholic tradition, see Jules Toner, *The Experience of Love* (Washington/Cleveland: Corpus Books, 1968); Giovanni Volta, "Per un indagine razionale sull'amore," in Carlo Colombo, *et al.*, *Matrimonio e Verginità* (Milan: La Scuola Cattolica, 1963), pp. 9-49.

[4] For an adequate historical summary and for further bibliographical references, see Édouard Hamel, S.J., "L'Usage de l'Ecriture Sainte en théologie morale," *Gregorianum*, XLVII (1966), 56-63; J. Etienne, "Théologie Morale et renouveau biblique," *Ephemerides Theologicae Lovanienses*, XL (1964), 232-241.

primarily with the sinfulness of particular acts. At best Scripture was employed in a proof text fashion to corroborate arguments that were based on other reasons. In the 17th and 18th centuries there was a call for a more scriptural approach to moral theology, but the attempts along this line failed because they were entwined in the polemic of the rigorists and probabiliorists against the laxists and probabilists. A more biblically oriented approach to the whole of moral theology first appeared in the Tübingen school in Germany and is best exemplified in the manual of Bernard Häring which, despite its necessarily transitional character, stands as the greatest contribution to the renewal of moral theology since the 16th century.[5]

Perhaps the major contribution of the biblical renewal in moral theology has been the insistence that Christian morality is a religious ethic. Rudolph Schnackenburg in his influential book *The Moral Teaching of the New Testament* insists on seeing the moral teaching of Jesus as part of the entire God-man relationship. The ethical teaching of Jesus must always be seen in the light of the good news. The manuals of moral theology by wrenching Christian ethics away from its relationship with the full Christian mystery of the saving act of God in Christ very often fostered a Pelagian mentality. The biblical renewal together with the ecumenical dialogue with Protestants has rightly emphasized the primacy of the saving intervention of God and thus avoided the one-sided approach of the past, which pictured man as saving himself by his own effort and actions.[6]

---

[5] Bernard Häring, C.SS.R., *The Law of Christ,* 3 vols. (Westminster, Md.: Newman Press, 1961, 1963, 1966).

[6] Rudolf Schnackenburg, *The Moral Teaching of the New Testament* (New York: Herder and Herder, 1965), pp. 13-53. The original German edition of his very influential work appeared in 1954.

*The Model of Relationality and Responsibility*

The insistence on a religious ethic in the context of the entire God-man relationship has helped alter the basic structure or model of moral theology itself. The Christian is viewed as one who responds to the activity and the call of God. The theological emphasis on the Word only accentuates the dialogical structure of the Christian life. The Christian moral life is man's response to the saving word and work of God in Jesus Christ. The important biblical concept of covenant reinforces the primacy of response and of the dialogical structure of the Christian life.[7]

Ethicists in general and Christian ethicists in particular have discussed three general types of ethical models which depend on the basic understanding of the structures of the moral life: teleological, deontological and responsibility ethics. Teleological ethics conceives the ethical model primarily in terms of the end or goal. Actions are then good or bad insofar as they help or hinder this movement to attain the end. Deontological ethics sees ethics primarily in terms of duties, obligations or imperatives. The model of responsibility understands man as freely responding in the midst of the multiple relationships in which he finds himself.[8]

In commenting on the use of the Bible in Christian ethics Edward LeRoy Long, Jr. employs such a threefold typology.[9] The Bible has been used in a prescriptive sense as the revelation of God's will. In a more fundamentalistic approach, some see the Bible as a book containing the revealed will of God. Others such as Calvin and Dodd also accept this

---

[7] J. L'Hour, *La morale de l'alliance* (Paris: Gabalda, 1966).

[8] For a description of these three different types of ethical models and arguments in favor of the responsibility model, see H. Richard Niebuhr, *The Responsible Self* (New York: Harper and Row, 1963).

[9] Edward LeRoy Long, Jr., "The Use of the Bible in Christian Ethics," *Interpretation*, XIX (1965), 149-162.

basic model but employ it in a more nuanced way. Dodd, for example, speaks of precepts that give a quality or direction to our actions. The second model sees the Scriptures as supplying principles or ideals which the Christian tries to attain in his daily life. Such an approach obviously corresponds to the teleological approach. Long sees the third model of responsibility and relationality in the ethics proposed on the basis of the Scriptures by Joseph Sittler and Paul Lehmann.

One could interpret the very perceptive study by James M. Gustafson on ethics and the Bible in much the same way.[10] Gustafson sees the Bible as being used by the Christian ethicist in two different ways—either as revealed morality or as revealed reality. Conservative, evangelical Protestants exemplify the revealed morality approach, for they see in the Scriptures the revealed will of God for man. Such a model obviously employs deontological language and imagery. Liberal Protestants adopted a variation of the revealed morality approach by taking biblical notions such as the kingdom of God and making them the ideal or the goal for the social life of man. Reinhold Niebuhr and John C. Bennett followed somewhat the same path by making love the ideal or the goal towards which the Christian strives. Notice the teleological model in such ethics.

Gustafson points out that a revolution has occurred in biblical theology, especially under the influence of Karl Barth, so that the Bible is not the revelation of a morality but the revelation of the living God and his activity. "In the place of moral teachings particularized or generalized, the new theology put God in his living, free activity. Thus Christian ethics had to think not about morality reduced to propositions, but about God and how life ought to be rightly related to his power and his presence."[11]

---

[10] James M. Gustafson, "Christian Ethics," in *Religion,* ed. Paul Ramsey (Englewood Cliffs, Prentice Hall, 1965), pp. 309-316.

Gustafson then shows how such an understanding of the Scriptures leads to the relationality and responsibility motif as the primary model for the understanding of Christian ethics. Man constantly responds in his freedom to the concrete action of God working in this world.[12] I believe that the biblical renewal for the reasons mentioned earlier has brought about the same emphasis on the model of relationality and responsibility in Catholic moral theology without necessarily accepting all the presuppositions of a Barthian theology of the Word.[13]

The scriptural renewal not only emphasized the primacy of the relationality motif but also argued against the primary insistence on either the teleological or deontological models in Christian ethics. There is no doubt that in popular Catholic life and thought the deontological model was primary. The moral life of the Christian was seen in terms of law and the will of God. The biblical renewal with its emphasis on covenant and the love of God runs somewhat counter to the supremacy of the deontological model.[14]

Even more importantly, in Catholic theology the biblical renewal pointed out the secondary role of law in the life of the Christian. The ten commandments were now viewed not as laws in themselves, but within the context of the covenant as expressions of personal commitment and relationship with God.[15] The renewal of biblical theology showed the

---

[11] *Ibid.*, p. 316.

[12] *Ibid.*, pp. 316-320.

[13] It is precisely the antiphilosophical stance and the theological actualism in Barthian thought that I cannot accept.

[14] Albert Gelin, *The Key Concepts of the Old Testament* (New York: Sheed and Ward, 1955). In this and the following paragraphs references will be made to works which seem to have been influential within the Roman Catholic world. There are obviously other studies which are of equal and even more importance that were done within the Protestant community.

[15] Philippe Delhaye, *Le Decalogue et sa place dans la morale chrétienne* (Bruxelles: La Pensée Catholique, 1963); Matthew J. O'Connell, "Commandment in the Old Testament," *Theological Studies*, XXI (1960), 351-403.

subordinate and relative position of law not only in the Old
Testament but also in the New Testament. The ethical teaching of Jesus was seen primarily in terms of conversion, *agape*,
or the following of Christ and not primarily in terms of
law.[16] Scripture scholars exercised considerable influence
by showing the true nature of the law of the Spirit in Paul
which is not primarily a written or propositional law, but the
love of the Spirit poured into our hearts.[17]

The Thomistic understanding of the moral life employed
the teleological model—God as the last end of man. The biblical witness, however, does not picture God primarily as the
ultimate end but as the person who invites man to share in
the fullness of his life and love through the Paschal Mystery.[18] In Protestant liberal theology there had been the
tendency to adopt some scriptural ideal such as the kingdom
of God as the goal for the social life of Christians. Catholic
theology was never tempted to accept some biblical concept
as the goal or ideal of social life, since Catholic social ethics
was based almost exclusively on the natural law concept of
the common good as the controlling idea in social ethics.

---

[16] Examples of these different approaches in Catholic theology with considerable emphasis on the biblical themes include: Bernard Häring, "Conversion," in P. Delhaye *et al., Pastoral Treatment of Sin* (New York: Desclee,
1968), pp. 87-176; Ceslaus Spicq. O.P., *Agape in the New Testament*, 3 vols.
(St. Louis: B. Herder, 1963, 1965, 1966); Fritz Tillmann, *The Master Calls,*
(Baltimore: Helicon, 1960). Again note the European origin of these influential works in Roman Catholic theology even in the United States.

[17] Perhaps the most influential article in this area was: Stanislas Lyonnet,
S.J., "Liberté du chrétien et loi de l'Ésprit selon saint Paul," *Christus,*
(1954) 6-27. This article has been translated into numerous languages and
has appeared in many different places. See also Philippe Delhaye, "Liberté
chrétienne et obligation morale," *Ephemerides Theologicae Lovanienses,*
XL (1964), 347-361; Florence Michels, O.L.V.M., *Paul and the Law of Love*
(Milwaukee: Bruce, 1967).

[18] In this context E. Hamel seems to present a position that has not fully
integrated moral theology into a newer perspective derived from the biblical
approach. He wants to maintain the existing tracts in moral theology; e.g.,
*de fine ultimo,* but give them a biblical perspective. Hamel, *Gregorianum,*
XLVII (1966), 76.

There are also reasons inherent in contemporary biblical scholarship itself which argue against using deontological or teleological models for the development of biblical moral theology or Christian moral theology. Biblical scholars acknowledge the cultural and historical limitations imposed on the written word of the Scriptures. Thus parts of the Scripture cannot be wrenched from their original context and applied in different historical and cultural situations without the possible danger of some distortion. What might be a valid and true norm in biblical times might not be adequate today. Thus one cannot without further refinement take biblical norms and automatically see them as always obliging in different contexts of our historical lives. The same reasoning also argues against finding goals and ideals in the Scripture which can then be proposed without any modification for our contemporary circumstances.

The breakthrough book in Catholic moral theology, Bernard Häring's *The Law of Christ,* well exemplifies the dialogical understanding of man the moral responder in the context of the covenant relationship. The title of Häring's book, however, illustrates the transitional character of the work, for the primary model of law, even though understood in terms of the law of Christ, bespeaks a primacy of deontological categories. In contemporary Catholic moral theology the responsibility and relationality motif has emerged as most fundamental.[19] There are important philosophical reasons also supporting such a choice, but the original impetus in the historical development came from the scriptural renewal. In my understanding of Christian ethics the primary model should be that of responsibility and relationality, but there remains a need for some teleological and deontological considerations even though they are of secondary importance.

---

[19] Albert R. Jonsen, *Responsibility in Modern Religious Ethics* (Washington/Cleveland: Corpus Books, 1968).

## OTHER BIBLICAL CONTRIBUTIONS

A third important contribution of the scriptural renewal in moral theology has been the realization that all Christians are called to perfection. An older theology reserved the gospel call to perfection to those who received the vocation to follow the evangelical counsels, whereas the majority of Christians merely lived in the world and obeyed the commandments and precepts (primarily of a natural law character) required of all. The biblical teaching did not inspire such a neat distinction between precept and counsel, but rather called for the total response of the Christian to the gift of God in Christ Jesus.[20] This important attitude changed the purpose and format of Catholic moral theology. which could no longer be content with the partial goal of training judges for the sacrament of penance to distinguish between mortal and venial sin and between sin and no sin. Moral theology now considers the life of Christians who are called to be perfect even as the heavenly Father is perfect.

The realization that all Christians are called to such perfection in their change of heart and moral response led to a fourth contribution of biblical morality to moral theology. Growth, development, and creativity became important ideas for contemporary moral theology. The Christian life no longer could be viewed in terms of passive conformity to minimalistic laws obliging all. A closer study of Old Testament ethics forced Catholic moral theology to be more open to the realities of growth and development in the moral life. A few years ago Catholic commentators reflected on the problems proposed for moral theology in the light of the

---

[20] For an illustration of the approach of biblical theology in this area, see Ignace de la Potterie, S.J., and Stanislas Lyonnet, S.J., *La Vie selon Ésprit* (Paris: Éditions du Cerf, 1965). For a theological development based on the scriptural evidence, see John Gerken *Toward a Theology of the Layman* (New York: Herder and Herder, 1963).

ethical teaching of the Old Testament which in many ways exemplied the reality of growth and development.[21] In theoretical areas such as the understanding of conscience or man's response to the call of God there was a development in the understanding which gradually placed more emphasis on the interiority of the personal response. God calls his people through conscience or the innermost part of the person and not through extrinsic means or persons such as angels.[22]

In practical moral matters the Old Testament created questions for moral theology precisely because some of the values and norms proposed by moral theology today were not accepted in the Old Testament. To explain the Old Testament attitudes to questions of marriage and sexuality it was necessary to accept some concept of growth and development. Logically moral theology would also see the need to apply the same attitude toward growth and development to some contemporary situations.[23]

The emphasis on growth and development in the light of the call to perfection called for a greater appreciation of the active virtues and the creative aspects of the Christian's response to God. The model of responsibility without denying the place of goals and norms also gives priority to the more active and creative aspects of the Christian life.

A fifth important contribution of the biblical renewal in moral theology was the importance given to historicity. Biblical studies indicated the importance of salvation history,

---

[21] Philippe Delhaye, "Le récours à l'ancien testament dans l'étude de la théologie morale," *Ephemerides Theologicae Lovanienses,* XXXI (1955), 637-657.

[22] Antonio Hortelano, *Morale Responsabile* (Assisi: Cittadella editrice, n.d.), pp. 19-27.

[23] The importance of growth in the moral life was emphasized by Louis Monden, S.J., *Sin, Liberty and Law* (New York: Sheed and Ward, 1965), pp. 87-144.

which gave a more central role to eschatology. Many differences in moral theology can often be traced to different understandings of eschatology which so profoundly color our understanding of man and his life in this world.

The centrality of history in biblical thinking was in contrast with the lesser importance attributed to history in the manuals of Catholic moral theology. From a philosophical perspective it was only natural that theories giving more importance to the historical aspects of existence should come into prominence in Catholic thought. The biblical renewal exercised another influence in the area of historicity. Biblical scholars used the tools of historical research in examining the Scriptures because of the historical and cultural limitations inherent in the Scriptures and other historical documents. The need to understand and interpret the Scriptures in their historical context easily led to a study of the moral teachings of the Catholic Church in the light of their historical contexts. The way thus opened up for a constant reinterpretation and reevaluation of past teaching in the light of changing historical circumstances.

A sixth important contribution of the biblical influence on moral theology concerns the stress on interiority and the total person with a corresponding lesser emphasis on the individual, external act itself. The Scriptures view man primarily in terms of his faith relationship to God and neighbor with individual acts seen as expressing the basic attitude of the person and his relationships. Contemporary theologians elaborated on the biblical theme of conversion as the fundamental response to the call of God. Conversion as the basic change of heart interiorizes the moral response of the total person but at the same time has a social and a cosmic dimension.

The reasons contributing to the primacy of the relationality and responsibility motif also give greater importance to interiority in the Christian life. The teaching on the law of the Spirit as the primary law of Christian morality insists on

the moral life embracing the heart of the person with the external act seen as an expression of this fundamental orientation of the person. The biblical theology of sin put great
emphasis on interiority, the change of heart and the breaking
of man's multiple relationships with God, neighbor and the
world.[24] Theologians on the basis of the scriptural data and
in the light of other philosophical data developed the theory
of the fundamental option as a better understanding of the
reality of sin in the life of the Christian.[25]

The biblical contribution to moral theology in the last few
years has not only affected the important aspects mentioned
thus far, but has also had some influence on the approach to
particular moral questions. One illustration is the teaching
on private property and the goods of creation. Studies of
both the Old Testament and the New Testament have under-
lined the communal dimension of property.[26] The goods of
creation exist primarily for all mankind. Old Testament leg-
islation such as the Jubilee Year indicates a way to safeguard
the communal aspect of the goods of creation. The prohibition against usury or interest on a loan was based on the fact
that an Israelite should not take advantage of a brother's
need to make money from him. Again these biblical attitudes
together with other considerations such as the increasing
socialization of the time brought about renewed emphasis in
Catholic theology on private property and the goods of
creation.

---

[24] *Théologie du Péché,* ed. Philippe Delhaye (Tournai: Desclée et Cie,
1960).

[25] For a recent and representative article with pertinent bibliography, see
John W. Glazer, S.J., "Transition between Grace and Sin," *Theological
Studies,* XXIX (1968), 260-274.

[26] P. Christophe, *L'usage chrétien du droit de propriété dans l'Écriture et
la tradition patristique* (Paris: Lethielleux, 1964); P. Grelot, "La pauvreté
dans l'Écriture Sainte," *Christus* VIII (1961), 306-330.

The influence of the scriptural renewal in moral theology has been enormous. Many significant changes which have occurred in moral theology in the last two decades owe much to the fact that Scripture was taken as the soul of theology and the starting point for systematic reflection on the Christian life. Obviously other factors such as philosophical considerations and signs of the times also played an important part in the renewal of moral theology, but the starting point of the renewal was the return to the Scriptures. However, moral theology has also become aware of the inherent limitations of the Scriptures in moral theology.

## II. LIMITATIONS IN THE USE OF SCRIPTURE IN MORAL THEOLOGY

The most succinct summary of the limitations of the Scriptures in moral theology is the statement that biblical ethics is not the same as Christian ethics. This point is readily acknowledged today by both Catholic and Protestant ethicians. The biblical renewal has emphasized the historical and cultural limitations of the Scriptures so that one cannot just apply the Scriptures in a somewhat timeless manner to problems existing in different historical circumstances. In addition the Scriptures were not really confronted with many of the moral problems we face today. Even among biblical theologians there are those who admit that the Scriptures teach little or no social morality.[27] There has been in theology an embarrassment about the attitude towards slavery and woman in certain parts of the Scriptures, especially Paul. Also the teaching of the Scriptures is often colored by eschatological considerations which make it difficult to apply

---

[27] "Jesus no more intended to change the social system than he did the political order. He never assumed a definite attitude on economic and social problems." Schnackenburg, p. 122.

them directly to any contemporary situation. The hermeneutic problem arises precisely because biblical morality and Christian morality are not the same.

From this basic understanding of the limitation of biblical ethics in the discipline of Christian ethics one should be cautioned about possible dangers in the use of the Scriptures in moral theology. A perennial danger is the use of Scripture as a proof text. An isolated scriptural text is used to prove an assertion for the present time without realizing the vast difference which might exist between the biblical and the contemporary contexts. Likewise there is the constant danger that the individual biblical text may be taken out of its own proper biblical context. Sacred Scripture cannot be legitimately employed in a proof text manner.

Too often the manuals of theology did employ such a use of the Scriptures. The conclusion was arrived at on other grounds, and then one text from Scripture was given as a proof of the assertion. Even today there continue to exist in both Catholic and Protestant theology some glaring examples of a proof text approach to the Scriptures in moral theology.

Bo Reicke translates the first Epistle of Peter, 2:18 as: "You workers, be submissive to your masters with all respect, not only to the good and reasonable ones, but even to the difficult ones."[28] Reicke in his commentary defends his choice of workers rather than slaves so that the passage will have meaning for contemporary Christian workers. The meaning of the passage according to Reicke is clear. "Regardless of provocation Christian workers should not rebel or fail in respect towards their employers."[29] Christ is the model of every suffering worker. "He did not stoop, as many

---

[28] Bo Reicke, *The Anchor Bible: The Epistles of James, Peter and Jude* (Garden City, New York: Doubleday, 1964), p. 97.
[29] *Ibid.*, p. 98.

oppressed people on earth, to reviling and threatening, v. 23, but committed his case to the righteous Judge. No striving after personal liberty or antisocial behavior or opposition to the existing order can be allowed to impair the Christian workers' imitation of Christ."[30] He later comments that Christianity will bring about a social revolution but through spiritual means.[31] However, I do not think that one can use the Scripture in this way to argue against the possibility of a legitimate strike by Christian workers.

## Eschatological Influence

Another vexing aspect of the hermeneutic problem concerns the eschatological coloring of the teaching of Jesus especially the Sermon on the Mount. In opposition to the liberal Protestant theology which saw the Sermon on the Mount as a blueprint for bringing about the presence of the kingdom of God in this world, Schweitzer and others maintained that such an intention was far removed from Jesus who was just proposing an interim ethic for the short time before the coming of the end of the world.[32] There has been much theological discussion about the ethical teaching of the Sermon on the Mount, but in one way or another eschatological considerations must enter into the picture.[33] Thus one cannot simply transpose the ethical teaching of the Scripture to the contemporary scene without some attention to eschatological considerations.

The biblical teaching on marriage and celibacy calls for

---

[30] *Ibid.*, p. 99.

[31] *Ibid.*, p. 100.

[32] Albert Schweitzer, *The Quest of the Historical Jesus* (New York: Macmillan, 1948). The famous second edition of this volume was first published in Germany in 1913.

[33] For a summary and evaluation of approaches to the eschatological aspect of Jesus' teaching with arguments against realized eschatology, see Richard H. Hiers, *Jesus and Ethics* (Philadelphia: Westminster Press, 1968).

some such interpretation, for eschatological considerations apparently downplayed the importance which marriage should have.[34] One major problem in Catholic life and moral theology at the present time, the question of divorce and the pastoral care of divorced people, is seen in the context of the teaching on the indissolubility of marriage in the New Testament. In my view such a teaching can be interpreted in the light of eschatology so that the absoluteness of Catholic practice and teaching should be somewhat relaxed.

Catholic teaching upholds the indissolubility of *ratum et consummatum* marriages and frequently invokes scriptural references including Mt. 19:9, as well as Mt. 5:32. However, some problems arise even within the Catholic tradition for only *ratum et consummatun* marriages are declared absolutely indissoluble while other marriages can be dissolved. There is no explicit warrant within the scriptural tradition for this. Paul in his letter to the Corinthinians allows some exceptions in the case of the indissolubility of marriage despite the absoluteness of the saying of Jesus. In fact, even the famous exception clauses in Matthew (except for the case of πορεια) have always proved somewhat difficult to interpret in the light of the present teaching of the Catholic Church.[35]

Many different interpretations have been proposed for the exception clauses in Matthew. The more traditional solution among Catholic exegetes interpreted Matthew to allow separation but not remarriage. A more modern interpretation indicates that the exception clauses refer to a marriage which is not valid from the very beginning. One cannot debate here the merits of the various solutions which have been pro-

---

[34] Gerken, pp. 37-54.

[35] For recent bibliography on the question, see William W. Bassett, "Divorce and Remarriage: The Catholic Search for a Pastoral Reconciliation," *American Ecclesiastical Review*, CLXII (1970), 100-105; Richard A. McCormick, S.J., "Notes on Moral Theology," *Theological Studies*, XXXII (1971), 107-122.

posed, but I would conclude that even in the New Testament times of Paul and the redactor of Matthew some exceptions were apparently made in the absolute teaching proposed by Jesus. Likewise the teaching of Matthew on divorce is also found in the context of the Sermon on the Mount where eschatological considerations are of considerable importance. I propose that the indissolubility of marriage is proposed as an ideal, but that in the world between the two comings of Jesus it is not always possible to achieve the fullness of that ideal.[36] Another important factor to mention concerns the practical problems involved in coming up with pastoral solutions to the question of divorces so that one can maintain the ideal, protect innocent persons and still realize that in this world it is not always possible to live up to the fullness of the ideal.

## *Problems of Systematization and Selection*

In general the limitations of the use of biblical ethics in Christian ethics arise from the differences between the two. However, problems exist even within the context of biblical ethics itself which also serve as a limitation and possible danger in the use of biblical ethics in Christian ethics. Two different possible approaches to biblical ethics are illustrated by the two most widely acknowledged contributions by Catholic authors to biblical ethics. Rudolf Schnackenburg adopts an historical or chronological approach to the moral message of the New Testament by considering the moral teachings in the synoptics, in the early Church in general, in John, in Paul and in the other New Testament writers.[37]

---

[36] Among exegetes who accept such an approach are: Bruce Vawter, C.M. "The Biblical Theology of Divorce," *Proceedings of the Catholic Theological Society of America*, XXII (1967), 223-243; Wilfrid Harrington, "Jesus' Attitude Towards Divorce," *Irish Theological Quarterly*, XXXVII (1970), 199-209.

[37] Schnackenburg, *The Moral Teaching of the New Testament*.

Ceslaus Spicq in his well documented two volume study ar-
ranges the moral teaching of the New Testament around ten
major themes each of which includes some subsidiary
themes.[38]

Spicq himself is well aware of the difficulty of presenting
any synthetic or systematic understanding of biblical morality.[39] Within the Scriptures different books treat the same
matter with different emphasis (e.g., the concept of love).
Likewise any attempt at systematization or synthesis involves an interpretation of the biblical teaching. The fact
remains that there is great divergence even within the biblical message itself which makes it most difficult to arrive at
a satisfying synthesis of biblical teaching or biblical morality.
In a somewhat larger context Roland Murphy argues that the
notion of "the unity of the Bible" should be interred precisely because of the diversity existing within the Scripture.
"In every case the rubric of unity turns out to be incomplete,
whether it be covenant, *Heilsgeschichte,* or promise-fulfill-
ment. Every such category, while it has a value in itself, is
simply too limited to deal with the variety offered by the
biblical material."[40] I would argue that even in the area of
biblical morality such a unity or perfect synthesis remains
impossible of achievement. There exists even within the
Scriptures a plurality of understandings of the moral life.
Thus even within the Scriptures themselves there remains an
inherent limitation in developing a systematic biblical
morality.

A more noticeable limitation arises from the fact that the

---

[38] Ceslaus Spicq, O.P., *Theologie Morale du Nouveau Testament.* 2 vols.
(Paris: Gabalda, 1965). For a discussion of the different approaches to
biblical morality itself, see Franco Festorazzi, "Il problema del metodo nella
teologia biblica," *La Scuola Cattolica,* XCI (1963), 253-276.

[39] Spicq, 9-16.

[40] Roland E. Murphy, O.Carm., "Christian Understanding of the Old
Testament," *Theology Digest,* XVIII (1970), 327.

Scriptures themselves even in moral matters are in need of interpretation. Whether implicitly or explicitly the theologian will bring his own presuppositions to his interpretatons of biblical morality. The danger is that we often forget the existence of such interpretations and presuppositions and uncritically acclaim the biblical approach of a particular author.

Spicq, for example, in summarizing his massive two volume work obviously shows his own theological presuppositions. Spicq insists that the Christian life does not primarily consist of obedience to rules but is a living out of the life of the new creature in Christ Jesus. The moral life follows from an ontology of the new creature. Spicq obviously interprets the biblical message in the light of the Catholic teaching on the transformation of the individual by God's redeeming grace. The Christian now has a regenerated nature which becomes the source of his life and actions.[41] Roger Mehl on the basis of his theological presuppositions takes issue with Spicq's interpretation. God's gift is his presence, but his presence never becomes a nature or a structure. Such an ontology or substantialist philosophy according to Mehl can never truly present the biblical understanding of the God-man relationship.[42]

Two different interpretations of Paul's understanding of the Christian life also illustrate the different theological presuppositions of the two authors. George Montague's study of Pauline morality exhibits on its cover jacket the basic presupposition of his thesis. The full title is: *Maturing in Christ: Saint Paul's Program for Christian Growth.*[43] The cover jacket then cites one Pauline text: "If anyone is in Christ, he

---

[41] Spicq, II, 756-761.

[42] Roger Mehl, *Catholic Ethics and Protestant Ethics* (Philadelphia: Westminster Press, 1971), p. 112.

[43] George T. Montague, S.M., *Maturing in Christ: Saint Paul's Program for Christian Growth* (Milwaukee: Bruce, 1964).

is a *new creature*." Montague's thesis maintains a basic transformation into the new creature taking place in the life of the
Christian.[44] Victor Paul Furnish in his study of Pauline
ethics denies the two fundamental presuppositions of Montague. First, Furnish refuses to accept the concept of a mystical union of the Christian with Christ. The being of the believer is not merged with the being of Christ. "The categories
used to describe the believer's association with Christ are all
*relational* not *mystical* categories."[45] Logically, Furnish also
denies at the end of his book any possibility of progress in the
life of the Christian according to Paul. Paul's preaching insists that the "fullness of life is not attained but given, and
that Christian obedience is not an expression of man's effort
gradually to realize his own innate possibilities, but an ever
repeated response to the ever newly repeated summons of
God."[46] Montague's basic thesis is thus denied by Furnish
although Montague would not positively explain his thesis
in the same terms in which Furnish denied the possibility of
progress in the life of the Christian.

Another example of differing interpretations of biblical
teaching is illustrated in James Sellers' choice of the concept
of promise and fulfillment as the basic stance in Christian
ethics. "The Judaeo-Christian faith then affirms a distinctive
understanding of what is happening to man; he is moving
from promise to fulfillment."[47] Paul Ramsey also argues from
the Judaeo-Christian tradition and from the concept of covenant, but he emphatically denies Sellers' emphasis on fulfillment. Precisely on the basis of eschatology and of covenent
fidelity Ramsey rules out the primacy of fulfillment in any

---

[44] *Ibid.*, especially pp. 101-110.
[45] Victor Paul Furnish, *Theology and Ethics in Paul* (Nashville: Abing-
don, 1968), p. 176.
[46] *Ibid.*, pp. 239-240.
[47] James Sellers, *Theological Ethics* (New York: Macmillan, 1968), p.
63.

understanding of the Christian moral life. Ramsey consistently opposes a teleological approach to Christian ethics precisely because of the fact that fulfillment or the attainment of the goal is not always possible for the Christian.[48]

A related danger in the use of the Scriptures in moral theology involves the selective use of the Scripture in keeping with one's own presuppositions. The Social Gospel approach to Christian ethics, for example, concentrated on the teaching of the prophets in the Old Testament and the teaching of Jesus in the New Testament, since these two sources are most consonant with the theological presuppositions of the Social Gospel approach. Walter Rauschenbusch in his *Christianity and the Social Crisis* well illustrates such an approach.[49]

The first of Rauschenbusch's seven chapters considers the teaching of the prophets, while the second chapter deals with the teaching of Jesus. In the third chapter he treats the more difficult problem of the social impetus of early Christianity. Rauschenbusch realizes there is not much social teaching in Paul whom he describes as a radical in theology but a social conservative. But Paul was not as apathetic towards social conditions as is generally presumed. In this context Rauschenbusch praises the social concerns of the Epistle of James, which had been rejected in the strict Lutheran tradition.[50] His attempts to prove the social implications in the teaching of the early Church are often exaggerated and unacceptable. "The Christian Church was of immense social value to these people. It took the place in their life which life insurance, sick benefits, accident insurance, friendly societies, and some features of trade-unions

---

[48] Paul Ramsey, *Deeds and Rules in Christian Ethics* (New York: Charles Scribner's Sons, 1967), pp. 178-192.

[49] Walter Rauschenbusch, *Christianity and the Social Crisis*, ed. Robert D. Cross (New York: Harper and Row Torchbook, 1964), pp. 93-142.

[50] *Ibid.*, pp. 98-99.

take today."[51] There are other exaggerated claims made to support his basic contention.[52] Thus one can see the dangers of selectivity in the choice of the scriptural parts which are used and the twisting of other parts of the Scriptures to fit in with the presuppositions.

Obviously those who make Christ the center of the moral life of the Christian tend to be quite selective in their use of Scripture and place importance on those texts which support their positions while passing over much of the biblical materials (especially the Old Testament) in silence. Bonhoeffer understands the foundation of the Christian life in terms of formation, or better, conformation with the unique form of Him who was made man, was crucified and rose again. Man does not achieve this formation by dint of his own efforts, but Christ shapes man in conformity with himself.[53] The Scripture employed by Bonhoeffer includes many important Christological texts in the New Testament—Gal. 4:19; 2 Cor. 3:18; Phil. 3:10; Rom. 8:29, 12:2; Phil. 1:21; Col. 3:3.[54] Again the critical ethician realizes the selectivity involved in such a use of Scripture. Obviously some selectivity must be employed, but the critical ethician needs to probe the implicit presuppositions behind the selection of certain aspects of the Scriptures.

Another somewhat related danger arises from the selection of one biblical theme as primary and as coloring one's whole approach to Christian ethics. Reference has already been

---

[51] *Ibid.*, p. 132.

[52] Rauschenbusch's summary of the attitude of the primitive Church is exaggerated (pp. 139-142). The Spirit of Christianity stirred women to break down restraints, caused some people to quit work, awakened in slaves a longing for freedom, disturbed the patriotism and loyalty of citizens. "All of its theories involved a bold condemnation of existing society. . . . Christianity was conscious of a far-reaching and thorough political and social mission" (p. 140).

[53] Dietrich Bonhoeffer, *Ethics* (New York: Macmillan, 1962), 17-23.

[54] These Scripture texts are cited by Bonhoeffer, pp. 17-19.

made to Sellers' choice of promise and fulfillment as the most basic aspect in Christian ethics. Again, it will always be necessary to choose some basic starting point in Christian ethics; but some themes which have been chosen do not seem to be that basic or central. Thus such a selection tends to distort the Christian ethics built around it. Today some theologians are developing a theology of liberation based also on biblical categories.[55] Difficulties arise, however, when this becomes the primary and even the exclusive emphasis in moral theology, for other important considerations go unheeded. In the field of social ethics order and security are other aspects of the question even though some theologians may have overemphasized these aspects in the past. Especially in the light of the fads which have existed in theology in the past few years there remains the constant danger of taking one aspect of the biblical message and making it so central and exclusive that the full biblical message is not properly understood.

## III. TWO METHODOLOGICAL QUESTIONS

There are two important foundational questions concerning the use of the Scriptures in moral theology which relate to the question of methodology. The first question concerns the precise way in which Christian ethicians have employed or should employ the Scriptures. The second question centers on the exact relationship between the content of the ethical teaching of the Scriptures and the content of nonbiblical ethical teaching.

In examining the different ways in which moral theology employs the Scriptures, I believe that the fundamental difference stems from one's basic understanding of the relation-

---

[55] e.g. Gustavo Gutierrez M., "Notes for a Theology of Liberation." *Theological Studies,* XXXI (1970), 243-261.

ship between Christian ethics and other forms of ethics especially philosophical ethics. Is Christian ethics just a certain type or species, if you will, of ethics in general? Does the methodological approach to Christian ethics depend on considerations common to all forms of ethical discourse? Or is the methodological approach to Christian ethics different from all other ethical methodologies precisely because of the distinctive aspect of Christian ethics? If the methodology of Christian ethics differs from the methodology of other forms of ethics because of the distinctive nature of Christian ethics, the ultimate reason must be found in the relationship of Christian ethics to revelation, grace and the Scriptures.

## A Fundamental but Limited Question

Note the limited yet very fundamental aspects of the question being pursued. The answer to this question will not solve all the methodological questions about the use of the Scriptures in moral theology, but it will indicate the first steps that should be taken in constructing such a methodology. At least logically there are two different methodological approaches which could be taken in response to our question. The one approach derives its content from the Scriptures, revelation and the other sources of ethical widsom for the Christian. In this approach one could use the Scriptures to argue for a particular methodological approach (e.g. a responsibility model rather than a deontological model), but the methodological structure would be common to all possible forms of ethics. The second approach would be a methodology which is peculiar to Christian ethics because of the distinctive character of Christian ethics which must bear some relationship to its scriptural basis.

With these two possibilities in mind one could set out to examine the different generic approaches which have been employed by moral theology or Christian ethics in the past to determine if there have been too such generic approaches to the methodology of Christian ethics. Such a thorough review is impossible here, but one can use the research of others in this area. James M. Gustafson has analyzed two different approaches in Christian theological ethics.[56] Gustafson briefly describes the one approach as the more intuitional and the other as the more rational approach. Gustafson cites Paul Lehmann as an example of the intuitional approach, for Lehmann maintains that Christian ethics responds to the question of what God is doing in the world to make and keep human life more human. Lehmann generally does not spell out criteria for discerning this humanizing activity of God, but he often appeals to intuition. The second approach is more rational in its methodology and allows for more ethical agrument in discussing what should be done.

One could argue that the difference between these two generic approaches comes from different philosophical understanding of ethics. The one would follow an intuitional, philosophical method and the other a more rational, philosophical method. However, I propose that the ultimate reason for the two different methodological approaches mentioned by Gustafson does not come from two different philosophical approaches as such but rather derives from a philosophical approach which employs a rational methodology which could be common to any and all forms of ethics and from an approach which sees Christian ethics as so distinctive that it even has a methodology which is distinctive from all other ethical methodologies.

Those who employ the approach Gustafson describes as intuitional are in general those Christian ethicians who see Christian ethics as essentially distinct from other forms of ethics and thus posit a distinctive methodology for Christian ethics. This distinctive methodology bears some relationship

---

[56] James M. Gustafson, "Two Approaches to Theological Ethics," *Union Seminary Quarterly Review,* XXIII (1968), 337-348.

to the revealed character of Christian ethics. Gustafson cites
Lehmann as an example of the intuitional approach, but
Lehmann willingly admits there is neither identity nor an
intrinsic relationship between Christian ethics and philosophical ethics, but rather there is an ultimate chasm and
even opposition between Christian ethics and philosophical
ethics. "The radical incompatibility between Christian and
philosophical ethics is the irreconcilability of their respective
views of human self-determination."[57] Lehmann adopts the
Barthian position by asserting that for philosophical ethics
man makes ethics, but for Christian ethics, God makes ethics,
for God initiates and establishes the humanity of man. Lehmann then cites Barth again to prove his fundamental assertion that the grace of God protests against every humanly
established ethic as such. The specifically and formatively
ethical factor cannot be given rational generalization.[58]

Lehmann thus indicates that a Barthian approach to theology accepts a distinctive methodology for Christian ethics
which differs from every other ethical methodology. The
Bible tells us of the actions of the living God, and it is with
the actions of the living God that Christian ethics must begin
and not with any philosophical understanding of man. Barth
in no way accepts a fundamentalistic approach to the Scriptures. The Word and concrete command of God are not the
same as the written word of Scripture. The role of Scripture
in moral theology is secondary, but through analogy man
may arrive at his decision in the light of the Scripture.
Barth's Christian social ethics with its emphasis on analogy
has been challenged precisely because of its seeming lack of
rational structure. There are few criteria given to indicate
how the analogy occurs, and many of the analogies which

---

[57] Paul L. Lehmann, *Ethics in a Christian Context* (New York: Harper
and Row, 1963), p. 274.
[58] *Ibid.*, pp. 268-284.

Barth draws seem to be quite arbitrary. Barth cannot accept rational criteria for establishing any movement by analogy from the Word of God to concrete ethical problems.[59]

Barth and Lehmann both illustrate the first approach which views Christian ethics as an altogether distinctive type of ethics precisely because of the theology of revelation, the Word and Scripture. The distinctive aspect of Christian ethics stems from their theology of the Word and the concrete command of God. Since such an approach rejects a biblical fundamentalism, the written word of God does not have the primary place in their ethic but somehow or other as the record of the acts of the living God does bear on the concrete situation here and now. Although Lehmann and Sittler in the United States seem to adopt such a generic approach, there can be no doubt that such an approach with its Barthian roots is much stronger in continental, European Protestant thought.[60]

A. Dumas raises the precise problem of how Christian social ethics goes from Sacred Scripture to contemporary problems.[61] Dumas points out the difficulties in the approach of liberalism which tried to reduce the gospel message to the essential core which would be true in all circumstances. On the other hand the Orthodox approach tries merely to repeat perhaps in different language the revealed word of the Scriptures. Both approaches are wrong because in trying to assure a universalism to the word of God they fail to come to grips with the existentialism and singularity of the biblical message. Dumas proposes a hermeneutic of

---

[59] Karl Barth, *Community, State and Church,* introduction by Will Herberg, (Garden City, Doubleday Anchor Books, 1960), pp. 171-186. For an analysis and critique of Barth's use of analogy, see Herberg's introductory essay, "The Social Philosophy of Karl Barth," pp. 31-38.

[60] Joseph Sittler, *The Structure of Christian Ethics* (Baton Rouge: Louisiana State University Press, 1958).

[61] A. Dumas, "De l'archétype à la parabole," *Le Supplément,* XXIII (1970), 28-46.

explicitation in which the contemporary Christian and the Christian ethicist see the Bible not as an archetype but as a parable which is normative for the present circumstances. However, there exists little or nothing in terms of rational criteria or even debatable criteria for discerning how precisely the Bible functions as a parable for normatively directing Christian ethics today.

The editors of *Christianisme Social* describe the function of Christian ethics not as applying principles derived from other historical and cultural circumstances to questions of the present times but rather as interpreting for our times a Word which had been a living word in a different setting. The editors of this journal try to find a direct relationship between the concrete biblical word and the precise social situation of the present.[62] Again, little or nothing is said about the criteria for developing this hermeneutic, and no criteria which can be rationally debated or discussed are proposed. In somewhat the same vein, F. Florentin speaks of a certain discernment which contemporary man receives from the Scriptures, but the process of how this discernment takes place is not developed.[63]

I personally cannot accept this generic approach to the methodology of Christian ethics, which sees it as distinctive from all other ethical methodology. Although the proponents of this generic approach do not make the written word of the Scriptures normative in itself without further interpretation, their use of the Scriptures in terms of analogy, parables, etc. does not seem to furnish an adequate methodology for Christian ethics in general and for the use of Scripture in Christian ethics in particular.

In general I would opt for a methodology in Christian ethics which is common to the ethical enterprise and is not

---

[62] "Au lecteur," *Christianisme Social,* LXXIV (1966), 281-283.

[63] Françoise Florentin, "L'ethique sociale et l'étude biblique," *Christianisme Social,* LXXIV (1966), 297-302.

distinctive. The methodology of Christian ethics exists in continuity with the ethical methodology in general. This position is in keeping with the Catholic theological tradition and is also accepted by many contemporary Protestant ethicians. Obviously this is a very generic approach and there can be many different methodological approaches within this generic option. This essay is considering just the most fundamental and basic of the questions confronting methodology in Christian ethics. Christian ethicians adopting such a generic approach that sees Christian ethics in continuity with the general ethical enterprise will generally admit the Scriptures are not the sole source of ethical wisdom for the Christian, but that Christian ethics also derives wisdom and knowledge from other human sources. This generic approach will thus rely on human wisdom and reason as well as on the Scriptures, a factor that will greatly influence the role and function of the Scriptures in moral theology.

Once one has opted for a methodology common to all ethical theory, there remains almost an infinite variety of such theories which one can choose. One must try to establish on the grounds of ethical thinking and Christian understanding what is the best type of theory to employ. Obviously this paper cannot consider all the different possibilities. The consideration will be limited to one brief observation and then a sketch of a possible development of the methodology to be employed in Christian ethics and the way in which it would use the Scriptures.[64]

The brief observation concerns the danger of oversimpli-

---

[64] For a very similar approach which also strives to be more comprehensive than most approaches, see James M. Gustafson, "The Place of Scripture in Christian Ethics: A Methodological Study," *Interpretation*, XXIV (1970), 430-455. Gustafson exemplifies his methodological use of the Scripture in Christian ethics by considering one particular problem. For a study of the methodological use of the Scriptures by Rauschenbusch, see James M. Gustafson, "From Scripture to Social Policy and Social Action," *Andover-Newton Quarterly*, IX (1969), 160-169.

fication. Some methodological approaches to Christian ethics appear to be erroneous precisely because they fail to consider all the elements that should enter into the ethical consideration. Perhaps no mention is made of the decision process itself, or the attitudes and dispositions of the subject, or the values and goals in the Christian life. In general an ethical approach must try to be as comprehensive as possible by considering all the elements that go into ethical considerations even though some will obviously have priority and be of greater importance. The Scriptures as well as human wisdom can be of help in all these areas.

Perhaps the most fundamental question in ethics is that of stance, horizon or posture. The horizon or ultimate way in which the Christian looks at reality is in my judgment in the light of the Christian mysteries of creation, sin, incarnation, redemption and resurrection destiny. Obviously, such a posture includes its own presuppositions. The stance is not defined in terms of any one value, disposition or goal, precisely because any one such value, ideal or goal with its specific content does not seem apt to serve as a basic stance. The basic stance proposed here is more formal in the sense that it indicates the structure of the Christian experience. This tries to give a formal intelligibility rather than a content intelligibility. Such a choice obviously indicates a distinct emphasis on the subject pole of human experience.

The second most fundamental ethical question concerns the general model for understanding the Christian moral life. Earlier, mention was made of the three general approaches of ethics to this question, and the model of relationality and responsibility was chosen in the light of the biblical understanding of man.

There are at least four other important considerations which should be present in ethics: 1) values, goals, or ideals; 2) dispositions and attitudes of the subject, or virtues, if you prefer; 3) norms; 4) the process of moral judgments and de-

cisions. Obviously the question of moral judgments and decision will always be the most decisive consideration, but these
other aspects cannot be neglected.

In the more general question of stance and model the
scriptural input will be more important, but it will not be the
only aspect of the question. There are ethical presuppositions
in my own decision to see the stance not in terms of content
but as a way of structuring the way in which the Christian
intends reality and the world in which he lives. On the other
more specific ethical considerations, with the emphasis on
the judging and decision making process, the role and function of the Scriptures will be less. The precise way in which
the Scriptures can contribute in all these areas is both partial
and limited in view of the hemeneutic question itself. This
has only been a brief sketch of a possible development of
methodology in Christian ethics once one answers the basic
question by seeing the methodology of Christian ethics in
terms of ethical theory in general and not as something distinctive to Christian ethics. Obviously, within this generic
approach there remain many possible options. In all these
the input of the Scriptures will be limited because of the historical and cultural limitations of the word of God as found
in the Scriptures, and will be interpreted in the light of the
ethical methodology chosen.

## A CONTENT QUESTION WITH
## METHODOLOGICAL OVERTONES

In the midst of the ethical and religious pluralism in which
we live there arises not only the question of the ethical
methodology employed by moral theology and its use of the
Scriptures but also the question of the content or the substance of biblical ethics and moral theology in comparison
with other religious and philosophical ethics. The generally
accepted approach of the past affirms a great difference be-

tween the revealed morality of the Bible and the nonrevealed morality of other ethics. Today there appears to be a tendency, with which I concur, to disagree with the older approach.[65] This question obviously has important methodological implications for Christian ethics.

In the past, the question of the relationship between Christian ethics and other ethics was phrased in terms of the existence of a source of ethical wisdom and knowledge which the Christian shares with all mankind in addition to the revealed wisdom of the Scriptures. An affirmative response to the question led to the further question of the exact relationship between the revelational and the nonrevelational sources of ethical wisdom and knowledge for the Christian. Precisely under the impact of the consciousness of religious and ethical pluralism as well as the apparent lack of ethical superiority in Christian ethics and in the Scripture, the question now takes on a different aspect: is there any great difference in content between Christian ethics, with revelation and the Scripture as the reason for its possible distinctive character, and other human ethics?

One way to approach the problem is to institute a comparison between biblical ethics and nonrevealed ethics. Some significant work has been going on in this area and is illustrated by the question of the decalogue in the Old Testament. Christians generally have the image that God revealed

---

[65] Charles E. Curran, "Is There a Distinctively Christian Social Ethic?" in *Metropolis*'s *Christian Presence and Responsibility,* ed. Philip D. Morris (Notre Dame, Ind.: Fides Publishers, 1970), pp. 92-120. A French translation appeared in *Le Supplément,* XCVI (1971), 39-58. A brief summary of the conclusion appears on p. 114: "The explicitly Christian consciousness does affect the judgment of the Christian and the way in which he makes his ethical judgments, but non-Christians can and do arrive at the same ethical conclusions and also embrace and treasure even the loftiest of proximate motives, virtues, and goals which Christians in the past have wrongly claimed only for themselves." See Chapter 1, p. 16.

his law to the people of the Old Testament even if they are sophisticated enough to realize there was no historical apparition or revelation to Moses amid thunder and lightning. The developing research in this area is most interesting, for the trend shows an ever growing awareness of the lack of distinctivenesss between the biblical law of the Old Testament and the nonrevealed law of the contemporaries of Israel.

Albrecht Alt in 1934 distinguished two types of law in Israel, the apodictic and the casuistic and acknowledged that the casuistic law was common to all people in the Near East, but the apodictic law was unique and peculiar to Israel. Such a position bolstered the notion of the distinctive and unique qualities of the revealed morality.[66] More contemporary scholarship, however, disputes the conclusion proposed by Alt and realizes that apodictic law was also common to other peoples in the Near East. Even the general covenant form is not something unique, but exists also in the Hittite Suzerainty treaties.[67]

In this context the question has been raised about the origin of the decalogue as we know it today. Obviously there is a connection between the form of the decalogue and its use in worship, so that some commentators have concluded that

---

[66] Albrecht Alt, "The Origins of Israelite Law," *Essays on Old Testament History and Religion* (Garden City: Doubleday Anchor Books, 1958). In this section I am heavily dependent on the following summaries of recent biblical interpretations: Alexa Suelzer, S.P., *The Pentateuch* (New York: Herder and Herder, 1964). This book gives a fine history of the development of thinking on the Pentateuch especially in Roman Catholic thought, but it is now too dated to include the results of more recent scholarly investigations. Johann Jakob Stamm with Maurice Edward Andrew, *The Ten Commandments in Recent Research* (Studies in Biblical Theology, Second Series, n. 2; Naperville, Ill.: Alec R. Allenson, 1967); Edward Nielsen, *The Ten Commandments in New Perspective* (Studies in Biblical Theology, Second Series, n. 7 Naperville, Ill.: Alec R. Allenson, 1968); Carroll Stulhmueller, "The Natural Law Question the Bible Never Asked," *Cross Currents,* XIX (1969) 55-67.

[67] Stulhmueller, *Cross Currents,* XIX (1969), 60-61.

the form of the decalogue as we have it today probably arose within the context of the cult. However, Gerstenberger and others claim that the apodictic law of the decalogue had its origin not in the treaty or in the cult but in the clan.[68] Again notice in these theories a tendency away from a distinctiveness concerning the circumstances of the decalogue.

J.J. Stamm appears to accept the conclusion that the content of the revealed morality of the Old Testament "came about in a much more secular way than is often supposed."[69] Gerstenberger maintains that one cannot conclude that Israel's law is better or more moral than that of her neighbors or that it is unique because it is revealed. Israel's law when brought into the context of the covenant comes to express fully what was already inherent in it: the necessity of the framework of relationship which breaks through that which is merely moral.[70] Thus the Old Testament gives the new context of the covenant with Yahweh for a law which was not unique, and even this general covenant context is somehow or other inherent in the law.

Carroll Stuhlmueller in the light of recent biblical studies (primarily relating to the Old Testament but also including some studies about the New Testament) specifically asks the question about the relationship between revealed morality and the so-called natural law. Stuhlmueller concludes that the origins of the revelation to Israel will be recognized not as a lightning bolt from above but as God's living presence with all men of good will.[71] "Biblically, the world at large

---

[68] Stamm and Andrew, pp. 66-68.

[69] *Ibid.*, pp. 73-74.

[70] *Ibid.*, pp. 74-75. Note that these authors here report and generally accept the conclusions of Gerstenberger. They do express the wish that Gerstenberger had repeated near the end his earlier emphasis on the distinctive context of the covenant and the Sinai revelation.

[71] Stulhmuller, *Cross Currents*, XIX (1969), 63.

contributes what men of faith can then identify as the presence of God speaking His will for human well-being."[72] At this juncture I would only add the cautionary note that human experience also reflects the limitations and sinfulness of men so that not everything that appears in human experience is necessarily good and to be accepted uncritically.

One could continue such a comparative study down through all the Scriptures including the teachings of the prophets, the wisdom literature, Jesus, Paul, John, and the early Christian community as compared with their contemporaries and others. This area provides a fertile field for possible future development and research. Interestingly, recent studies tend to be very modest in claiming any superiority for the biblical morality. Seán Freyne in a recent study of biblical morality in both the Old and the New Testaments admits that the content of biblical morality is similar to the content of nonrevealed morality.[73] The contribution of the prophets to the moral teaching of Israel does not derive from any special revelation of content from God, but the prophets merely refined the traditional morality.[74] Freyne comments that what is striking in the teachings of Jesus is his agreement with and acceptance of the better insights and formulations of the late Jewish moral thinking. As far as the content of the moral life is concerned Jesus inherited and refined rather than innovated.[75]

Freyne does, however, admit a purifying influence of faith on the insights of secular morality.[76] Freyne staunchly argues for a different motivation and context for biblical ethics,

---

[72] *Ibid.*, p. 59.
[73] Seán Freyne, "The Bible and Christian Morality," in *Morals, Law and Authority*, ed J. P. Mackey (Dayton: Pflaum Press, 1969), p. 7.
[74] *Ibid.*, p. 10.
[75] *Ibid.*, p. 19.
[76] *Ibid.*, p. 25.

but "the actual content of their morality will thus be often similar to that of their surrounding neighbors, at least in the more lofty formulations of these."[77] The difference he sometimes mentions in content between biblical and nonbiblical morality is that of refinement and purification. Perhaps this coheres with the caveat expressed earlier that human experience will also always contain the limitations and sinfulness which mark our human existence, but the loftiest aspects of human experience will often correspond with the best of the biblical ethic.[78]

One can also examine the question of the relationship between biblical or Christian and nonrevealed morality in a more systematic and theological approach. Is there a distinctively Christian ethic? A growing number of studies indicate that on the level of ethical conclusions and proximate values, norms and dispositions there is nothing distinctive about the Christian ethic. John Macquarrie maintains that the distinctively Christian criterion coincides with the criterion which is already guiding, at least implicitly, the moral aspiration of all men—the idea of an authentic or full humanity. Macquarrie finds the distinctiveness of Christian ethics not in the ultimate goals or fundamental principles but in the special context within which the moral life is considered.[79] Interestingly, Macquarrie links Christian and non-Christian ethics not on the basis of redemption but of creation.[80]

In Chapter 1 I denied the existence of a distinctively Christian ethic with regard to ethical conclusions and proximate dispositions, goals and attitudes; but the reason for the iden-

---

[77] *Ibid.*, p. 34.

[78] I would tend to disagree with Freyne's comment (pp. 34-35) that the added element in biblical morality is the assurance that what they are doing is God's will for them.

[79] John Macquarrie, *Three Issues in Ethics* (New York: Harper and Row, 1970), pp. 87-91.

[80] *Ibid.*, p. 88.

tity was not creation but redemption. It seems to me that Josef Fuchs takes much the same approach. Fuchs first distinguishes between the level of the transcendental or intentionality and the level of the categorical. On the level of the categorical Christ did not really add anything new. The distinctively Christian appears on the level of the transcendental and intentionality. Near the end of the article Fuchs also admits that the humanist operates not only on the level of the categorical but also on the level of the intentional, the transcendental and the unthematic.[81]

If one were to interpret Fuchs in the light of Rahner, which is acceptable in the light of Fuchs' own writings, the difference on the level of the transcendental or unthematic could possibly be only the difference between the explicit and the implicit, and not necessarily a difference of greater and lesser. In accord with Fuchs' article one could also conclude that the specifically Christian aspect does not add anything to the "proximate dispositions, goals, and attitudes" of Christians. Yes these dispositions, goals, attitudes and values would be considered in an explicitly Christian context, but non-Christians too can and do cherish "self-sacrificing love, freedom, hope, concern for the neighbor in need, or even the realization that one finds his life only in losing it."[82]

In the above paragraphs I am trying to clarify and further a dialogue begun by Richard A. McCormick, S.J.[83] McCor-

---

[81] Josef Fuchs, S.J., "Gibt es eine spezifisch christliche Moral?" *Stimmen der Zeit*, CLXXXV (1970), 99-112.

[82] I am here interpreting Fuchs as being in accord with my conclusions, p. 16.

[83] McCormick, *Theological Studies*, XXXII (1971), 71-78. I am guilty of complicating the discussion by not correcting an earlier version of my manuscript which I had sent to Father McCormick. The final version differs somewhat from that which McCormick used, since I tried to clarify my thought as a result of helpful discussions with McCormick and others at the symposium where the paper was originally given.

mick argues that the gospel should bring about distinctive attitudes and intentions. He then appeals to both Fuchs and Gustafson as supporting or being close to his position. McCormick finds support in Fuchs because Fuchs refers to "transcendental norms (e.g. the following of Christ, leading a sacramental life, the life of faith, etc.)."[84]

Perhaps the following of Christ can illustrate the question. I am interpreting Fuchs as agreeing with my conclusion: "The explicitly Christian consciousness does affect the judgment of the Christian and the way in which he makes his ethical judgments, but non-Christians can and do arrive at the same ethical conclusions and also embrace and treasure even the loftiest of proximate motives, virtues and goals which Christians in the past have wrongly claimed only for themselves."[85] Certainly the Christian explicitly reflects on the imitation of Christ, but the proximate attitudes, values and goals that come from this are the same attitudes that other people can arrive at in other ways. Chapter 1 spelled out some of these attitudes as self-sacrificing love, freedom, hope, concern for the neighbor in need or even the realization that one finds his life only in losing it.

Another way of trying to express the same reality was to say that Christians and non-Christians "can and do share the same general ethical attitudes, dispositions and goals."[86] "General" in this case refers to such a concept as self-sacrificing love which the Christian could share with other men in general, but see it in terms of explicit reference to Jesus Christ, which thus modifies the general concept not necessarily by adding to its content but by explicitly referring to Jesus Christ. In this way the following of Christ motif leads the Christian to the same conclusions and proximate attitudes that others can arrive at on other grounds and through

---

[84] *Ibid.*, p. 77.
[85] Chapter 1, p. 16.
[86] *Ibid.*

other conceptualizations. Obviously I am not saying that all non-Christians do arrive at these dispositions, but they can come to them. Likewise all Christians do not live up to such lofty ideals.

Gustafson has not directly asked the question as posed here, but he appears to assume that there is a greater difference between Christian and non-Christian ethics than the solution proposed here. Gustafson does stress the "differences that faith in Jesus Christ *often does make, can make,* and *ought to make* in the moral lives of members of the Christian community."[87] The question must eventually go back to the theological discussion of the relationship between the Christian and the non-Christian. Since in my opinion this difference can at times be only the difference between explicit and implicit, then one can maintain the conclusion proposed above.

*The Pastoral Constitution on the Church in the Modern World* proposes a methodology of viewing reality in terms of the gospel and human experience. Accepting this formulation, I would conclude that the gospel does not add a power of knowledge which *somehow or other* is not available in the consciousness of man called by God with regard to ethical conclusions and proximate dispositions, goals and attitudes. The gospel does make explicit and explicitly Christian what can be implicit in the consciousness of all men who are called by God. Precisely because the link between the Christian and the non-Christian is not based only on creation but also on redemption, then the redemptive power and knowledge that the Christian has in the gospel are also available somehow or other to all men. The difference in the specific area of ethics mentioned above is between explicit and implicit and not between more or less.

Human experience thus can have implicitly what is expli-

---

[87] James M. Gustafson, *Christ and the Moral Life* (New York: Harper and Row, 1968), p. 240.

citly found in the gospel and also cherish the same proximate ethical ideals, dispositions and decisions; but human experience also reflects the limitations and sinfulness of man (as the Scriptures do also). This realization will also have important repercussions on the way in which moral theology uses the Scriptures. I still see the important role of the Scriptures in terms of explicitly allowing us to reflect on who the Christian is and what his attitudes, dispositions, goals, values, norms and decisions are. However, in no sense can the Scriptures be used as a book of revealed morality precisely because of the hermeneutic problem. The Scriptures do furnish us with information about the self-understanding of the people who lived in convenant relationship with God and how this helped shape their lives and actions. The Christian and the Christian ethicist today must continue to reflect on this experience as recalled in the Scriptures, but they must also reflect on the experience of other men as they try to determine how they should live and respond to Jesus Christ in our times.

This section has not attempted to develop a complete methodology for the use of the Scriptures in moral theology, but rather has considered perhaps the two most fundamental questions involved in constructing such a methodology. The methodology of Christian ethics is not distinctive but is based on ethical methodology in general as viewed in the light of the gospel message and human experience. Secondly, the ethical wisdom and knowledge portrayed in the scriptural experience remains quite similar to the ethical experiences of all mankind. The primary difference is the explicitly Christian character of the gospel which will not affect the proximate ethical dispositions, attitudes and goals as well as concrete conclusions, but will color the explicit self-understanding of the Christian and the decision process he employs.

# 3

## Dialogue with Science: Scientific Data, Scientific Possibilities and the Moral Judgment

The relationship between theology and science has not been peaceful as the historical record of many frictions, misunderstandings, and problems attests. This essay will concentrate on the more specific question of the relationship between moral theology and science. There are many possible ways in which such a subject could be developed and treated. One could take the relationship between moral theology and a particular science or between moral theology and a certain type of science such as the behavioral sciences or the physical sciences.

With the realization of the different scientific methodologies pertinent to the different kinds of sciences and the fact that within any one science there often is no agreement on methodology (especially in terms of the behavioral sciences), this essay will consider the general question of the relationship of moral theology and the sciences from two different aspects. Traditionally the primary question concerning this relationship has been phrased in terms of the way in which moral theology understands and employs the data of the sciences in arriving at moral judgments or conclusions. The second aspect of the question to be treated here responds to an even more crucial question which has arisen more in the last few years: How is man going to control the future development of himself and his world? Thanks to the power derived from science and technology man now has the ability to drastically change and perhaps even remake himself and his world.

## THEORETICAL OPENNESS TO
## SCIENTIFIC DATA

Until the last few years Catholic moral theology has generally not been known for its use of scientific data in arriving at moral judgments, but in theory it seems that Catholic moral theology has traditionally proposed a stance or posture which is open to the importance of the data of the sciences in the moral judgment. From the theological perspective moral theology has never excluded the human and the rational from its considerations. In contrast, some forms of Protestant ethics have downplayed the role of the natural, the human, the rational, and consequently the data of science in the Christian moral judgment. An assumption that everything human stands under the corrupting influence of sin would also argue against the theological use of the data of the sciences.[1]

The history of Roman Catholic thinking especially in the area of the relationship between Christian ethics and human

---

[1] One example of a Protestant approach to Christian ethics which does not give enough importance to the data of science is the Christian ethics proposed by Karl Barth. Barth's position will be developed more specifically in Chapter 6.

ethics shows a willingness to enter into coalition with various forms of human and rational ethics.[2] The same basic acceptance of the human and the natural is illustrated by the concept of love in Catholic theology which has generally included the notion of human longing and fulfillment.[3] Lately there has been much criticism of the wedding of Catholic theology to Greek thought, which obviously has occasioned many problems especially in the light of more contemporary philosophical understandings of man. However, the coalition of Catholic theology with rational Greek philosophy shows the openness of such theology to the insights of reason and the sciences. A theology which is open to the insights of reason is thus in principle open to the data of science. In many ways Greek, and not Hebrew, thought with its emphasis on the ability of man to know the world through reason was the basis for the rise of science in Western civilization.[4]

The philosophical presuppositions of Catholic moral theology also show a theoretical openness to scientific data. Contemporary theologians realize the ambiguity of the term natural law and the fact there are many different philosophical methodologies which have employed that name. In the Catholic tradition the general thrust of the natural law teaching maintains that by his reason man can know the purpose and order which God has put into the world. The judgments of reason do depend upon sense data as a starting point so that empirical data should enter into the final intellectual judgment about the order implanted by God in the universe.

---

[2] Joseph Fuchs, *Human Values and Christian Morality* (Dublin: Gill and Macmillan, 1970).

[3] Martin C. D'Arcy, *The Mind and Heart of Love* (New York: Meridian Books, 1956). Compare this approach from within the Catholic tradition with Anders Nygren, *Agape and Eros* (New York: Harper Torchbooks, 1969).

[4] For one example of the failure to give sufficient credit to the Greek influence, see Harvey Cox, *The Secular City* (New York: Macmillan, 1965).

Likewise, nature as the principle of operation in every living organism is manifested in the activities of the thing itself.

## PRACTICAL SUSPICIONS OF SCIENTIFIC DATA

Despite a theoretical openness to science, Roman Catholic theology in general and moral theology in particular have too often in the past neglected the data of the sciences and expressed positive hostility to science. In the nineteenth century the scientific findings on evolution seemed to contradict the traditional Catholic teaching on creation. In general the spirit of the hierarchical magisterium of the nineteenth century was against the new developments that were taking place in science, politics and philosophy. In the political realm the encyclicals of Gregory XVI and Pius IX, especially the *Syllabus of Errors*, seemed at times to deny any validity to the new political and cultural developments.[5] All must admit that the liberalism of the time was far from perfect, but the solution for the Church should not have been a total repudiation of the present and an attempt to turn back the clock to an earlier period of history.[6]

The letter of Pius IX to the Archbishop of Munich in 1863 expressed reservations about the Congress of Catholic intellectuals organized by Döllinger, who hoped to bring Catholic teaching into contact with modern philosophy and science.[7] Later there would be many other warnings from the hierarchical magisterium about the dangers involved in such an attempt to bring Catholic teaching abreast of the contempo-

---

[5] The famous last proposition of the *Syllabus* reads: "Romanus Pontifex potest ac debet cum progressu, cum liberalismo, et cum recenti civilitate sese reconciliare et componere" (*Enchiridion Symbolorum*, ed. H. Denzinger, *et al.* [32d ed.; Barcelona: Herder, 1963], n. 2980).

[6] Étienne Borne, "Le problème majeur du Syllabus: vérité et liberté," *Recherches et Débats*, L (1965), 26-42.

[7] *Acta Sanctae Sedis*, VIII (1874-75), 436-442.

rary developments in science and philosophy. The later Roman insistence on Thomas Aquinas as the patron of Catholic philosophy and theology and the insistence that Catholic theology be taught according to the approach, teaching and principles of Thomas Aquinas was another attempt to make sure that Catholic thinking was removed from contact with contemporary philosophical and scientific advances.[8] No one can deny that good effects have resulted from the Thomistic revival, such as the papal teaching on social justice which has been an important contribution on the part of the Roman Catholic Church. However, the insistence on following Thomist thought in Catholic theology and philosophy was in reality an attempt to safeguard Catholic thinking against the prevailing philosophical and scientific thought. The seminary situation in which Catholic theology existed also contributed to its isolation from contemporary thought. Ironically, the popes in the last two centuries have used Thomas Aquinas for exactly the opposite of what he himself tried to do in his own lifetime, for Thomas attempted to understand the Christian message in the thought patterns which were then contemporary.

The twentieth century witnessed a continuation and fortification of the approach taken by the hierarchical magisterium in the nineteenth century. The modernist crisis, which was never really resolved except in a juridical way, illustrated the continuing tensions in Catholic life and thought. The clash with science and scientific data reverberated especially in the area of scriptural studies. Protestant Scripture scholars in the nineteenth century began to apply to biblical studies the tools of historical scholarship which had been employed in other historical disciplines with the result of dramatically changing the Christian's understanding of the

---

[8] Leo XIII, *Aeterni Patris,* August 5, 1879, *Acta Sanctae Sedis,* XII 1879), 97-115. For a reference to the major papal statements on the authority of St. Thomas, see Denzinger, especially n. 3601-3624 with the editor's introduction.

Word of God in the Scriptures.[9] Generally speaking the replies of the Biblical Commission, plus other disciplinary action, forced Catholic Scripture scholars, at the very minimum, to be very wary of employing the tools of historical criticism.[10] Catholic Scripture scholars finally received some encouragement to use this historical criticism from the Encyclical of Pius XII, *Divino afflante Spiritu* of 1943.[11]

In the area of moral theology the greatest source of tension has been in the relationship of moral theology to psychology and psychiatry. Just a few years ago there was a widespread opinion in psychology and psychiatry that Catholic thinking did not really accept their sciences.[12] The tensions experienced by someone like Marc Oraison, who has attempted to work in an interdisciplinary way with moral theology and psychology and psychiatry, indicate the problems existing in this area. As late as 1961, a Roman Congregation expressed a definite mistrust of psychoanalysis.[13] However, Catholic theologians have lately been working in this area to show there should be no conflict between theology and psychology or psychiatry, although one might strongly disagree with the metaphysical presuppositions of a particular school of psychoanalysis.[14] This healthy attitude of cooper-

---

[9] John Dillenberger and Claude Welch, *Protestant Christianity* (New York: Charles Scribner's Sons, 1954), pp. 189-198.

[10] Thomas Aquinas Collins, O.P., and Raymond E. Brown, S.S., "Church Pronouncements," *Jerome Biblical Commentary*, eds. R. E. Brown, S.S., J. A. Fitzmyer, S.J., R. E. Murphy, O.Carm. (Englewood Cliffs, N.J.: Prentice-Hall, 1968), pp. 624-632.

[11] *Acta Apostolicae Sedis*, XXXV (1943), 309 ff.

[12] Lawrence K. Frank, "Psychology and Social Order," in *The Human Meaning of the Social Sciences*, ed. Daniel Lerner (New York: Meridian Books, 1959), p. 237.

[13] *A.A.S.*, LIII (1961), 571.

[14] John C. Ford, S.J., and Gerald Kelly, S.J., *Contemporary Moral Theology* (Westminster, Md.: Newman Press, 1958), I, pp. 174-352; Louis Beirnaert, *Expérience chrétienne et psychologie* (Paris: Éditions de L'Epi, 1964).

ation and dialogue with science and even with contemporary philosophical thought seems to be in keeping with the best in the Roman Catholic tradition which had always admitted that there could not be a conflict between the truths of faith and the truths of reason. Unfortunately various circumstances brought about an approach on the part of the Catholic Church which was not in keeping with the best of its own tradition.

## CONTEMPORARY OPENNESS TO SCIENTIFIC DATA

Today the attitude of Catholic moral theology bespeaks an openness to the data of science and underscores the need for interdisciplinary approaches to particular moral problems. The Second Vatican Council speaks gratefully of the contribution of the sciences: "Thanks to the experience of past ages, the progress of the sciences, and the treasure hidden in the various forms of human culture, the nature of man himself is more clearly revealed, and new roads to truth are opened. These benefits profit the Church. . . ."[15] The Council goes on to apply the basic Catholic teaching that there cannot be a true conflict between faith and reason and thus argues for the legitimate autonomy of culture and the sciences because of which the sciences should have the freedom to develop in accord with their own scientific principles.[16]

What explains the greater openness to the data of science in the work of theology today? There are both theoretical reasons and more practical circumstances that explain the present emphasis even in the statements of the hierarchical magisterium on the harmonious relationship between faith or theology and science. From a theoretical viewpoint con-

---

[15] *Pastoral Constitution on the Church in the Modern World*, n. 44.
[16] *Ibid.*, n. 59.

temporary theology stresses a greater continuity between this world and the next and gives a greater significance to man's life in this world so that theology can look more positively upon human accomplishments and the scientific findings of reason. Perhaps the most important methodological change bringing about a greater awareness of the role of the sciences in theology has been the shift from the classicist worldview to a more historically minded worldview. A more historically conscious worldview, as described for example by Bernard Lonergan, sees reality more in dynamic terms of growth, development and change and employs a more inductive methodology. Greater attention is given to time and history as well as to the particular, the individual and the concrete.[17] Such a worldview with its corresponding methodology would be more appreciative of the role of the sciences in contributing to our understanding of man and the world and the ways in which men should act. In the past Catholic theology has not always avoided a somewhat *a priori* and deductive approach which was accentuated by an overly inflated argument from authority and tradition.

The more historically minded worldview has given a theoretical justification for the understanding of change and development in the moral teaching of the Church. Changing empirical data obviously calls for a change in the norms and even the values of a particular historical time. John Courtney Murray invoked the understanding of historical consciousness to explain the change in the teaching of the Church on religious liberty, and the relationship between Church and State. Murray willingly affirmed that the older teaching was true in the historical circumstances of the nineteenth cen-

---

[17] Bernard Lonergan, S.J., "A Transition from a Classicist World View to Historical Mindedness," in *Law for Liberty: The Role of Law in the Church Today*, ed. James E. Biechler (Baltimore: Helicon Press, 1967), pp. 126-133.

tury, but the teaching of the Church on religious liberty was situated in a "given historical-social-political context."[18] Murray understands the crucial development of this debate in the following terms of historical consciousness: "The link between religious freedom and limited constitutional government and the link between the freedom of the Church and the freedom of the people—these were not nineteenth century theological political insights. They became available only within twentieth century perspectives, created by the signs of the times. The two truths were not forged by abstract deductive logic but by history, by the historical advance of totalitarian government, and by the corresponding new appreciation of man's dignity in society."[19]

Personally, I think Murray used this device somewhat too facilely to protect the teaching of the Church from being in error at any time. In the nineteenth century there were available more than just the two solutions of accepting the liberalism of the day or turning back the clock to an older period of history. However, the methodological approach employed by Murray and frequently used by Catholic theologians arguing for change in other areas of Catholic teaching does give normative importance to the changing and contingent historical reality which is the subject matter of the sciences. A recognition of the change in other areas of the Church's teaching, for example, usury, and the arguments proposed for other changes such as contraception also invoke the changing understanding of reality as known often through the sciences.[20]

---

[18] John Courtney Murray, S.J., *The Problem of Religious Freedom* (Westminster, Md.: Newman Press, 1965), p. 85.

[19] *Ibid.*, p. 100.

[20] John T. Noonan, Jr., *The Scholastic Analysis of Usury* (Cambridge, Mass.: Harvard University Press, 1957); Noonan, *Contraception: A History of Its Treatment by the Catholic Theologians and Canonists* (Cambridge, Mass.: Harvard University Press, 1965); Noonan, "Authority, Usury and Contraception," *Cross Currents*, XVI (1966), 55-79.

The traditional Catholic approach to moral theology, as outlined above, in principle and at its best has been open to the data of science not merely as the material to which it applies its moral norms and values but also as entering into the very meaning of moral values and norms. Despite the openness in theory to the data of science, a classicist approach, an authoritarian Church structure and official teaching office, a fear of the findings of science, and an overprotective attitude with regard to Catholic truth and the sheep of the flock have all contributed to the fact that Catholic moral theology until recently did not see the role and importance of the sciences in forming moral norms and judgments.

What is the precise relationship between moral theology and the sciences? How do the other sciences relate to the final moral judgment? The question exists not only in terms of the relationship between moral theology or ethics and the data of the sciences, but also within the context of the self-understanding that the sciences, especially the human sciences, have of themselves. Until recently the empirical sciences such as sociology claimed only a neutral attitude towards morality, since sociology only observed phenomena and data. "In contrast to the normative sciences, empirical social study, like all empirical science, is neutral and non-tendentious in method."[21] Some contemporary social scientists are no longer content with such a view of their own method, and a ferment is rising especially among younger sociologists calling for a more normative approach to the discipline.[22]

From the viewpoint of moral theology an older approach could perhaps find a strict division between moral theology

---

[21] Wilhelm Korff, "Empirical Social Study and Ethics," *Concilium,* XXXV (1968), 7-23.

[22] Alvin W. Gouldner, *Coming Crisis in Western Sociology* (New York: Basic Books, 1970).

with its values and norms and the sciences with their interest in facts and observable data. In theory an older Catholic theology would not necessarily have made such a sharp distinction, for a Thomistic approach realized that observation helped us to discern the order of God in the world, and human understanding and judgment are in some way dependent upon the data of sense experience. Today there appears to be among both Catholic and Protestant ethicians a growing awareness that such a simple division between moral theology and the sciences is not possible. Robert Springer maintains that the social sciences are in some ways normative in themselves and in their relationship to moral theology. While encouraging the need for a closer dependence of moral science on empirical science, Springer does not want to make a total identity between them as is evident from such expressions as "in some ways normative" or "in some sense normative."[23]

Karl Rahner strongly insists on the need for future dialogue between theology and the sciences. Rahner maintains that in the past the decisive partner in the dialogue with theology was philosophy, and this philosophy was one philosophy despite inner tensions and controversies. Today the real partner in the dialogue with theology is the sciences, and this partner is no longer mediated through philosophy.[24] There remains some ambiguity in this statement, but it does not seem that Rahner is saying that ethical norms can be simplistically reduced to the findings of the empirical sciences. It seems more accurate to interpret Rahner as arguing that philosophy no longer furnishes the intellectual framework within which the sciences function and from which

---

[23] Robert H. Springer, "Conscience, Behavioral Science and Absolutes," in *Absolutes in Moral Theology?*, ed. Charles ·E. Curran (Washington/ Cleveland: Corpus Books, 1968), pp. 19-56.

[24] Karl Rahner, "Philosophy and Philosophizing in Theology," *Theology Digest*, XVI (Sesquicentennial issue, 1968), 28-29.

they derive their fullest meaning. Rahner certainly would not deny that the moral judgment involves a critical heremeutical principle by which the ultimate moral judgment is made in the light of the evidence including the scientific conclusions, but the moral judgment does not necessarily and always coincide with the conclusion of any one science.

The realization of the import and role of the empirical sciences in the moral judgment is not limited to one school of Catholic theologians or even to those who are arguing for change in some of the previous teachings of the hierarchical magisterium. Germain Grisez has developed a concept of natural law which leads him to the conclusion that artificial contraception is intrinsically wrong, but of more interest to our purpose is the emphasis that Grisez places on the role of the empirical sciences in making the final moral judgment.[25] Grisez holds that the first prescription of practical reason, which is not derived from any facts, is that good should be pursued and that actions appropriate in that pursuit should be done while actions which interfere with or do not help that pursuit should be avoided.[26] This first basic principle really contains no specific content as to the goods that man must attain. One must begin by examining man's basic inclinations. "What are all the inclinations with which man is endowed prior to acculturation or any choice of his own? This question requires and can be settled only by empirical enquiry."[27] Grisez then develops a list of these basic goods or inclinations in the light of psychology and anthropology.

The ecumenical aspect of Christian ethics today indicates growing convergences between Catholic and Protestant theology, although some forms of Protestant theology especially in the approach of Protestant liberalism have con-

---

[25] Germain G. Grisez, *Contraception and the Natural Law* (Milwaukee: Bruce, 1964).
[26] *Ibid.*, p. 62.
[27] *Ibid.*, p. 64.

sistently been open to the sciences and scientific data. Perhaps the greatest difference in contemporary approaches is the insistence frequently found in Catholic theology on an ontological understanding of man and the role of the sciences in discovering the being of man. Protestant theology generally places less emphasis on an ontological understanding of man and thus formulates a slightly different methodological approach to the place of the sciences in the moral judgment.

Max L. Stackhouse of Andover Newton Seminary proposes such an approach to ethics which attempts to formulate middle level normative statements, provisional norms and penultimate ends. These middle level norms are not derived deductively nor inductively, but rather they are analytically derived from the ethos. Stackhouse sees this as a redefinition of ethics and its methodology in the light of the importance of the data of the social sciences. This analytic ethic works by "defining the ethos and the historical conditions that influenced it with regard to competing norms of meaning, purpose, and righteousness in ways that lead to action." Stackhouse realizes the error in saying that the normative is derived merely from the prevailing ethos and the norms statistically present in that ethos. The ethicist does not merely respond to what he finds, but rather he "critically attempts to discern those structural and functional moral principles or norms that are in operation."[28] In his analytical task of trying to validate some norms against others, the ethicist needs a meta-ethical model which is also dependent upon technical data. Stackhouse admits a great dependence of the "ought" on the "is," but the explicit "oughts" are not, or need not be, mere reflections of the "is"; they can be rearranged consciously into new provisional "ought" patterns and tested

---

[28] Max L. Stackhouse, "Technical Data and Ethical Norms: Some Theoretical Considerations," *Journal for the Scientific Study of Religion,* V (1965-66), 196.

against the historically changing situation.[29] Perhaps there still remains too great a role for the "is" in such a theory, but Stackhouse in principle stoutly guards against a simplistic reduction of the "ought" to the "is."

Today theologians, both Protestant and Catholic, acknowledge the importance of the sciences and the fact that the data of the sciences, especially the human and behavioral sciences, enters into the establishment of moral values and norms. But there are also limitations connected with these sciences concerning their contribution to the moral norms. Just as it is poor moral methodology to exclude the sciences from contributing to the moral norms so it is poor moral methodology to simplistically reduce the moral norm to the findings of science especially the empirical sciences which describe the present state of human existence.

## LIMITATIONS OF THE SCIENCES

The limitations of the sciences in contributing to moral judgments stand out in the light of the total Christian mystery. As a result one can never make morally normative what is de facto present in any one moment of existence. The ethical is not the same as the statistical norm. The Christian vision sees the present in the light of the full Christian mystery which also embraces the future. The eschatological pull of the future is a negative critique of every existing reality and structure. Christian eschatology calls for a constant attempt to transform the present in the light of the future which has become proleptically present in the Paschal Mystery of Jesus Christ. Sciences and the empirical sciences which deal with present reality cannot of themselves come to grips with the transforming and future oriented aspect of the Christian vision of man and his world. Christian ethics

---

[29] *Ibid.*, p. 197.

must view reality in terms of an eschatological tension, but
one cannot eliminate the tension by reducing all things to
what is currently existing or by naively positing a future
utopia in the present. Insofar as the sciences merely tell us
about the present they cannot adequately and completely
fulfill a normative function. Likewise Christian eschatology
would not necessarily see the future as just an extrapolation
from the present, but the "in-breaking" future calls for some
discontinuity between the present and the future even in this
world.

The Christian vision furnishes another important theological reason for not making the present reality as viewed
through science, especially the social or human sciences,
normative for man. Sin is an important but all too often for-
gotten reality in our world, as is evident in some of the theological writing in the early part of the last decade. History
reminds us of the imperfections and even sinfulness as manifested in the ethos of earlier societies. One has to think only
about slavery, the denial of basic human rights to women,
the exploitation of the poor, the failure to adequately divide
the goods of creation so that all men may have what they need
for human existence. The pull of the future and the limitations
and sinfulness of the present are two important theological
reasons arguing for the limitations of all present reality in
furnishing moral norms for man and his world. Somewhat
connected with these theological reasons is the debate in
philosophical ethics about the relationship between the "is"
and the "ought." Ethicists point out the error in going from
the "is" to the "ought."[30] The present can never be simply
identified with what is normative for the Christian.

There are other limitations of the sciences despite their

---

[30] The Problem of "is"-"ought" in relationship to natural law is discussed in a number of studies in *The Natural Law Forum*, IV (1959); V
(1960), and subsequent responses by Bourke and Nagel.

importance in contributing to the establishment of moral norms and the "ought." The theological reasons mentioned above are based on the concept of transcendence. There is also a philosophical aspect to transcendence which argues for the limitations of science and the scientific approaches. This transcendent aspect corresponds to the wonder and awe that man experiences. There is something about man that does transcend the cold rationality of science. In this connection some theologians stress the importance of a Dionysian theology which gives more importance to this aspect of man.[31] Some theologically negative approaches to the sciences and technology emphasize this transcendent aspect of man and see the rational sciences as not corresponding to the fullness of man and the human. I would not see science and technology itself as opposed to the truly human, but the transcendent human aspect appears in the need for man to control and direct the sciences to properly human values and goals. Some would argue that the discontent of many with our contemporary society stems from an overimportance given to science and cold rationality and not enough emphasis given to the seemingly more transcendent dimension of man. At the very least one can and should conclude that the human can never be totally identified with the totality of the scientific.

## LIMITATIONS OF A PARTICULAR SCIENCE

The limitation of any individual science, whether social or a natural science, arises from the fact that an individual science by its very nature does not encompass all aspects of the human reality. Any particular science sees only a particular

---

[31] Sam Keen, "Manifesto for a Dionysian Theology," *Cross Currents*, XIX (1969), 37-54; Keen, *Apology for Wonder* (New York: Harper and Row, 1969).

aspect of reality and cannot be equated with the total human perspective. The conclusions of any one science can never be automatically equated with the moral conclusion. The moral judgment must take into consideration all the different aspects and perspectives of the question especially as these are known through the sciences. The conclusions of any one science are both particular and relative with regard to the universal and final moral judgment. The moral judgment must consider all the different aspects of the question and then reach its final judgment often with the realization that in our complex world nothing is going to be perfect from every particular aspect or perspective. The judgment of any one science is thus relative in the sense that it must be seen in the light of other perspectives and the total human perspective which transcends and thus judges all the more limited judgments which remain always relative to the final, synthesizing moral judgment.

In the past it seems that Roman Catholic theology has erred by identifying the human act with the physical, biological structure of the act, a question that emerges in some aspects of sexual ethics. This does not mean that the biological and physical are not important aspects of reality, but one cannot simply identify the human act with the biological structure of the act itself without considering other aspects of the total human perspective. I would see this inadequate approach behind the teaching against artificial contraception and the generic gravity attached to all sins directly against chastity.

Many of the questions existing in moral theology today, especially in terms of the situation ethics debate, focus on the existence of absolute norms. I deny the existence of "negative absolute norms," i.e. absolute norms in which the forbidden action is described only in terms of the physical structure of the act. I am not asserting that the physical and biological aspect of the act may not be identified with the moral human act, but one has to give other reasons to support this identity of the moral act with the physical or biological structure of the act.

A very important question in contemporary moral discussion is abortion and the crucial problem of the beginning of human life. There is much genetic and biological evidence arguing for the existence of individual human life from the formation of the genotype. Paul Ramsey has competently marshalled this biological evidence, but Ramsey does not seem to explicitly develop the argument that the human or the moral judgment in this case coincides with the biological and genetic judgment.[32] It appears that many people would accept such biological conclusions but do not see this as a convincing argument for the existence of a human person at that time. Ramsey does bring in more than biological criteria when he argues from the impossibility of determining any other time in the course of fetal development through birth at which one could argue that human life begins. In practice I tend to agree with Ramsey's conclusion, but it seems that there is a methodological need to explicitly show that the human moral judgment encompasses more than the biological considerations even though ultimately the moral judgment may be identical with these conclusions.

Germain Grisez carefully distinguishes in theory between the biological or genetic judgment and the moral judgment about the beginning of human life. Grisez acknowledges that the question whether the embryo or the fetus is a human being is perhaps the most important single question in the whole ethical controversy over abortion.[33] This embraces

---

[32] Paul Ramsey, "Points in Deciding about Abortion," in *The Morality of Abortion: Legal and Historical Perspectives,* ed. John T. Noonan, Jr. (Cambridge, Mass.: Harvard University Press, 1970), pp. 60-100; Ramsey, "The Sanctity of Life," *The Dublin Review,* 511 (Spring 1967), 3-23.

[33] Germain G. Grisez, *Abortion: The Myths, the Realities and the Arguments* (New York/Cleveland: Corpus Books, 1970), p. 273.

two different questions. The first question is the factual one about when does the human individual come into being, which is solved by biology. The metaphysical or theological question is quite distinct although the biological facts and conclusions of the first question are relevant. "This further question is: Should we treat all living human individuals as persons, or should we accept a concept of person that will in fact exclude some who are in fact human, alive, and individuals, but who do not meet certain additional criteria we incorporate in the idea of person."[34] I do not agree with the way Grisez states the two different judgments, but such a methodological approach seems more correct because it explicitly makes the necessary distinction between the biological or genetic judgment and the moral judgment. It is also interesting to note in passing that Ramsey usually uses the word individual and not the term person to describe the humanity of the fetus, whereas Grisez explicitly distinguishes between biological individuality and human personhood.

Since the scientific perspective in general is not identical with the human perspective, one can imagine the existence of possible conflicts between the two. The conflicts become even more apparent in the difference between the perspective of a particular science and the human perspective. One illustration of the dangers of making the perspective of one science identical with the human perspective can be seen in some of the comments of the late Nobel Prize winner, Herman J. Muller.[35] Muller, a geneticist, advocated the use of A. I. D. and the establishment of sperm banks both to prevent the deterioration of the human gene pool and to improve the human species. Muller argued that other possible approaches such as genetic engineering are not yet feasible,

---

[34] *Ibid.*
[35] For a collection of Muller's articles written before 1961, see *Studies in Genetics: The Selected Papers of H. J. Muller* (Bloomington, Ind.: Indiana University Press, 1962).

but mankind today should use the means that are available. "The obstacles to carrying out such an improvement by selection are psychological ones based on antiquated traditions from which we can emancipate ourselves, but the obstacles to do so by treatment of the genetic materials are rooted in the inherent difficulties of the physico-chemical situation."[36]

Such a statement of the question already indicates a view that fails to consider all the aspects of the question. There may very well be moral obstacles in the way of widespread use of A. I. D. Muller here even seems to use the term psychological to indicate that psychology could easily convince people to change their minds and adopt this procedure. But such a practice would raise questions for a number of other scientific disciplines such as anthropology and sociology as well as psychology. What effect would this have on the family structure or the husband-wife relationship? Many other factors merit consideration before a truly human and moral judgment could be properly arrived at. The fact that biology can totally separate the procreative and love union aspects of sexuality does not mean that mankind should necessarily adopt such an approach. Recent comments by Robert Francoeur, also a professional and highly competent biologist, seem too easily to accept the fact that man should adopt whatever biology makes possible without taking into account the many other perspectives which the human judgment must include.[37]

---

[36] Hermann J. Muller, "Means and Aims in Human Genetic Betterment," in *The Control of Human Heredity and Evolution*, ed. T. M. Sonneborn (New York: Macmillan, 1965), p. 100.

[37] Robert T. Francoeur, "Morality and the New Embryology," *IDOC, International*, North American Edition, VIII (August 15, 1970), 81-96. Francoeur does consider other aspects of the question but his last sentence is revealing: "Reproductive technology has demolished practically all our models and patterns in these areas; new models, symbols and patterns must be evolved if man is to survive."

The inherent limitations of any one science in relation to the human also appear in discussions about the limits to be placed on scientific experimentation. Edward A. Shils perceptively points out in the case of sociology that "the creation of techniques for the direct observation of living persons and contemporary institutions, the deepening of intellectual curiosity about the motives and the very tissue of social life, the diminution of inhibitions on intrusiveness into other persons' affairs, and the concomitant formation of techniques for perceiving these deeper and subtler things have precipitated problems of ponderable ethical significance."[38] The ethical values endangered by such new scientific methods are human dignity, the autonomy of individual judgment and action, and the maintenance of privacy.

Shils indicates that an interviewer can deceive his interviewee in such a way that might benefit the objectivity of his science, but it would still be morally improper to elicit information by deception. Likewise attempts to manipulate the person so that he reveals more about himself than he wants to reveal or knows he is revealing seem to be morally questionable. Shils in his concluding paragraphs discusses some of the factors operating against moral restraint in these areas. "On the other side is the *scientific* attitude and the impatience with imperfection, which are also parts of our cultural inheritance from Bacon, Condorcet, Comte, Marx, down to Bernal and Skinner, and which envision men of science ruling society, bringing it into order, overcoming man's imperfections by the application of scientific knowledge."[39]

The question of scientific experimentation brings into clear relief the inherent imperfections and limitations of the ap-

---

[38] Edward A. Shils, "Social Inquiry and the Autonomy of the Individual," in *The Human Meaning of the Social Sciences*, ed. Daniel Lerner (Cleveland/New York: Meridian Books, 1959), p. 117.

[39] *Ibid.*, pp. 151-152.

proach of any one science. There are human moral concerns which place definite limits on scientific experimentation and thus make it more difficult or even impossible to obtain helpful scientific knowledge. The moral limitations on experimentation are very evident in the areas of medicine, biology and genetics. Here again the basic reason stems from the possible conflict between the rights of the individual and the increase of scientific knowledge or the betterment of the whole human race. Since man cannot dispose of his life and existence in any way he might see fit, there are inherent limitations on experiments he can even voluntarily undergo for the good of the human species. At the very minimum there must be a fit proportion between the risk involved and the good to be obtained. The question of consent and of the real freedom of the patient to consent in certain circumstances has occasioned discussion in the literature.[40] There are also questions about the right of parents to give consent for their children to undergo some forms of experimentation especially when these children are confined to institutions.[41] In general, recognition of man's dignity is illustrated by the different way in which the researcher deals with human beings and with non-human subjects of experimentation. There are definite limitations placed on scientific methodologies and investigations because of the inherent human dignity of the person which can be violated because of the narrow perspective of any one of the sciences.

Another limiting factor in the role of scientific data in forming moral norms comes from the lack of agreement within a particular discipline which is particularly true in the behavioral and human sciences but not lacking even in the

---

[40] John Fletcher, "Human Experimentation: Ethics in the Consent Situation," *Law and Contemporary Problems,* XXXII (1967), 620-649.

[41] Paul Ramsey, *The Patient as Person* (New Haven and London: Yale University Press, 1970), pp. 11-58. Ramsey's discussion includes the general question of consent and its application in the case of children.

natural sciences. Geneticists, for example, are not in agreement on the extent of the deterioration of the human gene pool due to the deleterious effects of gene mutations.[42] Political scientists debate the validity of the "domino theory" which has played an important role in the United States foreign policy in Southeast Asia. The psychological and psychiatric evidence on the normality of homosexual behavior is conflicting so that different authorities can be cited for and against the fact that homosexuality is regarded as abnormal or pathological.[43] In contemporary society juries are frequently faced with conflicting testimony of different experts in their psychiatric evaluation of the same person. Somehow the human and moral judgment must be made in the light of this conflicting testimony but also in the light of many other perspectives. There is need for a moral hermenuetic which can not only bring together the different perspectives of all the sciences but also deal with the disagreements existing within the same scientific perspective.

## DANGER OF IDENTIFYING THE SCIENTIFIC AND THE ETHICAL

The great importance and the limitations of the sciences in contributing to moral judgment create the tension involved in the use of the sciences in contributing to moral norms. Moral theology should, in my judgment, avoid the extreme solutions of those who do not give any place to the sciences,

---

[42] Compare, for example, Hermann J. Muller, "Better Genes for Tomorrow," in *The Population Crisis and the Use of World Resources,* ed. Stuart Mudd (The Hague: Dr. W. Junk Publisher, 1964), p. 315, and Theodosius Dobzhansky, "Changing Man," *Science,* CLV (1967), 409.

[43] For a symposium which places more emphasis on the favorable judgment of the sciences to homosexuality, see *The Same Sex,* ed. Ralph W. Weltge (Philadelphia/Boston: Pilgrim Press, 1969). This is developed at greater length in Chapter 6.

especially the empirical sciences, in determining moral norms and those who too simplistically reduce the moral judgment to the conclusions of the sciences. There are indications in the writings of John Giles Milhaven that he does at times appear to endorse this type of reductionism. Milhaven has made important contributions to contemporary moral theology not only by his insistence on the importance of the sciences but also by other historical and systematic research.[44] Perhaps in his insistence on the role of the sciences he fails at times to nuance the precise role of the sciences in the moral judgment.[45]

In an essay on homosexuality Milhaven asserts that the Christian proponent of the new morality turns to the experience of the community, preeminently the critical experience of the psychologists, psychiatrists and analysts.[46] On the basis of such evidence, although there is contrary evidence favorable to homosexuality which Milhaven judges to be fragmentary, Milhaven concludes: "In one sense, therefore, the Christian of the new morality condemns homosexual behavior more severely than a Christian of the old.[47] Milhaven's discussion of homosexuality will be considered at greater length in Chapter 6.

Milhaven appears at times to reduce the moral judgment to the conclusions of the empirical sciences. "Hopefully preceding pages have made clear that for contemporary ethics the use of the behavioral sciences is morality."[48] On earlier

----

[44] John Giles Milhaven, *Toward a New Catholic Morality* (Garden City, N.Y.: Doubleday, 1970), especially Chapters Nine and Ten.

[45] *Ibid*, p. 62. In an article in *Theological Studies* in 1971 which he graciously sent to me, Milhaven compares the moral judgment with the esthetic judgment. I consider this to be a welcome emphasis in his thought and hope it will overcome his seeming overemphasis on the role of the behavioral sciences.

[46] Milhaven, p. 63.

[47] *Ibid.*, pp. 66-67.

[48] *Ibid.*, p. 125.

pages Milhaven made the following statements: "What *ought* a homosexual do? The answer could well be: what the psychiatrist tells him to do. Since the new Christian ethic holds no absolute principles, even in the sexual domain, but aims solely at that fullness of personal living concretely possible for the given individual, the ethical goal for the individual need not differ from the goal a good psychiatrist would have for him."[49] His discussion of promiscuity and theft a few pages earlier seemed incomplete precisely because the discussion focused on the levels of personal involvement, but sociological aspects such as the effects on society or on other individuals were not mentioned.

Milhaven asserts that the ethical importance of professional and scientific experience severely limits the contribution of the general moral theologian or Christian ethicist. In fact there will no longer be ethical generalists but only specialists who will need extensive formation in the pertinent behavioral sciences or in corresponding professional training and internship. Milhaven does maintain there are strictly theological elements of Christian ethics which are most important, but they are fewest in number.[50]

In discussing the questions of medical ethics Milhaven claims that the human values at stake are not difficult to discern and one need be neither ethicist nor doctor to recognize them. "But one does need scientific experience and knowledge to answer the ethical question—how can the values be incarnated in the day-by-day practice of the hospital? How should a new drug be tested before use . . . ?[51] But a number of the questions posed by Milhaven in this series of questions do require and presuppose reflective moral reasoning and more than just scientific knowledge and experience. The

---

[49] *Ibid.*, p. 120.
[50] *Ibid.*, p. 121.
[51] *Ibid.*, p. 54.

original title of one essay by Milhaven, "Exit for Ethicists," implies that by the year 2000 there will be no further need of ethicists. "Since they more reliably and extensively bring to light constants of human behavior, the behavioral sciences and any professional or trained experience will more and more give answers to the new kind of ethical question."[52]

There are, however, indications that Milhaven does not want to make a complete identity between the moral norm and the empirical discoveries of the behavioral sciences. He speaks of the behavioral sciences as "transforming and in good part constituting the methodology of Christian ethics."[53] In response to the criticism of his statement that good medicine is good morality Milhaven clarifies his understanding of good medicine "not merely in a technical sense, but in a sense of the humane, moral, dedicated practice of medicine that is the ideal of the good doctor."[54] This explanation seems to introduce moral and ethical notions to serve as a critique and guide for medicine. Milhaven also briefly compares the moral judgment with the judgment of the artist and the aesthete.[55]

Milhaven emphasizes the change in ethical methodology because the ethical question is significantly changing to the means by which we can accomplish our ethical goals. In our contemporary society we so often agree on the goals of justice for all or a share of the goods of creation for all men, but the important question concerns the means of obtaining these goals. I would agree that these questions will be more prevalent in the future and that Catholic theology (e.g. papal social encyclicals) in the past has generally avoided the important questions of how to bring about the desired

---

[52] *Ibid.*, p. 52.
[53] *Ibid.*, p. 125.
[54] *Ibid.*, pp. 53-54.
[55] *Ibid.*, pp. 50-51.

changes. Likewise, the sciences will be of great help in this matter, but there will still be a need for reflective moral reasoning on the ways in which men make their ethical and human judgments on the goals they choose, and on the means to attain the goals.

Milhaven correctly sees the need for a much greater role of the empirical sciences in the formulation of moral judgments and norms. Even if he does not totally reduce the ethical judgment to the scientific judgment, his theory still places too much emphasis on the role of the behavioral sciences so that his methodological approach lacks that transcendent, creative and critical aspect that must be a part of the methodology of Christian ethics. There are indications that Milhaven does not want to lose this aspect, but his theory does not seem to allow enough room for it.

There is no doubt that in the future the sciences will play a greater role in determining and contributing to ethical norms. Even now the knowledge explosion coming from the findings of the sciences has created a human problem as man tried to find human meaning and intelligibility in the midst of so much data. But the human problem remains that of finding human meaning and intelligibility in the midst of such complexity. The sciences in the future will only add to the complexity of the data and make even more crucial men's search for meaning and intelligibility.[56]

## FROM "CAN" TO "OUGHT"

The relationship between moral theology and science in the past has focused primarily on the question of how the conclusions and findings of science will enter into the moral judgment. Today there is a new and even more important

---

[56] *Collection: Papers by Bernard Lonergan*, S.J., ed. F. E. Crowe, S.J. (New York: Herder and Herder, 1967), pp. 252-267.

question emerging: If man has the knowledge and power to do something, should it be done? Should we ever say "no" to the possibilities that some science places before us? The other question involved the relationship between the "is" and the "ought"; this question involves the relationship between the "can" and the "ought." Ought we do whatever is scientifically possible? In general I deny that man ought to do whatever is scientifically possible.

It has become almost trite to say that we are living in revolutionary times, but there are many indications which point in this direction. Through the knowledge and application of science man now possesses extraordinary powers over his life and his future. Man is now able to some extent to guide and direct his own evolution. The problem has been discussed in the theological literature of the past few decades in terms of man and his technology. The same basic question confronts man as he assays the knowledge that science gives him to plan his own future. Some theologians such as Jacques Ellul see technology as a threat to Christian values and a true Christian understanding of reality; whereas Victor Ferkiss argues that man can use technology and science to accomplish truly human goals.[57]

Ferkiss maintains that technological man has not yet come into existence, but this constitutes the challenge for modern man. By definition he sees technological man as man "in control of his own development within the context of a meaningful philosophy of the role of technology in human evolution . . . . Technological man will be man at home with science and technology, for he will dominate them rather than be dominated by them; indeed he will be so at home that the question of who is in charge will never even arise."[58]

---

[57] Jacques Ellul, *The Technological Society* (New York: Vintage Books, 1967); Victor Ferkiss, *Technological Man: The Myth and the Reality* (New York and Toronto: New American Library, 1970).

[58] Ferkiss, pp. 202-203.

Ferkiss realizes that man transcends his technology and must direct it to truly human goals so that "man can abandon the age old fight against nature for survival and accept nature as a companion so that man can then turn to his real purposes which are play and the cultivation of the inner space of the individual and society.[59] Although man may have all these new powers (and here Ferkiss is too optimistic about man's being able to rationally control these powers), Ferkiss earlier in the book realized that these new powers would not overcome the beast within man.[60]

Ferkiss includes in his understanding of technology all the scientific advances of the present including cybernetics and the new biology. Cybernetics as a science is only about two decades old, but it already promises to bring about great changes in man's control and communication of knowledge. Computers have a memory and an ability to perform some types of calculations which far exceed man's own powers. The development of cybernetics raises in an even more acute way the problem of the relationship between man and the machine.[61]

Perhaps the best illustration of man's scientific power to direct and change his own future comes from the biological revolution.[62] People debate whether or not such changes can truly be called a revolution, but such knowledge and power can definitely be revolutionary in its effects on human exis-

[59] *Ibid.*, p. 212.

[60] *Ibid.*, p. 34.

[61] Norman Wiener, *The Human Use of Human Beings: Cybernetics and Society* (Garden City, N.Y.: Doubleday Anchor Books, 1954); Ian G. Barbour, *Science and Secularity: The Ethics of Technology* (New York: Harper and Row, 1970), pp. 95-115.

[62] For summaries of the possibilities of the new biology and some ethical discussions, see Barbour, pp. 76-94; Francoeur, *IDOC*, VIII (August 15, 1970), 81-96; Leroy Augenstein, *Come, Let Us Play God* (New York: Harper and Row, 1969); Paul Ramsey, *Fabricated Man* (New Haven and London: Yale University Press, 1970).

tence. Geneticists have now cracked the genetic code. Genetic engineering will make it possible to change a particular molecule in the complex structure of the gene and thus eliminate deleterious effects or bring about the desired good effects by altering presently inherited and programmed physiological and psychological processes. In the very near future man will have the power not only to know but also to determine the sex of his children. Medical science will have the technical know-how to make the thousand year old man a prospect.

There is already talk of freezing human life to keep it in existence for an indefinite future. Artificial processes may substitute for the whole process of reproduction so that fertilization will take place in vitro, and the embryo will develop outside the womb of the mother thus completely severing reproduction from sexuality if man so desires. Cloning, the replication of a genetically identical individual from the cells of a complex, multicellular living organism will be a possibility. It will be possible to replicate a very large number of identical twins of people who have proven to be successful and outstanding human beings. Through nerve gases and germs it will be possible to destroy virtually all human and animal life in the world. Even today through A. I. D. and sperm banks man can embark on a genetic program to improve the human species. These questions from just one science spotlight the problem of man's control of and responsibility for shaping the future of the human race. However, just because man has the knowledge and power to do such things, it does not follow that he morally ought to do them.

In view of the major thrust of this paper concerning the important but limited role of the sciences in the moral judgment, there is a clear need for a human control of scientific and technological advances. In principle one can conclude that there are things which man can do that he ought not do.

The inherent limitations of science can be seen in terms of the new capabilities of biology and genetics. Is it human to clone man? What psychological, sociological and antropo!ogical effects will occur? Should we separate procreation from sexuality and marriage? Should we increase the time span of human life? What effect will this have on the generation gap which seems so prominent in our contemporary society? The perspectives of any one science are thus limited by the perspectives of the other sciences and by the totally human perspective. Man also knows only too well that science can not overcome the hardness of the human heart which Christian theology has called sin. The history of mankind sadly chronicles the fact that men have used economic power, political power, ecclesiastical power and nuclear power for selfish gains and as means of exploiting others. The fact that men might abuse genetic power does not mean that mankind must necessarily avoid ever having such power, but it does realistically call for concern about the control of such power.

Contemporary experience also points to the need for some human control over technology or a particular science. The present concern over ecology and the needs of the environment testify to the fact that man cannot interfere with nature whenever and wherever some particular end might be achieved. The great industrial and technological advances of the last few years have not been unambiguous precisely because of the harmful human consequences that have accompanied them. The needs of the environment serve as a constant reminder that man must take into consideration more than the narrow perspective of a particular science when he is deciding what constitutes truly human progress.

Another important factor in the development of science and technology springs from the question of social priorities on a national and international scope. Any nation only has a limited amount of resources which must be used to advance the more important human concerns. It seems that in the

past human needs have suffered because of excessive spend-
ing for military, industrial and scientific purposes. Limited
resources call for rigorous moral judgment about the alloca-
tion of limited resources for the good of human society.

The fact that there are limitations on the development of
the sciences and that man necessarily ought not do what a
particular science can do does not mean that one has to be
opposed to human and scientific progress. By no means. One
can believe in and work for human progress (understood in
a sense to be explained later) without baptizing all possible
advances of particular sciences. The challenge for theology
and Christian ethics is to establish models, principles and
themes which will adequately appreciate the reality of human progress with all its accompanying ambiguity and critically judge the contributions of the particular sciences to
such progress. A realistic approach realizes that at times one
might have to say no to the capabilities of a particular science in the name of the truly human.

It seems that theology in the last decade has produced
some theological models which are not truly critical. Perhaps
Catholic theology has too often been in dialogue with its own
past and not with the contemporary problems of the day.
There is no doubt that an older Roman Catholic theology
tended to be suspicious of the sciences and did not give
enough importance to human progress, growth, change and
development. But now, especially in terms of the dialogue
with the contemporary world, there is the need to be more
critical about the whole concept of human progress and
scientific development. In general, the approach should be
one that is open to human progress but realizes that human
progress does not necessarily coincide with the advance of
every particular science, and the model for human progress
does not necessarily coincide with the models of the progress
of technology or of a particular science. In the search for
more adequate models to deal constructively and critically

with the question of man's control of his own future, a number of different theological models and themes will be considered.

## THEOLOGICAL CONSIDERATION OF MAN

The understanding of man is a most fundamental theological concept. Nobody can deny that today man does have the power to direct and to a certain extent determine his future. Man today through his scientific knowledge and power shares more and more in the creative power of God insofar as he is called upon to help build the new heaven and the new earth. In this context some theologians today describe man as a self-creator, because now his power over nature and the world corresponds more closely to his spiritual freedom of responding to the call of God and thereby responsibly creating his own destiny. Karl Rahner, as well as Milhaven and others, accepts this description of contemporary man as a self-creator and also understands man primarily in terms of his freedom.[63]

In Rahner's essay on "Experiment: Man," the translation frequently uses the expression, man as self-creator, although in the original German Rahner usually uses the term self-manipulator.[64] If the term self-creator is taken literally and strictly it seems to say too much about man and fails to acknowledge the human limitations and finitide which are part and parcel of our human existence. Creation as the making

---

[63] Karl Rahner, "Experiment: Man," *Theology Digest,* XVI (Sesquicentennial Issue, 1968), 57-69. Milhaven (p. 116) very succinctly describes the supreme value, the absolute value that is the source of all other values, as core freedom, the self as self-creating. But later (p. 122) Milhaven criticizes those who hold a too optimistic view of human freedom, for human freedom is a spark affecting only in small part the onrush of human life.

[64] Karl Rahner, "Experiment Mensch: Theologisches über die Selbstmanipulation des Menschen," *Schriften zur Theologie,* VIII (Einsiedeln: Benziger, 1967), 260-285.

of something out of nothing implies the unlimited ability to create whatever the person might responsibly decide to create, and that there exist no other limitations on what the person can do. However, man does not have that type of creative power in dealing with himself and his world precisely because of his given existence as man in this particular world. We are all conscious of the limitations of time, history, geography, fatigue, knowledge, and courage which we have perceived in our own lives. The existing human being realizes there are given limitations within which he operates as he responsibly attempts to help shape his own future.

An anthropology which views man exclusively or even primarily in terms of freedom (without insisting on the other aspects of man) suffers from the same shortcomings as the view of man as self-creator, for there is no articulation of the limits within which man finds himself. I use the word "limits" here to refer to the fact that man exists in a definite situation with relationships to a particular time, space, to other people and to the whole world. Man's freedom is situated or limited by reason of the other aspects of his human existence. To see man exclusively in terms of freedom does not seem to give enough importance to the bodily aspects of man and his relationship to other people and to the world, which marks his human existence. In the past, an overemphasis on the freedom of man produced a theological individualism which can be seen, for example, in *laissez-faire* capitalism. Modern questions raised by particular sciences, technology, and ecology remind man that he exists in a web of relationships and cannot be defined solely in terms of his freedom.

Victor Ferkiss implicitly points out the inadequacies of understanding man uniquely or even primarily in terms of freedom when he tries to develop a meaningful philosophy of the role of technology in human evolution to help man control and guide his development. Ferkiss explains that there are three elements in this new philosophy: a new naturalism which asserts that man is indeed part of nature rather than apart from it, but that nature is not the rigid, mindless, determinate machine that earlier eras conceived it to be; a new holism which emphasizes how interconnected things are; a new immanentism which realizes that God is not wholly "up there" or "out there."[65] One does not have to accept totally the categories proposed by Ferkiss to see the inadequacies of an anthropology which views man as a self-creator and defines him exclusively or primarily in terms of his freedom.

In general Rahner does employ the term self-manipulator which avoids some of the connotations of limitlessness connected with self-creator, and although he does speak about man in terms of his freedom he has elsewhere developed a theology of history and of the world.[66] The "Experiment: Man" article does speak about human limitations, especially death. Man has been his own creator and determined his orientation in the area of knowledge and faith, but the "power of self-creation, rooted in his spiritual freedom, has now grasped the physical, psychological and sociological dimensions of his existence."[67] All these various aspects of man's existence must come into consideration, since in a sense they are limitations or modifications of man as a self-creator viewed primarily in terms of his freedom. Rahner also realized the existence of man's nature as of overruling theological importance and sees that "human self-creation poses for the contemporary theologian the urgent question

---

[65] Ferkiss, pp. 205-207.

[66] In the series of lectures, which commemorated the sesquicentennial of St. Louis University and was published in the special issue of *Theology Digest*, XVI (Sesquicentennial issue, 1968), Rahner not only gave the paper, "Experiment: Man"; but he also delivered papers on "The Historical Dimension in Theology" (pp. 30-42) and on "Christianity and the New Earth" (pp. 70-77). Both of these studies also appear in *Schriften zur Theologie*, VIII, 88-110, 580-592.

[67] Rahner, "Experiment: Man," p. 62.

of what this nature of man really and truly is. It is this that determines the moral norms and limits to man's autocreation."[68] Although Rahner thus explicitly does recognize there are limits on the self-creative power and freedom of man, he does not carefully spell out these exact limits (perhaps because he is not really dealing with the critical ethical questions in which these limiting factors take on such great meaning).

When more attention is given to these limits, it must also affect the way in which one understands man. Man does have enormous power to shape his own future, and hence great responsibilities in this area; but self-creation does not seem the most accurate term to describe this reality precisely because self-creation does not consider the limitations which are man's by reason of his existence as creature and not as creator. One cannot doubt the fact that freedom distinguishes man from all other creatures, but at the very least this is a situated freedom and should be viewed in terms of the multiple relationships within which the individual finds his existence. These two criticisms directed at Rahner's emphasis on man as self-creator and as self-transcending freedom seem to share the same basic concern as the critique proposed by J. B. Metz in his attempts to develop a political theology.[69]

## A THEOLOGICAL MODEL OF HUMAN PROGRESS

A second important theological consideration centers on the question of eschatology, for eschatology furnishes the model for the understanding of human progress. Contempo-

---

[68] *Ibid.*, p. 63.
[69] Johannes B. Metz, *Theology of the World* (New York: Herder and Herder, 1969), pp. 107-124; Metz, "Foreword," in Karl Rahner, *Spirit in the World* (New York: Herder and Herder, 1968), xiii-xviii.

rary theological concerns express great interest in the future and see the human vocation in terms of taking responsibility for building the new heaven and the new earth. There is a decided emphasis on the continuity between this world and the next. Dialogue with Marxism, theologies of the future, theologies of hope all accentuate this trend.[70] Just as historical mindedness from a philosophical viewpoint has put renewed emphasis on change, growth and development, so contemporary understandings of eschatology reinforce this idea and see growth in terms of progress towards the absolute future or the eschaton.

A proper Christian understanding of eschatology, in my judgment, must include three different aspects—the teleological, the prophetic and the apocalyptic.[71] In the past theology overstressed the apocalyptic and consequently saw little or no continuity between this world and the next. The prophetic and teleological aspects of eschatology joined with the notion of cosmic redemption accentuate man's vocation to cooperate in building the new heaven and the new earth. A balanced eschatological outlook will embrace these three different aspects and affirm both continuity and some discontinuity between this world and the next. Some forms of contemporary theology adopt a too optimistic approach which overstresses continuity and fails to give due weight to discontinuity and to the reality of sin which will never be completely overcome or redeemed in this world.[72]

An adequate theological model for human progress tries to keep in tension the different aspects of eschatology and

---

[70] For an illustration of this type of theologizing, see *New Theology No. 5*, eds. Martin E. Marty and Dean G. Peerman (New York: Macmillan, 1968).

[71] Harvey Cox, "Evolutionary Progress and Christian Promise," *Concilium*, XXVI (1967), 35-47.

[72] For a critique of overoptimism in some forms of contemporary theology, see Roger Lincoln Shinn, *Man: The New Humanism* (Philadelphia: Westminster Press, 1968).

the resulting continuity as well as some discontinuity between this world and the next. In general I would maintain there has been and will be some truly human progress in the world, and man has the responsibility to contribute to building the new heaven and the new earth, but there will always remain some discontinuity and sin.[73] This theological model understands that human progress is not always unilaterally developmental and progressive. Man continues to bring about his own tragedies and disasters, for sinful man will always be tempted to abuse the power he has so that greater power and responsibility will not necessarily be progressively employed for more truly human purposes. This view recognizes there is human progress, but the development of such progress is slow and uneven, including reverses as well as progress.

Such a theological view of human progress differs from the technological and scientific (especially the natural sciences) model of progress. Technology progresses in a constantly steady, upward movement. One technological breakthrough builds on the other so that man has advanced from the wheel to the cart, to the car, to the airplane, to the rocket circling the moon. Scientific and technological progress give man the impression of an ongoing, always progressive development; but reflection on human experience confirms the theological model of progress. Perhaps much of the disillusionment and disenchantment of people in our society today comes from the fact that they earlier had accepted too naive a view of human progress. It remains much easier to build a moon landing craft or even to crack the genetic code than to bring about peace in the world or a better distribution of the goods of creation.

The technological view of progress sees every development as necessarily good and an improvement on what went

---

[73] For a balanced theological judgment on the existence of human progress in the world, see Christian Duquoc, OPP., *L'Eglise et le Progres* (Paris: Editions du Cerf, 1964).

before. The theological view of progress sees a greater ambiguity in newer developments, for such a model realizes that not every development is necessarily for the better. A critical and testing attitude towards newer developments in no way involves a return to an older theological model which saw human existence in terms of conformity to preexisting laws and denied the true creativity which belongs to man.

What is automatically a step forward in the field of genetics is not necessarily a truly human development. The proposed theological model avoids the two extremes of canonizing the past or the present and the opposite extreme of baptizing as a human development whatever is a possible development in technology or in one of the sciences. This theological model will also call into question the methodology of those who wish to prove a particular point merely by citing the Scriptures without realizing that the Scriptures themselves are historically and culturally conditioned documents which might not apply in the changed conditions of contemporary science. For example, one cannot claim to have a totally convincing argument against A.I.D. or cloning by appealing to the Genesis text which sees procreation in terms of the one flesh unity of man and wife.[74] Perhaps the Genesis text does indicate the way in which human procreation should still take place today, but other reasons must be adduced to show this as the meaning of human parenthood today.

The future serves both as a pull in the direction of human progress and also as a critical standard by which one realizes the imperfections of the present and of some proposed future developments. Karl Rahner frequently speaks of Christianity as the religion of the absolute future and envisions man as going forward toward that future, but in the same connec-

---

[74] Perhaps too much emphasis is given to the unnuanced scriptural argument from *Genesis* and from the New Testament by Paul Ramsey, *Fabricated Man*, pp. 36-39.

tion Rahner insists on discussing death which is the great limit situation and the sign of some discontinuity between now and the future.[75] It would be helpful to discuss the limiting factors in greater detail so that criteria could be developed for testing and discerning what truly constitutes human progress. An insistence on an unqualified openness to an absolute future creates many of the same difficulties as the concepts of man as self-creator or as self-transcending freedom.

## THE ETHICAL MODEL

A third important consideration for moral theology as it views the possibilities for human progress brought about by scientific advance and technological breakthroughs centers on the model chosen as the basic understanding of ethics. Traditionally philosophers have distinguished two different types of ethics—teleological and deontological. Lately the model of responsibility has been introduced as an alternative approach.[76] The teleological model with its emphasis on ends and the means to attain them fits in very well with the view of progress as unilaterally developing towards greater perfection and progress.

H. Richard Niebuhr has described the teleological approach in terms of man the maker. His perceptive description of this model is most appropos of our discussion. Morality is viewed analagously to man the maker, the artisan, the fashioner who constructs things according to an idea and for the sake of an end. There are many varieties of teleological ethics depending on what man accepts as his ultimate end. Idealists, utilitarians, hedonists and self-realizationists all fit under

---

[75] Rahner, "Experiment: Man," pp. 67-68.
[76] H. Richard Niebuhr, *The Responsible Self* (New York: Harper and Row, 1963), pp. 47-68.

the generic umbrella of an ethical model of man the maker. The very term indicates that such a model would be congenial in an industrial and technological world, as well as to some extent in the world of the natural sciences where men are always trying to improve and move towards further progress. Perhaps the description given by Niebuhr is itself pejorative, for man the maker indicates what seems to be only a partial view of man; and yet that is precisely part of the problem with this ethical model. Such a model is conducive to an understanding of man as one who has the power to direct his progress ever more towards his goal.

The difficulties proposed by Niebuhr from a philosophical perspective against such a model seem to be equally valid objections from the theological perspective. The image of man the maker views man primarily as a craftsman and interprets personal life as *techné*. Whereas in craftsmanship both the end and the means are relatively under our control, neither is at our disposal when we deal with ourselves as persons or as communities. Man the maker can reject material which does not fit his purpose; but the individual human being lives with his body, his personal relationships, his human communities, his historical period. Rather than planning his own end or future, man realizes that the favors or disfavors of fortune and nature often put him at the mercy of alien powers and forces so far as the completion of his life and the attainment of his goals are concerned.[77]

Theological considerations remind us that man is not a limitless self-creator with complete dominion over his life and future. No one can deny that man does have extensive power over his life and his future, but he will never have full control or total dominion precisely because he is a creature and not the Creator. The model of man the maker presupposes that man has materials to work with which he can change or dis-

---

[77] *Ibid.*, pp. 51-52.

card at will, but such is not true of the Christian view of man precisely because man is not a self-creator who can be adequately understood in terms of his unlimited freedom. The image of man the maker implies that the only obstacles that stand in the way of human progress can be overcome through knowledge and the power of scientific and technological discoveries. The Christian should know there are limitations and obstacles that are beyond the power of man's control and beyond the power of his science.

The model of man the maker, precisely when seen in the context of the theological presupposition of man as self-creator and in the context of an overly optimistic model of human progress as always developing in a positive manner, cannot explain the tragic dimension in human existence. Precisely because sin and death are outside the control of man, man will always experience the limits and imperfections of his existence and frequently be buffeted by forces outside his control. The Paschal Mystery which marks all Christian existence is incompatible with a view of human progress as one triumph upon another, for the Paschal Mystery knows only too well the reality of sin, suffering and death. However, the transforming power of the resurrection can change sorrow into joy and death into life. Human experience shows there is a great amount of tragedy in our lives, but a creative suffering and love can overcome such tragedy. The tragic as a specifically human phenomenon escapes the model of man the maker just as it also stands beyond the intelligibility of a purely technological viewpoint.

There is rightly much concern in contemporary society about the exploding population growth. The slogan of many who are fighting to bring the population growth down to zero is that every child should be a wanted child. There is some truth in this slogan especially when applied to areas in which man does have some control, but such a slogan cannot be accepted as an ultimate principle because there are many areas over which man does not have this type of control by which he can program and plan exactly what he wants. In fact, I think most human beings would find it uncomfortable to be living in such a world because there is no room for that transcendence which is man's distinctive feature and also there is no room for the tragic which is part and parcel of our human experience.

Reality reminds us that we do not always obtain what we want, for man has to live with the unexpected, the mystical, the tragic and the unwanted. Who for example, would want to be born blind? Who would want to have his or her child born defective? Who would want to have a child of 13 killed accidentally? I hope that in the future science will help to overcome or at least alleviate some of these tragic burdens, but man will always live with the sorrow of the tragic as well as with the joy of the unexpected and unplanned. In the face of the tragic the truly human aspects of creative love can reveal the depths of man's self especially in redemptive terms. In the midst of sorrow and suffering human love at times reaches its highest peak. Obviously man should plan what he can and strive to control as much as possible, but man will always live with the sudden, the abrupt, the unforeseen which can bring with it joy or sorrow and opportunities for creative and redeeming love that man could never plan.

The inadequacies of a teleological model of ethics especially when seen in terms of man the maker, do not necessarily call for the adoption of the deontological approach such as Paul Ramsey has proposed.[78] I would prefer a re-

---

[78] In this entire section on inadequate theological themes and models and throughout the chapter I am developing in a somewhat different way ideas and critiques which have appeared in the voluminous and thought-provoking writings of Paul Ramsey. At times, Ramsey seems to overreact in some of his criticisms. For my agreements and disagreements with Ramsey's specific teaching on genetics, see my *Contemporary Problems in Moral Theology* (Notre Dame, Ind.: Fides Publishers, 1970), pp. 189-224.

sponsibility model, for it is better suited to interpret the
reality of complexity and the fact that man does have great
creative powers and responsibilities for himself and his
world. Chapter 2 has proposed the primacy of the relationality and responsibility model in the light of the data of biblical morality.

A particular form of teleological ethics would base its ultimate moral judgments on consequences. John Giles Milhaven does propose such an ethical approach, but he seems
to see this as the same model which is functioning in the
empirical sciences.[79] One who believes there is a difference
between the methodological approach of ethics and the
methodological approach of the sciences must reject such an
approach. Such a model is generally consistent with the approach which views man as a self-creator with dominion over
things which he can do with what he wills because of his
self-transcending freedom. There have been many theological and philosophical reasons proposed against such a form
of consequentialism. The primary concern of this essay is
that the model which is adequate in judging the success of
technology and the natural sciences does not constitute an
adequate model for Christian ethics.

One of the problems indicating the limitations of the sciences was that the goal of scientific advancement might in-
fringe on truly human rights and values. In other words
man is not a means who can be subordinated to any scientific
goals. The technological model tends to view all reality as
means which man the maker can manipulate and control in
order to accomplish his own ends. This model of man the
maker which views morality primarily in terms of consequences does not do justice to all the aspects which deserve
consideration. The just war theory, for example, consistently
maintained not only the principle of proportionality, which

---

[79] Milhaven, pp. 27, 113.

is the legitimate question of weighing consequences, but also the principle of discrimination which prohibits the direct killing of innocent people no matter what the consequences. There are problems with the way in which the just war theory is understood and applied by some theologians, but the theory clearly and rightly maintains as a matter of principle that all morality cannot be reduced to consequences. Too often our technological power tempts us as a nation to violate this principle of discrimination as happened even in the bombing raids in 1944 with their direct killing of innocent people.

An ethic based on consequences not only is logically consistent with a purely technological view of man and an understanding of man as self-creator with almost unlimited powers, but also with the concept of man understood primarily or exclusively in terms of freedom. The consideration of the good is too easily reduced just to consequences when there is no structure (definitely not to be interpreted as a given that cannot be changed) or relational understanding of man that includes reality other than his freedom. Exclusive stress on freedom and self-creation leads to an extrincistist and voluntaristic approach which then can judge morality primarily in terms of intention or consequences alone. Once one acknowledges some structural understanding of man, which I would see in the multiple relationships in which he finds himself, then factors other than consequences, narrowly understood in accord with a technological model, must enter into consideration. Man is not just putty that the individual as self-creator in his freedom can manipulate to achieve certain good consequences.

This essay itself is somewhat unbalanced because the main thrust of the argument was directed against those who too easily identify the moral with the scientific. The question will become ever more acute as man actually does obtain the scientific power which now he can only envision as a great possibility. There can be no doubt that in general man will acquire much greater power in the future through the advances of science and technology. In the midst of growing complexity the human sciences will also provide man with great help. The challenge for man is to find the truly human meaning of these things and to direct science and technology for human progress, since he does have the vocation to cooperate with God in the attempt to build up even now the new heaven and the new earth, but with the realization there will always be sinfulness and limitations in this world, and not only continuity but also some discontinuity between this world and the next. There is some truly human progress taking place but the growth rate is slow and uneven. Science and technology can assist man in this struggle for human progress, but the limitations of science in general, and any one science in particular, mean that in principle man cannot always say yes to what one science makes possible.

# 4

# Dialogue with Social Ethics:
# Roman Catholic Social Ethics—
# Past, Present, and Future

This discussion of Roman Catholic social ethics will consider only the important statements of the hierarchical magisterium during the past century. Obviously there are other aspects to Roman Catholic social ethics, but these papal and conciliar statements dominated the theological reflection and the pastoral life of the Church in this area of social ethics. In the future a changed understanding of ecclesiology and the magisterial function in the Church will reduce the importance attached to similar statements of the hierarchical magisterium. The comparatively sparse theological literature generated by Pope Paul's encyclical *Populorum Progressio* published in 1967 appears to indicate a future trend.[1] Our purpose is to point out some changes and developments that have occurred in the methodological approach to social

---

[1] The indices to theological literature illustrate this fact. For the lack of courses on the papal encyclicals in Catholic colleges, see Benjamin L. Masse, S.J., "On Campus the Encyclicals are Out," *America*, CXXI (July 5, 1969), 5.

ethics as found in these documents and to indicate possible
areas of development and problems for the future.

## EMPHASIS ON CONTINUITY

Unfortunately there have been comparatively few critical
studies of the development of the papal social teachings.[2]
Most of the Catholic commentaries on these documents have
tended to explain the papal teaching and indicate some applications in different circumstances. Often the commentaries on the papal documents paralleled the biblical commentaries by concentrating on an exegesis of the papal text to
determine its precise meaning. Many commentaries employed a rather apologetic approach which did not enter into
critical dialogue with the papal teaching. Likewise, an evaluation of the social encyclicals generally skipped over the
historical *sitz im leben* which is so necessary for a truly critical appraisal.[3] Catholic commentaries on the papal encyclicals also stressed the continuity in the doctrine of the various
popes so that the papal teaching appeared as a number of
immutable principles which were applied to new situations
as they arose.

The popes themselves took great pains to stress continuity
with their predecessors even though in reality there were

---

[2] The best of these commentaries include: J. Y. Calvez, S.J., and J. Perrin,
S.J., *L'Église et société économique: l'enseignement social des Papes de
Leon XIII à Pie XII, 1878-1958* (2d ed.; Paris: Aubier, 1959); English
translation: *The Church and Social Justice* (Chicago: Henry Regnery Co.,
1961); John F. Cronin, S.S., *Social Principles and Economic Life* (Milwaukee: Bruce, 1959); Oswald von Nell-Breuning, *Die soziale enzyklika;
erläuterungen zum weltrundschreiben papst Pius XI* (Köln: Katholische
tat-verlag, 1932); English translation: *Reorganization of Social Economy:
The Social Encyclical Developed and Explained* (Milwaukee: Bruce, 1936).
All three of these commentators have published articles and other books
dealing with the later papal documents and other apsects of the social
question.

[3] Richard L. Camp, *The Papal Ideology of Social Reform: A Study in
Historical Development* (Leiden: E. J. Brill, 1969), pp. vii-viii.

many examples of discontinuity and change from one pope to the next. Piux XI in *Quadragesimo Anno*, for example, defines his scope as recalling the benefits derived from *Rerum Novarum* of Leo XIII, defending the teaching of Leo and passing judgment on the contemporary economic and social scene.[4] John XXIII in *Mater et Magistra* follows the same generic format in the four parts of his encyclical. The first part reviews the earlier papal teachings; the second part develops these earlier teachings; the third part treats new aspects of the question especially in terms of the imbalances present in our world; whereas the final part serves as a conclusion and summary to the whole encyclical. Pope John wrote *Mater et Magistra* "not merely to commemorate appropriately the Encyclical Letter of Leo XIII, but also, in the light of changed conditions, both to confirm and explain more fully what our predecessors taught, and to set forth the Church's teaching regarding the new and serious problems of our day."[5]

One of the obvious areas of development in the papal social teachings concerns private property. Leo XIII staunchly defended the right to private property but in terms of the needs of the individual person. Leo also did mention but did not emphasize the social aspect of property.[6] Later

---

[4] Pope Pius XI, *Quadragesimo Anno*, n. 15. Unless otherwise noted, the translations and paragraph numbers for the encyclicals of Pius XI are taken from: *The Church and the Reconstruction of the Modern World: The Social Encyclicals of Pope Pius XI*, ed. Terrence P. McLaughlin, C.S.B. (Garden City, N.Y.: Doubleday Image Books, 1957); *Acta Apostolicae Sedis*, XXIII (1931), 181.

[5] Pope John XXIII, *Mater et Magistra*, n. 50. Unless otherwise noted, the translation and paragraph numbers of this encyclical are taken from *Mater et Magistra*, tr. William J. Gibbons (New York: Paulist Press, 1961); A.A.S., LIII (1961), 413.

[6] Pope Leo XIII, *Rerum Novarum*, nn. 4-31. Unless otherwise noted, the translation and paragraph numbers of the encyclicals of Leo XIII are taken from: *The Church Speaks to the Modern World: The Social Teachings of Leo XIII*, ed. Etienne Gilson (Garden City, N.Y.: Doubleday Image Books, 1954); *Acta Sanctae Sedis*, XXIII (1890-91), 643-655.

papal teaching underscores the social aspect of property all the while recalling that Leo also mentioned this aspect in *Rerum Novarum.* Pius XI begins his consideration of private property by asserting: "First, then, let it be considered as certain and established that neither Leo nor those theologians who have taught under the authority and guidance of the Church have ever denied or questioned the twofold character of ownership, called usually individual or social according as it regards either separate persons or the common good."[7] On the question of the just distribution of capital or property, Pius argues for the "wise words of Our Predecessor" insisting that the earth serves the common interests of all.[8]

John XXIII begins his discussion of the social function of property with words that have almost become a caricature: "Our Predecessors have always taught that in the right of private property there is rooted a social responsibility."[9] John then cites Leo XIII to prove his point. *The Pastoral Constitution on the Church in the Modern World (Gaudium et Spes)* asserts the common purpose of created things and bases this assertion not on the Scriptures or the Fathers but rather on Pius XII and John XXIII.[10] Paul VI in *Populorum Progressio* envisions the universal purpose of the goods of creation as a cornerstone of his theology of development which he proves not by quotations from earlier statements of the hierarchical magisterium but rather from citing Scripture and from developing a theology of the goods of crea-

---

[7] *Quadragesimo Anno,* n. 45; A.A.S., XXIII (1931), 191-192.

[8] *Ibid.,* n. 56; A.A.S., XXIII (1931), 196.

[9] *Mater et Magistra,* n. 119; A.A.S., LIII (1961), 430.

[10] *Pastoral Constitution on the Church in the Modern World,* n. 69, footnote 221. Unless otherwise noted, the translation and paragraph numbers of the documents of the Second Vatican Council are taken from: *The Documents of Vatican II,* ed. Walter M. Abbott, S.J., translation ed., Joseph Gallagher (New York: Guild Press, 1966); A.A.S., LVIII (1966), 1090-1091. The original Latin text also has the same paragraph numbering as the English translation.

tion.[11] Even Paul's discussion of private property in the following paragraph is anchored in quotations from the Scripture and St. Ambrose with no mention made of the teaching of his predecessors.[12] Thus the style of the hierarchical magisterium especially before Paul VI indicates the intention of the authors to stress the continuity in the papal teaching.

But there are even more subtle indications of the magisterial preference for continuity with past teachings and a reluctance to give any semblance of discontinuity with the predecessors of happy memory. Pius XI, for example, in *Quadragesimo Anno* calls for a very thorough reconstruction of the social order; whereas Leo XIII forty years earlier did not envision the need for such a radical restructuring. John XXIII obviously abandoned Pius' plan for such a reconstruction and expressed a much more positive attitude toward the existing structures of political, social and economic life. However, the popes never mention such existing differences.

Richard L. Camp in his study of papal teaching on social matters points out that Pius XI neatly covered one of the weaknesses in Leo's exposition of the defense of private property.[13] One should note that Leo's defense of private property did not really meet the major objections which were directed not against the small property holdings of working men but rather against the great accumulation of wealth and property among a few people in the midst of much economic need and want. Leo's failure to justify private property by any other title than labor was also an obvious source of embarrassment in the discussion with socialists. Pius XI deftly

---

[12] *Ibid.*, n. 23; A.A.S., LIX (1967), 269.
[11] *Populorum Progressio*, n. 22. Unless otherwise noted, translations and paragraph numbers are from the Paulist Press booklet: *On the Development of Peoples*; A.A.S., LIX (1967), 268. The original Latin text also has the same paragraph numbering as the English translation.
[13] Camp, p. 66.

fills in the lacuna in such a way as to give the impression that he is merely quoting Leo. "That ownership is originally acquired both by occupancy of a thing not owned by anyone and or by labor, or, as it is said, by specification, the tradition of all ages as well as the teaching of our predecessor Leo clearly testifies.[14] No precise citation is given to Leo apparently because Leo did not explicitly mention this other title to property.

## I. THE THEOLOGICAL QUESTION INVOLVING NATURAL LAW

Undoubtedly the most important change in the teaching of the hierarchical magisterium in social ethics concerns the shift away from a strict natural law approach and methodology. Even in the last decade the social teachings of John XXIII invoked natural law as the basic methodological approach to social questions. John XXIII begins *Mater et Magistra* by summarizing papal teaching on the social question from the time of Leo XIII, who in *Rerum Novarum* "proclaimed a social message based on the requirements of human nature itself and conforming to the precepts of the Gospel and reason."[15] John then summarizes Pius XI's social teaching insisting on its "natural law character."[16] *Mater et Magistra* then quotes from Pius XII's Pentecost message of June 1, 1941, which based the social order on the "unchangeable order which God our Creator and Redeemer has fixed both in the natural law and revelation."[17]

*The Pastoral Constitution on the Church in the Modern World,* the longest document produced by Vatican II, which deals precisely with the questions of the economic, political,

---

[14] *Quadragesimo Anno,* n. 52; A.A.S., XXIII (1931), 194.
[15] *Mater et Magistra,* n. 15; A.A.S., LIII (1961), 405.
[16] *Ibid.,* n. 30; A.A.S., LIII (1961), 408.
[17] *Ibid.,* n. 42; A.A.S., LIII (1961), 410.

social and cultural order, employs the term natural law only three times in the entire document and then only in the second part of the Constitution, and studiously avoids any implication that natural law furnishes the methodological foundation upon which the entire document is based. *Populorum Progressio* uses the term natural law only once and then in a citation taken from Leo XIII.[18] Obviously the framers of these documents made a conscious and concerted effort to avoid the term natural law which indicates an unwillingness to accept the natural law methodology which had been associated with the older teaching of the hierarchical magisterium on social matters.

The natural law is a very ambiguous term and includes many different aspects. Basically one should clearly distinguish the philosophical and the theological aspects of natural law. The philosophical question concerns the precise understanding of nature and the way in which the theory develops moral norms in the light of its understanding of nature. From a philosophical viewpoint there have been many different understandings of natural law precisely because there are many different understandings of nature. This paper will prescind from the philosophical aspect of the question even though there are undoubtedly philosophical reasons behind the changing use in the documents of the hierarchical magisterium.

From a theological perspective natural law has been the general answer of Roman Catholic theology to the question: is there a source of ethical wisdom and knowledge for the Christian which exists apart from the explicit revelation of God in Christ in the Scriptures? Does the Christian share ethical wisdom with all mankind because of the common

---

[18] *Pastoral Constitution on the Church in the Modern World*, nn. 74, 79, 89; A.A.S., LVIII (1966), 1096, 1102, 1111. The Latin text uses the word *lex* in n. 74 and n. 89, while n. 79 employs the word *ius*.

humanity they share? What is the relationship between the
wisdom the Christian shares with all men and the specifically
Christian moral wisdom, between the natural and the supernatural? Recently the question has been posed in terms of
pure *agapism* versus mixed *agapism;* i.e., does Christian
ethics rest solely on the distinctively Christian aspect here
assumed to be *agape,* or is Christian ethical wisdom com-
bined with an ethical knowledge which exists outside the
pale of explicit Christianity? This section will discuss the
question of natural law from such a theological perspective.

The papal social encyclicals in line with the Roman
Catholic theological tradition firmly admit the existence of
an ethical wisdom and knowledge which the Christian shares
with all mankind. Perhaps the most explicit affirmation of
natural law as the primary basis of the papal social teaching
and the best illustration of its applications in social morality
are found in *Pacem in Terris.* (One can only surmise that at
a time when Catholics were beginning to question natural
law in other areas, the pope made a concerted effort to indicate that natural law was the basis for the widely acclaimed
social teaching of the Church and also took the pains to describe his understanding of natural law). The introductory
paragraphs of *Pacem in Terris,* after extolling the work of
creation, assert: "But the Creator of the world has imprinted
in man's heart an order which his conscience reveals to him
and enjoins him to obey: They show the work of the law
written in their hearts. Their conscience bears witness to
them."[19] By these laws men are most admirably taught how
to conduct their mutual dealings, how to structure relationships between the individual and the state, how states should
deal with each other, how men and political communities

[19] Pope John XXIII, *Pacem in Terris,* n. 5. Unless otherwise noted, the
translation and paragraph numbers of this encyclical are taken from: *Pacem
in Terris,* ed. William J. Gibbons (New York: Paulist Press, 1963); A.A.S.,
LV (1963), 258.

should be related to the world community. These four types of order and relationships serve as the structural foundation for the four basic chapters of the encyclical.[20]

Perhaps in no other papal teaching is there such an explicit affirmation of the natural law as the primary basis for the social teaching of the Church. Generally speaking the papal social encyclicals mention two different sources of knowledge and wisdom for the Church's social teaching—revelation and natural law. These two sources of wisdom in the gnoseological order correspond to the ontological order of nature and supernature. Commentaries on the papal social teaching underscore the methodological role of these two sources. "We see that the popes have customarily juxtaposed the two sources of the social doctrine of the Church; revelation and natural law."[21] Near the beginning of his first chapter, Guerry asserts that the concepts which make up the social teaching of the Church are drawn from revelation and the natural law.[22] One could point out frequent references in the encyclicals themselves to this twofold source of ethical wisdom—gospel and reason, divine revelation and natural law, supernatural and natural.

I personally agree with the recognition that all men because they share the same humanity also share a common ethical wisdom and knowledge which has been described in various theological terms such as natural law or common ground morality. For various theological reasons some Protestant theological approaches in the past have denied such a valid source of ethical wisdom for the Christian, either because a reliance on the Scriptures excluded all other possible sources of knowledge, or because sin affected or even destroyed the structures of creation, or because they were

---

[20] *Ibid.*, n. 7; A.A.S., LV (1963), 259.

[21] Calvez and Perrin, p. 40.

[22] Emile Guerry, *The Social Doctrine of the Catholic Church* (New York: Alba House, 1961), pp. 15-19.

unwilling to accept any natural theology or coalition ethics involving the Christian and the human.[23]

## Critique of the Pre-Vatican II Approach

The primary fault with the methodological approach of the papal encyclicals before Vatican II was the way in which reason or natural law was related to the whole ethical perspective. Either natural law and revelation or gospel were juxtaposed as Calvez describes the general approach, or else the natural law served as the foundational starting point for the entire structure of the ethical consideration of the social order with the supernatural then added on top. Such a concept of the natural viewed in isolation from the reality of sin, redemption and resurrection destiny failed to see the complexity of human reality in the proper Christian perspective and did not properly relate the area of the natural to the realities of sin and grace. The natural law or the area of the natural remains integral in itself and is not really affected or transformed by the supernatural which is merely added on top of an already constituted natural order. Thus in the gnoseological order natural law and revelation remain two different sources retaining their own autonomy and identity corresponding to the same type of distinction between nature and supernature.

In such a theory the transforming power of grace or redemption does not really affect the understructure of the natural; or, in the famous terminology of H. Richard Niebuhr, Christ is not seen as transforming culture.[24] A view of grace or Christian eschatology as transforming nature and culture furnishes a more dynamic foundation for Christian

---

[23] John C. Bennett, "Issues for the Ecumenical Dialogue," in *Christian Social Ethics in a Changing World,* ed. John C. Bennett (New York: Association Press, 1966), pp. 377-378.

[24] H. Richard Niebuhr. *Christ and Culture* (New York: Harper Torchback, 1956).

ethics. The eschatological fullness stands as a constant critique of all existing structures and institutions thus asserting in a positive fashion the need for continual change and improvement. An ethic which sees the natural as unaffected by the transforming power of the eschaton tends to be more conservative and to view existing structures as reflections of the immutable, eternal law of God. Obviously there are also philosophical presuppositions in the approach of the papal encyclicals which would reinforce this more conservative view of a somewhat static order reflecting the eternal and immutable order in the mind of God.

In fairness to the papal social teaching the popes did not hesitate to see and criticize the inadequacies of the existing social order in the light of the ideal of natural law and natural justice. Some popes, especially Pius XI, called for a seemingly thorough reconstruction of the social order.[25] However, the theological foundations of the natural law theory were somewhat inadequate especially in the area of social change which was manifested in some of the papal teachings. There was always the danger of identifying a particular order or structure as the immutable order of God when in reality it was only an historically and culturally conditioned attempt to respond as well as possible to the needs of a particular period and very often manifested the desires of the dominant power group in the society rather than the eternal order of God.

The response of the nineteenth century popes to the question of freedom in all its political, cultural and religious ramifications shows an undue preference for the forms of the past and an inability to come to grips with the problem of change. There was a tendency, for example, to see the union of Church and state as the ideal social order reflecting the eternal order of God, when in reality it was only a time con-

---

25 Camp, pp. 38-40.

ditioned reality. I for one would admit many of the problems with the concept of liberty proposed in the nineteenth century (Karl Marx was a severe critic of this individualistic liberty especially when applied to the economic area), but the solution to the problem was not to turn back to an older historical form as if this were the representation of the eternal plan of God.[26] Even Pius XI's severe critique of existing structures seemed to indicate that the older solution as found in the guilds was necessary in our own times.[27] Perhaps there was wisdom in his suggestion, but there still remains the danger of identifying the eternal plan of God with a particular historical order, and usually in the case of Catholic theology an order which existed in a previous historical period. An understanding of the transforming aspect of grace and the eschaton would avoid the danger of canonizing any historical order as an expression of the eternal order willed by God.

Catholic natural law teaching in general and the papal social encyclicals in particular also failed to give enough importance to the reality of human sinfulness. Obviously, no Christian theology can ignore the reality of sin. The papal social encyclicals do frequently mention sin and its effects, but sin and its power do not possess the significance they should have. *Pacem in Terris* well illustrates the failure of papal social teaching to give enough importance to the reality of sin. Even the very title of the encyclical implies that peace is a possibility here on earth, but a more sober reflection reminds us that sin and its effects will always be with us until the end of time and the consummation outside history.

A person reading the introductory paragraphs of *Pacem in Terris* today realizes the romantic and utopian view which

---

[26] Étienne Borne, "Le problème majeur du Syllabus: verité et liberté," *Recherches et Débats,* L (1965), 26-42.

[27] Calvez and Perrin, pp. 415-427; Camp, pp. 125-128.

finds in the heart of man an order and the laws by which men know how to regulate their lives. Our own contemporary experience reminds us of another important factor—the disorder which exists in the hearts of man because of which men do not know how to live in order and peace with one another, because of which tensions between individuals and the government have become escalated, because of which individual nations remain suspicious of one another and unwilling to give up their own power of autonomy to any supranational body. One could very easily take the four main parts of *Pacem in Terris* and, beginning from the sin and disorder existing in man's heart, show the opposite tendency to that which is alone emphasized in the papal document. One could argue that *Pacem in Terris* merely proposed an ideal based on reason, but a more realistic vision of peace and the world order calls for a greater realization of the existence of sin and its disruptive effects in human existence.

Catholic theology is vulnerable to the charge that it does not give enough importance to the reality of sin precisely because the area of the natural is not integrated into the full Christian perspective. In general Catholic theology, perhaps in an overly defensive posture to safeguard its valuable assertion that creation is good, did not give enough importance to the reality of sin. Even reconstructions of the notion of the natural such as proposed by Joseph Fuchs do not seem to give enough importance to the role of sin or of grace for that matter.[28]

Fuchs, in responding to Protestant critiques, points out that Catholic theology does not mean by nature that which corresponds merely to creation. Nature is that which is essential to man and present in all the different possible states of salvation; whereas Protestant theology sees nature in terms

---

[28] Josef Fuchs, S.J., *Natural Law: A Theological Investigation* (New York: Sheed and Ward, 1965).

124 Catholic Moral Theology in Dialogue

of creation and then argues that creation is affected by sin.[29] Fuchs' approach is obviously better than some other explanations which do seem to equate nature with creation; but even he must admit there is still a connection between creation and nature, even the more abstract concept of nature which he sees as present in all the states of man. Fuchs speaks of an essential human nature which then is modified in its application to the different aspects of the history of salvation. Thus the natural remains the primary concept which is affected in different ways by grace or sin but really not internally affected or transformed.

In some forms of Catholic theology with an even less adequate understanding of nature as grounded in the work of creation to which supernature is added, there remains the greater danger of not giving enough importance to the reality of sin. Sin can be easily and mistakenly viewed as the loss of the supernatural aspect which is merely added on to the natural order, but sin does not intrinsically affect the natural order. In one school of Catholic theology man after the fall is related to man in the state of pure nature as *nudatus ad nudum.*[30] There was a somewhat better aspect of Catholic theology in this matter, but unfortunately it was not always systematically applied throughout the area of theology. In theory Catholic theology held that man after sin was *vulneratus in naturalibus* (wounded in those things pertaining to nature), and also that grace was morally necessary for a man to observe even the substance of the natural law for a long time.[31] But too often in practice sin was viewed as the loss of the supernatural while the order of the natural remained intact.

---

[29] *Ibid.*, pp. 42-52.

[30] Josephus F. Sagües, S.I., *Sacrae Theologiae Summa* (Madrid: Biblioteca de Autores Cristianos, 1955), II, 988-998.

[31] Severinus Gonzalez, S.I., *Sacrae Theologiae Summa* (3d ed.; Madrid: Biblioteca de Autores Cristianos, 1956), III, 521-542.

Sin obviously has an effect on many existing social structures and institutions. Very often the papal social encyclicals leave the reader with the impression that reason alone is the only element in establishing the proper social order and reason alone is sufficient to bring about the necessary changes in this order. A failure to recognize the reality of sin plus an overly idealistic or rationalistic understanding of reality combine to give a somewhat inadequate view of the social order and of effecting social change. The existing social order is never the product of pure reason but results also from the power struggles existing within the society itself. Minorities are discriminated against in many societies precisely because of the power and thus even the tyranny of the majority who control the power and thus greatly influence the social structures. Likewise the struggles and the tensions within society are greater than a theory based solely on reason can account for. Sin obviously becomes incarnate in society in the struggles between rich and poor, developed nations and developing countries, capital and labor. An older papal teaching does not seem to take this reality seriously enough. On the other hand, the existence of sin in the world will mean that perfect justice is never attainable in this world no matter how hard man will strive to find it. The Christian vocation to struggle against the reality of sin serves as another motive for the Christian to engage in the struggle to strive for a more just social order and not merely to accept the present structures as the immutable order of God.

## Developments of Vatican II and Afterward

*The Pastoral Constitution on the Church in the Modern World* marks a decisive turning point in the understanding of natural law and tries to integrate the natural law more fully into the whole schema of salvation history. Both in explicit words and in theory the document generally avoids understanding the natural as a relatively autonomous order unaffected by sin and grace. The first three chapters of Part One of the Constitution illustrate the newer methodological approach which tries to integrate the reality of the natural or the order of creation into the total Christian perspective. Chapter One on man begins with the fact of creation because of which man is made in the image of God. A second paragraph asserts the reality of sin and the resulting fact that man experiences within himself a dramatic struggle between good and evil. After a discussion of many other aspects the chapter ends with a paragraph on Christ as the new and perfect man. Thus creation, sin and redemption together explain the meaning of man for the Christian. The same general structure also governs the following two chapters on human community and human action.

An important idea that appeared in the draft drawn up at Ariccia in 1965 is the notion of the truly or the fully human.[32] This term had appeared in the earlier drafts but refers to nothing more than what would correspond to the natural as distinguished from the supernatural. The draft proposed at Ariccia definitely tried to overcome the false separation between the natural and the supernatural order. In this draft Christ assumes a more important place than in the earlier drafts, and Christ appears especially as the perfect man, the fulfillment of the human.[33] For example, in the close of the third chapter the draft maintains that the history of humanity tends toward Christ who is the focal point of the

---

[32] This fact has been documented and explained by William J. Bergen, S.J., in his doctoral dissertation, "The Evolution of *The Pastoral Constitution on the Church in the Modern World:* A Study in Moral Methodology," which will shortly be completed at the Catholic University of America. I am grateful to Father Bergen for documenting the ideas summarized in this paragraph.

[33] "De Christo, Homine Perfecto" is the title of the final section of Chapter One of Part One of the Ariccia draft (Ariccia draft, Part I., Chap. I, n. 20).

desires of history and civilization.[34] The Spirit not only arouses a desire for the age to come, but He animates, purifies, strengthens those noble longings by which the human family strives to make its life more human and to render the whole earth submissive to this goal.[35]

The references added at Ariccia referring to the more human and the truly human must be interpreted in terms of this newer understanding of Christ as the perfect man and the Spirit working now in the hearts of man to develop his love which is the basic law of human perfection and brings the earth towards its goal. The terms truly human and fully human thus seem to be concepts that overcome the previous dichotomy between the natural and the supernatural in earlier statements of the papal magisterium. One should note that such concepts do not have a primary and foundational place in the final document, although it seems to me that many of the framers of the final draft did see this as a very fundamental concept.

*Gaudium et Spes* definitely avoids the term natural law. The pivotal paragraph introducing the second part of the Constitution with its consideration of five different practical areas employs a new phrase to describe its theological methodology. "To a consideration of these in the light of the gospel and of human experience, the Council would now direct the attention of all."[36] Obviously there are many reasons of a more philosophical nature involved in the shift from natural law to human experience. However, it would be wrong to see no importance from a theological perspective

---

[34] Ariccia draft, Part I, Chap. III, nn. 45-46. This does not appear as such in the final version of *Gaudium et Spes*.

[35] Ariccia draft, Part I, *Chap. I*, n. 20; Part I, Chap. IV, n. 49; Part II, Chap. V, n. 91. These references are substantially incorporated into the final version of *Gaudium et Spes*.

[36] *Pastoral Constitution on the Church in the Modern World*, n. 46; A.A.S., LVIII (1966), 1066.

in this change. In such a perspective human experience does
not mean the same thing as natural law. There is not a
dichotomy between gospel and human experience as there
was between gospel and natural law. Human experience is
not restricted merely to the natural.

Chapter One in its discussion of sin remarks that what
divine revelation makes known to us about the existence of
sin "agrees with experience." Examining his heart man finds
that he has inclinations to evil and is engulfed by evils which
do not come from the good Creator.[37] Human experience is
not impervious to the reality of grace, for the Constitution
speaks of all men of good will in whose heart grace works in
an unseen way. The ultimate vocation of all men is in fact
one and divine.[38] Thus human experience does not correspond to the natural order as distinguished from the supernatural, for grace and sin are not foreign to human experience even apart from the gospel as such.

Extrinsic evidence also supports the thesis that *Gaudium
et Spes* makes a decided shift away from the theological
understanding of natural law and the natural as pertaining
to natural theology and totally unaffected by the reality of
redemption. Canon Charles Moeller, the sub-Secretary of the
Vatican Congregation for the Doctrine of the Faith and one
of the drafters of the Pastoral Constitution, made this precise
point in a speech he gave as an official Catholic observer to
the meeting on Church and Society sponsored by the World
Council of Churches in Geneva in the summer of 1966.
Moeller explained that the terms nature and supernature
were not employed in the document because of ecumenical
reasons. The Orthodox use the term nature to describe what
Catholics call supernature; whereas in Protestant theology

---

[37] *Ibid.*, n. 13; A.A.S., LVIII (1966), 1034-1035.
[38] *Ibid.*, n. 22; A.A.S., LVIII (1966), 1043.

there are difficulties connected with a concept of a natural theology of human nature because such a concept cannot be found in the Scriptures.[39]

The Encyclical *Populorum Progressio* issued by Pope Paul VI in March 1967, again avoids the nature-supernature, natural law-gospel dichotomies and continues along the lines proposed in *Gaudium et Spes.* The central and foundational idea of the encyclical is development. The first part of the encyclical treats man's complete development, while the second part treats the development of the human race in a spirit of solidarity. Paul describes human life as the vocation of every man to fulfill himself. This self-fulfillment is obligatory for man who as a spiritual being should direct himself to God. "By reason of this union with Christ the source of life, man attains to new fulfillment of himself, to a transcendent humanism which gives him his greatest possible perfection. This is the highest good of personal development."[40]

In a technical age Pope Paul realizes that it is necessary to search for "a new humanism which will enable modern man to find himself anew by embracing the higher values of love and friendship, of prayer and contemplation."[41] In one important paragraph the encyclical proposes a united ideal of what true development means. More human conditions of life "clearly imply passage from want to the possession of necessities, overcoming social evils, increase of knowledge and acquisition of culture. . . . Then comes the acknowledgement by man of supreme values and of God their source and finality. Finally and above all, are faith, a gift of God accepted by man's will, and united in the charity

---

[39] Msgr. Charles Moeller, "Conference sur *L'Eglise dans le monde d'aujourd'hui,*" *La Documentation Catholique,* LXIII (1965), 1500.

[40] *Populorum Progressio,* n. 16: A.A.S., LIX (1967), 265.

[41] *Ibid.,* n. 20; A.A.S., LIX (1967), 267.

of Christ, who calls us all to share as sons in the life of the living God, the Father of all men."[42]

This new methodological approach does not deny the basic affirmation of the goodness of creation and the continuity between creation and redemption. However, the area of the natural no longer appears as merely extrinsically juxtaposed to the supernatural but rather creation is constantly affected by the drag of sin and the pull of grace. The concept of the truly human, the identification of Christ as the perfect man, and the assertion that Christianity furnishes a new and transcendent humanism which brings man to his fulfillment show that the Christian and the truly human are the same. Thus the newer approach of the hierarchical magisterium lends support to the thesis proposed in Chapter 1 which denies a distinctively Christian ethic as regards ethical conclusions and proximate attitudes, dispositions and values.

## Critique of the Newer Approach

The newer approach proposed originally in *Gaudium et Spes* still creates some theological problems. *The Constitution on the Church in the Modern World* does not really follow in practice the methodology proposed in the important introduction to the consideration of practical problems in the second part of the Constitution. Especially the problems considered in the last three chapters of Part Two (economic life, political life, peace among nations) do not receive a methodological discussion in the light of the gospel and human experience. Rather the approach is one based primarily on the dignity of the human person which is an extension of the older natural law approach. These chapters contain frequent references to past papal teaching but comparatively few

---

[42] *Ibid.*, n. 21; A.A.S., LIX (1967), 267-268. Also see Antonio Messineo, S.I., "L'Umanismo plenario e lo sviluppo integrale dei popoli," *La Civiltà Cattolica*, Part I, CXIX (1968), 213-226; Jean-Yves Calvez, S.J., "Populorum progressio," *Projet*, XV (1967), 515-530.

references to a broader history of salvation approach. Thus these three important chapters do not really implement the newer methodological approach proposed in theory at the beginning of Part Two.

Canon Moeller admits this diversity between the two parts of *Gaudium et Spes* and explains it in terms of a dialectic between biblical anthropology and the understanding of the human person. This dialectic or antinomy attempts to bring together in a vital tension the biblical and the human or the eschatological and the incarnational approach.[43] I cannot agree with Moeller's explanation which appears to be too apologetic. It seems to me that the first part of the document does try to maintain this tension within itself by constantly developing the principal chapters in a history of salvation approach which integrates creation, sin and redemption. The Introduction for Part Two, understood in the light of Part One, should now apply this particular methodological approach to the particular problems under discussion. The tension resulting from such an approach is precisely what is missing in the last three chapters of Part Two, since the approach is based almost solely on the dignity of the human person as known from reason. There is an obvious explanation of this lack of consistency. The chapters of Part Two were at one time intended only to be appendices to the real constitution. Later it was decided to incorporate them into the text, but in a true sense they were just juxtaposed with a text which from the fifth draft spelled out in theory a different methodological approach.[44]

---

[43] *La Documentation Catholique*, LXIII (1965), 1505.

[44] Mark G. McGrath, C.S.C., "Note storiche sulla Costituzione," in *La Chiesa nel mondo di oggi*, ed. Guilherme Baráuna, O.F.M. (Florence: Vallechi, 1966), pp. 141-156; Charles Moeller, "History of the Constitution," in *Commentary on the Documents of Vatican II*, Vol. V: *Pastoral Constitution on the Church in the Modern World*, ed. Herbert Vorgrimler (New York: Herder and Herder, 1969), pp. 1-76.

The Pastoral Constitution did try to integrate the natural into the total Christian perspective so that it was no longer seen as a relatively autonomous area not affected by sin and redemption. However, in the process it seems that other important aspects did not receive enough attention. In integrating the "natural" into the "supernatural," the document and other Catholic writing tend to forget about the finiteness and limitations of the creaturely which will always be present despite the basic goodness of creation. Secondly, the reality of sin, which was even somewhat neglected in the older approach, did not receive enough attention. This fault in the newer approach resulted in a too optimistic and even naive view of the world. Thirdly, the eschatological element was too easily collapsed.

With emphasis on Christ the perfect man, for example, in the last paragraph of Chapter One, the eschaton somehow becomes collapsed with too great a stress on realized eschatology.[45] Perhaps the whole reality of Christ should have been discussed after creation and sin and then followed by the other considerations with a closing paragraph considering the eschatological future both in terms of its continuity and its essential discontinuity with the present. In this way the structure of the first three chapters of Part One would present a more realistic understanding of the Christian's view of man, community and human action. The aspect of future eschatology is missing almost totally from the closing paragraph of the discussion on human community in Chapter Two.[46] Chapter Three does devote its last paragraph almost exclusively to the future and its different relationships to the present and thus presents a more adequate theological understanding of our pilgrim existence than the first two chapters.

---

[45] *Pastoral Constitution on the Church in the Modern World*, n. 22; A.A.S., LVIII (1966), 1042-1044.

[46] *Ibid.*, n. 32; A.A.S., LVIII (1966), 1051.

Precisely the first two criticisms mentioned above were also directed by many Council fathers at the draft drawn up at Ariccia.[47] These interventions at the fourth session of the Council objected to a tendency to forget the distinction between the order of nature and the order of grace and to an undue optimism arising from a lack of the sense of sin. There is no doubt that the framers wanted to overcome the rigid division of two orders, the natural and the supernatural, and two vocations which had characterized much of earlier Catholic teaching especially on a more popular level. I believe that these objections to the text of Ariccia were pointing out important defects in that draft and also in the final document itself. The solution is not to reinstate a rigid division between the two orders but rather to realize the existence of the creaturely with its goodness and also its limitations which is affected by the reality of sin, but gradually trying to be transformed in the times in between the comings of Jesus who will bring to completion the work he has begun, a perfection or completion or fullness which always lies outside history.

The three criticisms of *Gaudium et Spes* also have validity in assessing some of the theological literature commenting on this document. For example, a paper by Joseph Gremillion at the Notre Dame symposium on Vatican II in 1966 merits the same criticisms despite some perceptive comments about the changing approach of *Gaudium et Spes*.[48] The author correctly shows the different methodological approach in comparison with the natural law approach of the manuals, although most of his stress falls on the different philosophical implications and not the theological implica-

---

[47] Philippe Delhaye, "Histoire des textes de la Constitution Pastorale," in *L'Église dans le monde de ce temps*, ed. Yves Congar, O.P. (Paris: Édditions du Cerf, 1967), I, 267-273.

[48] Joseph Gremillion, "The Church in the World Today: Challenge to Theology," in *Vatican II: An Interfaith Appraisal*, ed. John H. Miller, C.S.C. (Notre Dame: University of Notre Dame Press, 1966), pp. 521-544.

tions treated here. However, Gremillion does not take up the question of eschatology and the tension between the imperfections of the present and the eschatological fullness to which we are all called in Christ Jesus. The article does mention sin; but the perfunctory treatment, which is primarily a long citation from the document itself, indicates that sin does not have a profound effect upon the world in which we live and struggle for justice and peace.[49]

*Populorum Progressio* at times shows a more critical attitude towards the present reality of the world and also realizes the effect of sin in our world. Pope Paul, however, seems to imply that the individual development of the person is possible and so is the complete development of a true communion among all nations possible of achievement. Paragraph 21 supposes that the new humanism embracing this total development is possible, and this paragraph appears to be a foundational section of the encyclical. No mention is here made of sin preventing such total development nor the realization that the final development will never come until the end of time and outside history through the saving intervention of the second coming of Jesus.

The foundational paragraph in the second part of the encyclical on the development of the human race in a spirit of solidarity speaks of the duty to form a true community among all nations based on a "brotherhood which is at once both natural and supernatural" and includes a threefold aspect: the duty of human solidarity, the duty of social justice, the duty of universal charity. Note that the terminology tries to overcome the division and separation between nature and grace, but there is in this foundational paragraph no mention of sin and of the fact that a "true communion" remains only an eschatological goal and hope.[50] Thus the later magisterial documents overcome the separation between nature and

---

[49] *Ibid.*, pp. 534-535.
[50] *Populorum Progressio*, n. 44; A.A.S., LIX (1967), 279.

supernature, but fail to integrate this into a total Christian perspective especially because they fail to appreciate the finitude and imperfections of creation, the reality of sin, and the eschatological as a future now trying to transform the present but capable of fulfillment only as God's gift at the end of time. Catholic social ethics in the future needs a more realistic view of man and his life in this world which does not forget the finitude, limitations and sinfulness of the present as man strives for the truly human or the full development which will ultimately come only as God's gift at the end of time.

## II. CATHOLIC SOCIAL ETHICS AND CHANGE

Change, even radical change, characterizes the present social, political, economic and cultural orders. In general in the past Roman Catholic social ethics has not been equipped to come to grips with the reality of change. There are signs in the last decade, however, that social ethics as taught by the hierarchical magisterium is adopting a methodology more apt to cope with the reality of social change. The theoretical inability to deal with change and development is multiplied when one enters the practical arena of proper strategies to bring about social change. The problem becomes more acute because many people today are aware of the great changes which must take place in national and international life.

The papal social teaching of the past was not unaware of the changing conditions of economic, social, political and cultural life. Leo XIII began *Rerum Novarum* by pointing out that the revolutionary spirit has influenced political and economic life.[51] To cope with these changes in the light of Christian teachings Leo wrote his many encyclicals. Pius XI

---

[51] *Rerum Novarum*, n. 1; A.S.S. XXIII (1890-91), 641.

realized that many changes had occurred since Leo's time, and he calls to judgment both the existing economic system and its most bitter enemy, socialism.[52] The very outline of *Mater et Magistra* indicates Pope John's realization of the importance of past papal social teaching but also the historical changes which have occurred since that time. Part Two of that encyclical explains and develops the older teaching in the light of changed conditions; whereas Part Three examines new aspects of the social question.

At the same time there is another strand in the papal social teaching which methodologically hampers this teaching from dealing with the fact of change. In his encyclical on the state Leo XIII traces out what should be the form and character of the state in accord with the principles of Christian philosophy. Leo proposes a union of two powers, the ecclesiastical set over the divine and the civil set over the human, with each supreme in its own sphere and working together in a harmonious relationship. Just as in lower nature a marvelous order and harmony reign so that all things fitly and aptly work together for the great purpose of the universe, so too there must be a harmonious relationship between Church and state.[53] Leo understands the union of Church and state in this manner as reflecting the ever changeless law.[54] He then condemns that harmful and deplorable passion for innovation which has invaded philosophy and thrown confusion into the Christian religion. This innovation brings about that unbridled license which is at variance with not only the Christian but even the natural law.[55]

The somewhat negative attitude towards change manifested by Leo obviously has many partial explanations

---

[53] *Immortale Dei*, nn. 13-14; A.S.S., XVIII (1885), 166-167.
[54] *Ibid.*, n. 22; A.A.S., XVIII (1885), 169.
[52] *Quadragesimo Anno*, n. 98; A.A.S., XXIII (1931), 209.
[55] *Ibid.*, n. 23; A.S.S., XVIII (1885), 170.

including the historical conditions of the time, but the methodological approach of natural law, seen now in its philosophical aspect, is a major contributing cause. The papal social teaching even in the encyclicals of John XXIII insists that the natural law proclaims an order for society in which all things should exist in harmony and unity. "Now an order of this kind, whose principles are universal, absolute and unchangeable has its ultimate source in the one, true God."[56] The natural law has these unchanging characteristics, and even the order shares in such characteristics. The impression arises that there is a hierarchically structured order in which all things form a harmonious whole with each having its proper function with regard to the whole. Such a notion of order with its correlative insistence on universality and immutability does not furnish an apt paradigm for change. A more adequate social ethic, while truly appreciating the need for order and structure, will reject a static approach which tends to deny the reality of change.

The danger also exists of identifying a particular historical ordering with this order in the mind of God whose principles are immutable and universal. This danger is heightened when theology loses the sense of the eschaton as calling into judgment every existing social order and institution as was mentioned in the first part of this chapter. Both theologically and philosophically the papal natural law methodology had difficulty coping with the reality of historicity and change. The tendency of social conservatism arises not only from the unwillingness to accept change because of an overemphasis on order but also because the changes brought about in the present seem often to contradict some past order which appears to be the order willed by God.

A methodology proceeding from the concept of an immutable order in the mind of God which has been implanted in

---

[56] *Pacem in Terris,* n. 38; A.A.S., LV (1963), 266-267.

the heart of man easily adopts an *a priori* and deductive approach. As late as 1963, *Placem in Terris* builds its entire argument on just such a notion. Leo XIII had earlier pointed out that the Christian organization of civil society was "educed from the highest and truest principles confirmed by natural reason itself."[57]

## A New Development

*Pacem in Terris,* however, also marks the beginning of a change which will ultimately embrace a more inductive methodology more open to change, development and even tension. The concluding paragraphs of the four main parts of the encyclical speak about: distinctive characteristics of our age, these requirements in our day, the fact that men are becoming more and more convinced of a certain reality, a commendation of the modern development of the United Nations Organization with its Universal Declaration of Human Rights.[58]

*The Pastoral Constitution on the Church in the Modern World* takes a further step toward a more inductive methodology more open to change, tension and perhaps even some disorder. *Gaudium et Spes* begins with an introductory statement, originally intended to be the first part of the Constitution, which records the signs of the times. Signs of the times was a favorite expression employed by John XXIII, but the phrase itself appears very rarely in the final version of *Gaudium et Spes* because some Council Fathers objected to the use of term in a manner different from its primary scriptural meaning.[59] The Council thus acknowledges the rapid changes taking place in the modern world and tries to speak

---

[57] *Immortale Dei,* n. 16; A.S.S., XVIII (1885), 167.
[58] *Pacem in Terris,* nn. 39-45, 75-79, 126-129, 142-145; A.A.S., LV (1963), 267-269, 278-279, 291, 295-296.
[59] *The Documents of Vatican II,* pp. 201-202, footnote 8.

to them in the light of the gospel and of human experience.[60] Each of the five chapters in the second part of the Constitution begins with a reading of the signs of the times in the particular area under consideration—marriage, culture, economy, politics, peace and international relations. Note that the signs of the times are now considered first and not last as in *Pacem in Terris.*

*Populorum Progressio* takes another step in this same direction, for Paul VI for the first time in a papal encyclical cites contemporary authorities from other fields, a sign that some type of dialogue is truly taking place.[61] The earlier literary genre of papal encyclicals with its lack of specific references to other areas of science and knowledge and its frequent citations of "Our predecessors of happy memory" reinforced the *a priori* and deductive type of methodology which is antithetical to change. In the later documents there is no longer any question of beginning with the order which God has imprinted in the hearts of men from which the principles and order of society can be deduced.

In the future Catholic theology must develop a methodology which can grapple with change and even radical change, but Christian theology and the Churches should never uncritically baptize every change which occurs. A sound theological and philosophical methodology cannot be totally inductive in the sense that there are no criteria outside the present situation by which to judge it. A naively utopian theological perspective together with an unwillingness to rationally assess possible changes is obviously quite rampant in our society. This would be just as inadequate an approach to the problem as the Catholic natural law ap-

---

[60] "Thus the human race has passed from a rather static concept of reality to a more dynamic evolutionary one." *Pastoral Constitution on the Church in the Modern World,* n. 5; A.A.S., LVIII (1966), 1029.

[61] See the references in the following footnotes of the official text: 15, 17, 22, 27, 29, 31, 44, 45, 46, 62.

proach which in the past could not cope with the reality of change.

*Strategies for Change*

Christian ethics or moral theology considers not only the more theoretical question of the norms, values and goals for Christian action but also the more practical question of the strategies for bringing about social change. Generally speaking Catholic theology, including the papal social teaching, has been very deficient in this area of strategies. Again there are implications in the older methodological approach militating against developing a suitable strategy for the implementation of moral ideals, goals, and norms in social life. Catholic natural law stressed the order of God reflected in the world in which all things fit together in a marvelous hierarchical coordination and subordination. Such an approach could not easily accept the fact of change.

On the level of structure such an approach again emphasized a hierarchical ordering in which authority and power were invested in the office holders in the society, and all direction in the society (and what little change there could possibly be in the light of such a model) came from the office holders. Order and ordering in the theoretical realm became law and structure in the practical realm. Obviously the structure of the Roman Catholic Church well illustrates this practical understanding. This point will be developed in the following chapter. Change is brought about primarily through order or reason in the theoretical realm and through reason and law or structure in the practical realm. Such a methodology has a built in prejudice against change in the theoretical realm and almost totally bypasses the question of practical strategy for social change, since this would be accomplished in an orderly way by the office holders.

In practice, one must admit that Catholic social teaching was cognizant of the need for strategies to bring about social change. The papal social teaching realized, despite its stress on hierarchical ordering, that there were also many tensions in society. The papal encyclicals were written primarily because of the disorders, imbalances and tensions existing in society either between the rich and the poor in a particular country or between the rich nations and the poor nations of the world.[62] Papal teaching realized that labor needed the right to strike as a means of trying to obtain justice from employers. The right to war has even been recognized often in Church documents. Even more recent writings of the hierarchical magisterium speak, although somewhat reluctantly, about revolution as a means of last resort to bring about social change, but caution against ever finding the proportionality commensurate to the harm caused by revolution.[63]

Changes in the theoretical approach to an understanding of Christian social ethics have already been mentioned. The emphasis on an *a priori* ordering involving a somewhat detailed plan of subordination and coordination of all the different parts as a reflection of the plan of God is beginning to disappear. More importance is given to historicity, change, tension, growth. These same changes will also affect the practical realm of strategies for social change. In the categories employed by Edward LeRoy Long, Jr., there will be a shift from a more institutional motif to a more operational motif on the level of strategy for the implementation of social justice. The operational motif gives less place to the role of structure or ordering and sees change coming about through the various seas of influence present in any society.[64] Such a view also has a more realistic understanding of the existing

---

[62] E.g., *Rerum Novarum*, n. 1; A.S.S., XXIII (1890-91), 641; *Mater et Magistra*, n. 122; A.A.S., LIII (1961), 431.

[63] *Populorum Progressio*, n. 31; A.A.S., LIX (1967), 272.

[64] Edward LeRoy Long, Jr., *A Survey of Christian Ethics* (New York: Oxford University Press, 1967), pp. 167-251.

social structures. Such institutions and structures are not necessarily a perfect reflection of the divine order produced by human reason but rather they very easily reflect the power and influence of those who do have power in the society itself. Law and structure very often incarnate discrimination and injustice as well as some attempt at justice. Not only a more operational motif but also a theological realization of the sinfulness of man despite his resurrection destiny would come to the conclusion that existing social structures are not merely a rational reflection of the order of God.

In the future Roman Catholic theology must develop a more operational motif which can more adequately handle the problem of strategies in bringing about social change. For many people today, especially in the area of living the Christian life, the more important question remains the strategies by which social change can be accomplished. Many Christians today are convinced of the general framework of social justice and charity which should exist but are frustrated in their attempts to bring about corresponding change.

Among the many questions that Catholic theology will have to address is that of power which obviously is an important factor in the reality of social change and the strategies to bring about such change. As pointed out, the papal magisterium realized the need for power in its general attitude to strikes and in its realization that revolution could never be absolutely ruled out despite the many concomitant problems. Interestingly, the final version of *Gaudium et Spes* in its consideration of the political community is less conscious of power as a means of social change than an earlier version. The 1964 Appendix I on man in society contained an entire section on public opinion. "More and more centers of moral power are cropping up in present day society; they exert influence on public opinion and change it.

The effect of this new type of power is that more and more people are able to participate in social life."[65] Unfortunately this section was dropped and not included in the final draft.

The final draft of *Gaudium et Spes,* however, does show some advantages over *Pacem in Terris* pointing in the direction of a lesser influence of the structural and hierarchical ordering in society. In reality many nineteenth and twentieth century Church documents on political life considered only the aspect of political authority. *Pacem in Terris* also gives first and primary consideration to political authority but points out that authority is a means in the service of the common good and the community.[66] *Gaudium et Spes* first discusses the political community itself before going into the topic of authority, since the community obviously embraces more than just authority. The Pastoral Constitution calls for the participation of all in the government.[67] Thus one can see a development towards a lesser role and function given to authority and structure in the understanding of society, which illustrates the emergence of a more operational motif.

In the future Roman Catholic social ethics must develop a more operational motif which includes power as a means of social change. Such a development should not totally deny the need for order and structure which has been the most significant aspect of Catholic social ethics in the past. The importance of both order and change must be recognized so that theology is truly critical about proposed changes. Likewise in developing a theology of power, power should not be seen primarily or exclusively in terms of sin. Catholic theology with its ontological presuppositions can see power as

[65] The text is cited by Jean-Yves Calvez, S.J., "The Political Community," in *The Church Today,* ed. Group 2000 (Westminster, Md.: Newman Press, 1968), p. 198.

[66] *Pacem in Terris,* nn. 46-79; A.A.S., LV (1963), 269-279.

[67] *Pastoral Constitution on the Church in the Modern World,* nn. 73-75; A.A.S., LVIII (1966), 1094-1099.

a necessary characteristic of being. A balanced theology of power will show that power stems also from the connection with the power of redemption. Power, understood in its relationship to the total Christian perspective of creation, sin and resurrection destiny, can never become the sole consideration of social ethics, but again must be integrated into the other elements of social ethics—justice, truth, love and freedom. These are the challenges facing the future of Roman Catholic social ethics.

## III. INDIVIDUAL AND COMMUNTY

A perennial ethical problem which will be of even greater importance in the future concerns the relationship between the individual and the community. The growing interdependency and complexity of human existence will heighten tensions and possible conflicts between the individual and the community. In the area of population growth the question arises about the rights of the government to impose limits on family size. Discussions in the area of genetics occasion questions about the role of the community in the genetic planning of the future of man. Catholic social teaching has lately admitted the legitimacy of government appropriation of large unused estates so that more people might share in the ownership of the land.[68] On an international level trade between nations cannot be dictated only by the market place because the rich nations of the world will continue to exploit the countries that export only raw materials.

On the other hand, many in our society are more conscious than ever of the rights of conscientious objection either to the policies of the government or the military draft or the immoral orders of a superior in the military. The cybernetic revolution has brought about a situation in which the government can easily obtain and preserve much data about

---

[68] *Populorum Progressio,* n. 24; A.A.S., LIX (1967), 269.

the private life of its citizens which seems to be an invasion of the privacy of the individual.

The teaching of the hierarchical magisterium on social ethics retains, as would be expected, the tension between the individual and the community, with a changing emphasis depending on changed historical and cultural circumstances. The older approach, however, did at least in theory lay heavy emphasis on the community, and especially the state.[69]

In general Catholic social ethics views man as political and social by nature. Society is a natural institution because of the very nature of man. This is a constant theme recurring in Roman Catholic social ethics, as exemplified in the following passage from *Gaudium et Spes:* "Individuals, families, and various groups which compose the civic community are aware of their own insufficiency in the matter of establishing a fully human condition of life. They see the need for that wider community in which each would daily contribute his energies toward the ever better attainment of the common good. It is for this reason that they set up the political community in its manifold expressions."[70]

The Protestant tradition generally sees the origin of the state in the sinfulness of man, whereas Catholic theology understands the state as a natural society based on the very nature of man. Between these views there is not only a theological difference about the importance attached to sinfulness (which as discussed previously does not receive enough attention in Catholic thought) but also a metaphysical or philosophical difference in the understanding of man. The more classical stand in Protestant theology would tend to view man primarily in terms of his freedom, so that the state

[69] Heinrich A. Rommen, *The State in Catholic Thought* (St. Louis: B. Herder, 1945).

[70] *Pastoral Constitution on the Church in the Modern World,* n. 74; A.A.S., LVIII (1966), 1095.

as a result of sin must compel man to act in accord with civic righteousness.[71] Catholic theology does not see man primarily in terms of freedom but rather as a being with a structure to which he must conform. In a sense freedom in such a Catholic view is only the freedom to correspond to and act according to man's essential structure. This is the primary reason Catholic social ethics did not originally stress the freedom of man.[72] The Catholic emphasis on order and structure thus understands the state as "an organic unit in which, under the preservation of their metaphysical, substantial equality and independence, the members of the moral organism in different, unequal, concrete functions form that organism. Thus the dignity of the person always exists even in the humblest function of the organic whole."[73] In this way Heinrich Rommen sees Catholic thinking overcoming a dichotomy or duality between the individual and society. Since the individual person is not understood primarily in terms of his liberty but also in terms of his natural relationship to the societal whole, there is not only an equality about man but also an inequality because each has different functions to fulfill in the social organism.

The above description of the state in Catholic thinking does reflect the papal teaching before Pius XI. In this context one can better understand the denial of the right of religious liberty even in the encyclicals of Leo XIII.[74] For the same reason, Leo XIII could call for the intervention of the state

---

[71] Jacques Ellul, "Rappels et réflexions sur une théologie de l'état," in *Les Chrétiens et l'etat* (Paris: Mame, 1967), pp. 130-137.

[72] For the contrast between the older view of responsibility and freedom and the newer view, see Albert R. Jonsen, S.J., *Responsibility in Modern Religious Ethics* (Washington/Cleveland: Corpus Books, 1968), pp. 11-27.

[73] Rommen, p. 299.

[74] Pope Leo XIII, *Libertas Praestantissimum*, especially nn. 18-47; *Acta Leonis XIII*, VIII (1888), 228-246; see also *Immortale Dei*.

to overcome some of the evils associated with laissez-faire capitalism.[75]

Although even the older Catholic teaching in the nineteenth century upheld the dignity of the human person and thus rejected the socialism of the day, it was Pius XI who gave even greater emphasis to the dignity and freedom of the human person in his social ethics. In conflict with the totalitarian states of fascism and communism, Pius XI staunchly proclaimed the dignity and freedom of the individual person who cannot be sacrificed to the end of the state.[76] Obviously such a new stress in different historical circumstances opened the way for a development or change in the hierarchical teaching on religious liberty, which Vatican II based on the dignity of the human person which "has been impressing itself more and more deeply on the consciousness of contemporary man."[77]

This changing emphasis in the social teaching of the hierarchical magisterium has also been lately incorporated into the theoretical understanding of man and society. Part Four of *Mater et Magistra,* for example, calls for a reconstruction of social relationships, indicates some false philosophical approaches, and then outlines the teaching of the Church on social matters as "having truth as its guide, justice as its end, and love as its driving force."[78] The heading of this final part of the encyclical, which is not a part of the official Latin text but is included in the translations supplied by the Vatican in other languages, reads: "Reconstruction of social relation-

---

[75]*Rerum Novarum,* nn. 32-42; A.S.S., XXIII (1890-91), 655-661.

[76] For the historical development in the teaching of the popes on the freedom of the individual, see John Courtney Murray, S.J., *The Problem of Religious Freedom* (Westminster, Md.: Newman Press, 1965).

[77] *Declaration on Religious Freedom,* n. 1; A.A.S., LVIII (1966), 929.

[78] *Mater et Magistra,* n. 226; A.A.S., LIII (1961), 454.

ships in truth, justice and love."[79] *Pacem in Terris* indicates
an important development by adding a fourth member—
freedom—to this original trio.[80] The fourfold basis for
Catholic social teaching as proposed in *Pacem in Terris* does
not merely constitute one other paragraph in the encyclical
but rather serves as a foundational point for the development
of the teaching itself. Part Three, for example, on the relations between states uses this particular fourfold schema to
develop its teaching. The section on liberty or freedom calls
for the developed countries to respect the liberty of the developing countries in the promotion of their own economic
development and progress.[81]

Perhaps somewhat paradoxically, the decade of the 60's
also witnessed a renewed realization of the intervention of
the state in the social order. *Mater et Magistra* recalls that
the multiplication of social relationships is one of the principal characteristics of our time. Greater complexity and interrelatedness calls for an added emphasis on man's role in
community and also calls for an expanded role of the government itself, as well as the functioning of other smaller groups
in the society. In this light Pope John developed his famous
teaching on socialization.[82] Later writings, especially *Populorum Progressio,* have extended this concept even to include
at times government expropriation of unused large estates.[83]

The social teaching of the hierarchical magisterium in the
1960's reflects an insistence on both the dignity and freedom
of the person and the complexities of contemporary existence
calling for a correspondingly larger role of the state in social

---

[79] *Ibid.,* n. 212; A.A.S., LIII (1961), 451.

[80] *Pacem in Terris,* n. 35; A.A.S., LV (1963), 265-266.

[81] *Ibid.,* n. 123; A.A.S., LV (1963), 289-290.

[82] *Mater et Magistra,* nn. 59-66; A.A.S., LIII (1961), 415-418. See Jean-
Yves Calvez, S.J., *The Social Thought of John XXIII* (Chicago: Henry
Regnery, 1966), pp. 1-14; John F. Cronin, S.S., *The Social Teaching of Pope
John XXIII* (Milwaukee: Bruce, 1963), pp. 8-12.

[83] *Populorum Progressio,* n. 24; A.A.S., LIX (1967), 269.

life. Catholic theology with its traditional stress on order, hierarchical structure and relationships has provided a theoretical basis for greater community intervention in the life of the society and of the individual person. The dignity of the person and the self-transcending characteristics of the individual have been incorporated into this original framework with a corresponding loosening of the way in which hierarchical ordering, structure and relationships are viewed. Interestingly, the freedom and dignity of the human person have thus accomplished the same general result as the realization of sin and the transforming power of grace mentioned in the first part and the historicity mentioned in the second part of this paper.

The presuppositions of the hierarchical teaching have not abandoned their emphasis on order and structured relationships, but other elements are added which introduce greater flexibility, historicity and even tension and some disorder into this Catholic social teaching. The hierarchical social teaching in its understanding of man and society has now incorporated the realization of man's freedom as an important foundation for its teaching, but man is not viewed in terms of his freedom alone. The very fact that truth, justice, love, freedom and power form the basis for the understanding of man's life in society indicates the tensions that will exist now and in the future. With this somewhat balanced basis, one can better approach the social problems of our complex future existence.

# 5

# Dialogue with a Theology of the Church: The Meaning of Coresponsibility

The theme of responsibility has come to the fore in Christian ethics and moral theology in the contemporary scene. A number of studies have appeared which try to explain the precise way in which responsibility has become a normative model and theme in Christian ethics.[1] The present essay will not repeat or even summarize these studies but rather, after indicating the centrality of responsibility as a normative model, will explore the foundations and the reasons explaining the importance attached to the model of responsibility.

---

[1] Two recent studies which discuss the question from different perspectives and include helpful bibliographical references are: Albert R. Jonsen, *Responsibility in Modern Religious Ethics* (Washington/Cleveland: Corpus Books, 1968) and Thomas W. Ogletree, "From Anxiety to Responsibility: The Shifting Focus of Theological Reflection," in *New Theology No. 6*, ed. Martin E. Marty and Dean G. Peerman (New York: Macmillan, 1969), pp. 35-65.

150

The reasons supporting the responsibility model show beyond all doubt that this model or something very similar to it does not involve a passing fad but corresponds to the emphases and themes which constantly recur in contemporary theological discussions. Chapter 2 has already discussed the scriptural reasons arguing for the primacy of the relationality and responsibility motif in moral theology.

The implications of the new emphasis on responsibility as a normative model are quite extensive especially on the level of the implementation of decisions or strategies, since the responsibility model is not compatible with a totally institutional motif which has traditionally characterized Catholic moral theology. Since the reasons influencing the importance of coresponsibility as a theme in ecclesiology appear to be basically the same reasons which support the theme of responsibility in moral theology, then the implications of this new model for moral theology also suggest implications in the areas of ecclesiology. The danger exists both in moral theology and in ecclesiology that one will try to put the new wine of responsibility into old wine skins, but the adoption of the normative model of responsibility calls not only for new theoretical approaches to particular problems but above all it calls for a drastic change on the level of strategies or implementation which affects ecclesiology on the level of institution and structure.

## I. CENTRALITY

Responsibility has recently emerged in a number of different contexts to become the dominant theme in Christian ethics today. Some might argue that moral theology and Christian ethics have always stressed responsibility, but there remains a great difference between the older approaches and the more contemporary approaches. Albert Jonsen in his study, *Responsibility in Modern Religious Eth-*

*ics,* willingly admits that moral philosophy often employed the concept of responsibility in ethics; but responsibility did not become a centrally normative theme, for it was limited to two different patterns of ideas.[2] The first pattern of ideas is associated with the attribution of responsibility and reflects the judge's concerns as to whether or not the individual is held accountable either for praise or for blame for the action that he has done. The second pattern of ideas is that of appropriation which is "concerned not with judging agents and actions as guilty or innocent, but with the process of how an agent takes possession of his action, moves from outer-directed to inner-directed, in short, becomes a properly moral agent."[3] Thus the responsible self as a moral agent must act with consideration, conscientiously and with commitment to pursue what he considers right. Responsibility as appropriation tends to be a formal concept without any specific content so that it could even apply to a responsible thief or a responsible liar, since the term does not connote any normative content.

What is new in the use of responsibility in Christian ethics today is that responsibility has become the central and normative motif for many theologians. The difference between an older use of responsibility and the more contemporary use is well illustrated, by a prolonged comparison which Jonsen makes between a modern seminarian and his superior, both of whom use the term responsibility but with different understandings of the term. In the older approach responsibility implies that the individual on his own internally accepts and lives up to the norms that have been established for right conduct; but in the newer approach responsibility implies that the individual lives in a network of different relation-

---

2 Jonsen, pp. 35-73.
3 *Ibid.,* p. 62.

ships in which there can be no minutely codified plans of
conduct, but in a creative way the individual determines, by
properly responding to all these demands upon him, the way
in which he should respond and live his life.[4]

Even a cursory glance at contemporary Christian ethics
reveals that the responsibility motif is both recent and becoming more important as a normative model or theme. In
the area of Christian social ethics, the term "responsible
society" came into existence in the discussions and literature
of the World Council of Churches in the years immediately
following the Second World War. In the volumes written in
preparation for the First Assembly of the World Council of
Churches meeting in Amsterdam in 1948, J. H. Oldham
wrote an essay entitled, "A Responsible Society," which,
after outlining the crisis of man and the crisis of culture, develops the elements that should be present in the social
order. These elements stress the freedom of the individual,
respect for persons, importance of interpersonal relations,
need for criticism of institutions, importance of setting restraints on institutional power, equitable distribution of material goods, and political freedom for all.[5]

The main theme of the 1948 Amsterdam Assembly was
"Man's Disorder and God's Design" which was considered
under four aspects: 1) "The Universal Church in God's Design," 2) "The Church's Witness to God's Design," 3) "The
Church and the Disorder of Society," 4) "The Church and
the International Order." The concept and implications of
the responsible society were discussed and made part of the
report of Section III. "The World Council of Churches has
employed the responsible society as a model for social ar-

---

[4] *Ibid.*, pp. 185ff.
[5] J. H. Oldham, "A Responsible Society," in *The Church and the Disorder of Society* (London: SCM Press, 1948), pp. 147-154.

rangement which maintains in dynamic equilibrium freedom and order, liberty and justice while barring the road to tyranny and disorder."[6] The 1954 Evanston Assembly of WCC explicitly declared the normative aspect of the responsible society which "is not an alternative social or political system, but a criterion by which we judge all existing social orders and at the same time a standard to guide us in the specific choices we have to make."[7]

In the area of personal ethics (realizing the problems in even insinuating a dichotomy between personal and social ethics), H. Richard Niebuhr introduced the model of man-the-responder.[8] Niebuhr points out the inadequacies of the two traditional models of teleology and deontology which he describes in terms of the models of man-the-maker and man-the citizen. Man-the-responder becomes for Niebuhr the symbol of responsibility which is an alternative and an additional way of viewing human existence. Niebuhr ascribes four elements to his notion of responsibility. "The idea or pattern of responsibility, then, may summarily and abstractly be defined as the idea of an agent's action as response to an action upon him in accordance with his interpretation of the the latter action and with his expectation of response to his response; and all of this in a continuing community of agents."[9]

Responsibility as a normative model appears in other theologians and in other contexts. In the debate over situation ethics responsibility has emerged as a basic term. Joseph

[6] Edward Duff, S.J., *The Social Thought of the World Council of Churches* (New York: Association Press, 1956), p. 191.

[7] *The Evanston Report: The Second Assembly of the World Council of Churches,* ed. W. A. Visser 't Hooft (New York: Harper and Bros., 1955), p. 113.

[8] H. Richard Niebuhr, *The Responsible Self* (New York: Harper and Row, 1963).

[9] *Ibid.,* p. 65.

Fletcher employs the concept of responsibility to describe his ethical approach which he distinguishes (in an overly simplistic manner) from the opposite extremes of legalism and libertinism. "Libertinism is controlled by the id, legalism is controlled by the superego, and situationism is ego control —which is what all analysis and therapy aim at. Ego control is responsibility."[10] Fletcher objects to a concept of responsibility understood in terms of conformity to established practices and conventional morality. "Responsibility means a free and critical 'conformity' to the fact first of all—the shifting patterns of situations—and then to the unchanging single norm or boss principle of loving concern for persons and the social balance."[11]

James Gustafson and James Laney have edited a volume of readings in Christian ethics under the title *On Being Responsible: Issues in Personal Ethics* which, as the title indicates, highlights the central and normative character of responsibility but avoids the overly simplistic approach proposed by Fletcher. Gustafson and Laney see responsibility as charting a course between an ethics of conformity to law or order that is given *a priori* and an ethic that merely reacts in utter openness to whatever is happening.[12] Perhaps in this phrasing these authors are setting up two straw men which no theologian today would defend, but their approach at least corroborates the fact that the model of responsibility has assumed a greater importance because of the contemporary debate over contextualism or situation ethics. Gustafson and Laney seem to approve the approach of the authors selected for their volume who appreciate, on the one hand,

---

[10] Joseph Fletcher, *Moral Responsibility: Situation Ethics at Work* (Philadelphia: Westminster Press, 1967), p. 237.

[11] *Ibid.*, p. 8.

[12] *On Being Responsible: Issues in Personal Ethics*, ed. James M. Gustafson and James T. Laney (New York: Harper and Row, 1968), p. 13.

openness, dynamism, interaction, freedom, responsiveness, creativity; but, on the other hand, also appreciate lines of continuity and direction, obligation, accountability and order in the proper understanding of the moral life.[13]

Responsibility also becomes a central model in Roman Catholic thought as Jonsen illustrated by his study of Häring and Johann.[14] I have employed the motif of responsibility but also raised the cautionary note that responsibility tends to be a term which all would favor but remains capable of many different interpretations.[15] For this reason in the future theologians might have to adopt more specific models which flesh out the more generic approach of the model of responsibility.

Another context in which responsibility appears as a major and controlling motif in contemporary theology concerns the attitude of the Christian toward his existence in this world and toward the structures and institutions of this world. Man does not merely conform to the existing patterns and structures of social, economic and political life; but Christian theology today asserts that now man has come of age and must assume a greater responsibility in making and keeping human life more human.[16] Some approaches of this type (e.g., in my estimation Harvey Cox's *Secular City*) fail to give enough importance to the reality of human limitations and to all the aspects of human sinfulness, but even limited

---

[13] Gustafson and Laney, p. 18. One should note here the fact that James M. Gustafson, who edited this book of readings, also has written the introduction to *The Responsible Self* and the Foreward to *Responsibility in Modern Religious Ethics*, which in its original form was a thesis written by Jonsen under Gustafson's direction.

[14] Jonsen, pp. 86-107; 153-171.

[15] Charles E. Curran, *A New Look at Christian Morality* (Notre Dame, Ind.: Fides Publishers, 1968), pp. 223-249, especially p. 231.

[16] E.g., Harvey G. Cox, *On Not Leaving It to the Snake* (New York: Macmillan, 1967).

and sinful man is called to cooperate with the creative power and redeeming forces that are striving to work towards the new heaven and the new earth.[17] This emphasis on responsibility as characterizing the Christian life in the world also calls for profound changes in the way Christians look upon the mission and function of the Christian Church.

In these three important areas of social ethics, personal ethics and the general attitude of the Christian towards his existence in this world, responsibility has become a primary normative theme in moral theology; but the term is very often used without any precise explanation of its meaning, and in some areas it tends to become a slogan which robs it of value and precision. It lies beyond our scope, however, to attempt a more systematic and probing consideration of responsibility as a normative motif in Christian ethics, for the next step in this essay tries to discover why responsibility has become a normative model in contemporary moral theology.

## II. FOUNDATIONS

Why has responsibility become so central a theme in moral theology today? Is this just a fad like a few other themes which arose in theology in the 1960's? This section will attempt to ferret out the theological reasons for the contemporary emphasis on responsibility and thus indicate that responsibility as the primary normative model in moral theology, despite the need for further clarification and systematic development, corresponds to the fundamental thrusts in contemporary theology. One could thus surmise that the same factors have played a part in the contemporary emphasis on coresponsibility in ecclesiology.

---

[17] Ogletree, *New Theology No. 6,* pp. 35-65, realizes that an ethic of responsiblity must take into consideration man's sinfulness.

## Contribution of Neo-Orthodoxy

From a theological perspective one factor influencing the concept of man-the-responder stems from the neo-Orthodox insistence on the transcendence of God and the power of the Word of God. Barthian theology, with its emphasis on the proclamation of the Word and the fact that man is pictured primarily as one who listens to and responds to the Word of God, played an important part in setting the theological scene for a further development of responsibility. Barth himself seems to have underestimated the human aspect at the expense of God's action and thus referred to man's action primarily in terms of obedience to the Word of God, but later theologians were able to develop within a neo-Orthodox context the understanding of man as responder.[18]

Emil Brunner adopted Buber's I-Thou relationship to explain the relationship between God and man and the nature of man as one who responds to the Word and work of God in Christ.[19] A good example of such an approach (with the drawbacks of not giving enough importance to the role of man and of his reason in discerning the criteria by which one can judge the very concrete action and command of God) is Joseph Sittler's *The Structure of Christian Ethics*.[20] Sittler's first chapter points out the confusion in contemporary Christian ethics and insists on the organic way in which the Bible views the God-man relationship so that Christian ethics becomes lived faith. The titles of the remaining two chapters well identify the approach taken by the author—Chap-

---

[18] For a summary and critique of Barth's approach in these matters, see James M. Gustafson, *Christ and the Moral Life* (New York: Harper and Row, 1968), pp. 13-60.

[19] Emil Brunner, *The Divine Imperative* (Philadelphia: Westminster Press, 1947).

[20] Joseph Sittler, *The Structure of Christian Ethics* (Baton Rouge, La.: Louisiana State University Press, 1958).

ter Two: "The Shape of the Engendering Deed" and Chapter
Three "The Content of the Engendered Response."

Not many theologians today would embrace the fundamental neo-Orthodox approach that was in vogue before the
1960's, but many still profit from the dialogical or respon-
sorial structure of the Christian life which could be derived
from such an approach. Bernard Häring in Roman Catholic
moral theology adopted a response and responsibility motif
precisely because of the dialogical structure of the Christian
life. The covenant relationship, which God initiated with his
people in the Old Testament and completed in the gift of His
Son in the New Testament, characterizes all of Christian
morality.[21] Häring views man as the one who responds to
the call of God's loving gift, and thus he develops such considerations as the importance of worship in the life of the
Christian and the concept of the *kairos* as a basis for an acceptable Christian ethics of the situation.[22] Häring integrates his understanding of the natural law into the same
pattern by viewing the natural law in terms of man's response to values.[23]

## A New View of Man

A second theological approach underlying the accent on
responsibility in Christian ethics stems from the way in
which theology today perceives man and his life in the
world. Theology today understands man in terms of his capacity, vocation and power to achieve his own existence and

---

[21] Bernard Häring, C.SS.R., *The Law of Christ* (Westminster, Md.: Newman Press, 1961), I, 35-39.

[22] Bernard Häring, C.SS.R., "The Biblical Notion of *Kairos*," in *Readings
in Biblical Morality*, ed. C. Luke Salm, F.S.C. (Englewood Cliffs, N.J.:
Prentice-Hall, 1967), pp. 110-127.

[23] Bernard Häring, C.SS.R., "Dynamism and Continuity in a Personalist
Approach to Natural Law," in *Norm and Context in Christian Ethics*, ed.
Gene H. Outka and Paul Ramsey (New York: Charles Scribner's Sons,
1968), pp. 199-218.

to better the world in which he lives. Man's life does not come to him as a completed whole but rather man has the task and the vocation of becoming more of a man and making more human the world in which he lives. As discussed earlier, in Chapter 3, Karl Rahner has even referred to man as a self-creator.[24] Man has the dignity of a free person with the task and the vocation of creating his own meaning and that of the world in which he lives. Thus man has responsibility for shaping his own life and his world.

Contemporary theology, in contrast to the neo-Orthodox approach, no longer insists in an exaggerated way on the ultimate limitations and sinfulness of man. An overemphasis on the transcendence of God naturally underrated the reality of man himself so that theology created a God of the gaps who filled in those things which limited man could not do for himself. Although some aspects of contemporary theology have overexalted man and romanticized the progress that man can make; nevertheless, one can easily agree with the often quoted remark that man today has come of age.[25] Human limitation and sinfulness, however, will always characterize human existence and serve as a sober antidote against the utopian dreams and unrealistic romanticism of those who too readily embrace an easy progressivism and an unduly optimistic evolutionism that seem to be based on an acceptance of the technological view of steady and ever increasing human progress.

Such a naive approach characterized both some theological approaches and also some attitudes of Christians in the last decade especially when it seemed that we as a world were winning the battle for equal rights of all men and for

---

[24] Karl Rahner, S.J., "Experiment: Man," *Theology Digest*, Sesquicentennial issue (1968), p. 58.

[25] A great impetus was given to this approach by the later writings of Dietrich Bonhoeffer.

peace on earth.[26] The naive bubble burst in the experience of an American society that now knows only too well domestic discord and international wars. Man, nevertheless, does have a vocation to work for the new heaven and the new earth; but the Paschal Mystery will always be present in his life and work. In this context one can agree that often the great sin of man is his apathy, sloth or failure to take responsibility for himself and his world. History also reminds us that man frequently has abused his power through pride and a lust for power, but we are more cognizant today of the fact that one of the most important sins of man is precisely the failure to take responsibility for himself and his world.[27]

One notes with interest that in his article on "A Responsible Society" in 1948, J. H. Oldham on two different occasions cites an article by the French Jesuit Henri De Lubac on "The New Man."[28] Man is not placed in this world as one thing among other things in a ready made world, but rather man is called to cooperate in transforming himself, his destiny and his world. Man as an individual must be protected against the abuses of institutional power and also given the opportunity to co-participate in the development of the responsible society.[29]

## Eschatology

A third theological factor influencing the primacy of the model of responsibility derives from an eschatology which gives more importance to man's existence in this world and sees it in greater continuity with the next world. I would

---

[26] For an example of this approach, see William Hamilton. "The New Optimism—from Prufrock to Ringo," in Thomas J. J. Altizer and William Hamilton, *Radical Theology and the Death of God* (Indianapolis: Bobbs-Merrill, 1966), pp. 157-169.

[27] Ogletree, *New Theology No. 6*, pp. 35-65.

[28] Oldham, *The Church and the Disorder of Society*, pp. 122 and 141.

[29] *Ibid.*, p. 122.

argue strenuously against those who would see total continuity between this world and the next, but there is not the total discontinuity which seemed to characterize much popular piety and even theology in the past.[30] The *Pastoral Constitution on the Church in the Modern World* laments the fact that in the past the daily life of the Christian was separated from his faith commitment.[31] A proper understanding of eschatology does not disparage man's life in this world but rather indicates that man does have a responsibility to cooperate in the work of bringing about the new heaven and the new earth.

Jonsen points out that Häring, Bonhoeffer and Johann all employ responsibility as a theological affirmation by which they attempt to draw into a unity the different parts of the Christian life which have too often in the past been dissected by some dualistic tendency. Häring uses the responsibility motif to overcome the dichotomy between nature and supernature so that all of Christian existence can be seen in terms of the call to perfection. Bonhoeffer's ethics of deputyship and responsibility centers on Jesus Christ the Reconciler who overcomes the false dichotomies of Law and Gospel, faith and works, and the two realms. Responsibility characterizes the Christian life as one takes on the form of Him who reconciled all things in heaven and on earth. Johann through his concept of responsibility tries to draw into a unity the multiplicity of responses and the response to the One who is Lord.[32] These three approaches thus presuppose an eschatology which sees some continuity between this world and the next.

Eschatology, which realizes both a continuity and some

---

[30] For a theological summary of the discussion in Roman Catholic theology from 1935-1955, see Bernard Besret, S.O.Cist., *Incarnation ou Eschatologie?* (Paris: Cerf, 1964).

[31] *Pastoral Constitution on the Church in the Modern World*, n. 43.

[32] Jonsen, pp. 174-184.

discontinuity between this world and the next, does not seek to take the Christian out of his present existence but rather to remind him of his Christian obligation to cooperate in the work of bringing about the new heaven and the new earth.[33] Such an eschatology includes the concept of cosmic redemption by which the Christian believes that all the world shares now in the redemption and looks forward in hope for the final coming. Eschatology properly understood embraces teleological, prophetic and apocalyptic elements so that it proclaims a future existence that will both surpass and fulfill man's existence and thus serves as a negative critique of all existing structures and institutions.[34]

The eschatological pull of the future constantly reminds the Christian of the imperfections of the present and the need to renew and change the structures and institutions now existing. In this perspective the Christian life can no longer be viewed in terms of conformity to the existing order, structures or institutions, for the Christian eschatological vision exerts a negative criticism on all existing orders and impels the Christian to attempt to transform them so they might better serve the needs of man.[35] This same eschatological understanding in ecclesiology has emphasized the pilgrim structure of the life of the Christian and the life of the Church so that it can never lose sight of the need for continual conversion. However, the Christian does not naively expect that renewal will ever be totally accomplished; but, precisely because of his hope that God will bring to com-

---

[33] For an appreciative critique of the Council's emphasis on realized eschatology and cosmic redemption, see George A. Lindbeck, *The Future of Roman Catholic Theology* (Philadelphia: Fortress Press, 1969).

[34] Harvey Cox, "Evolutionary Progress and Christian Promise," *Concilium*, 26, (June 1967), 35-47; M. C. Vanhengal, O.P., and J. Peters, "Death and Afterlife," *Concilium*, 26 (June 1967), 161-181.

[35] Edward Schillebeeckx, O.P., *God the Future of Man* (New York: Sheed and Ward, 1968).

pletion the work he has begun, the Christian remains committed to his vocation of bringing about the new heaven and the new earth despite all the frustrations and failures that are a part of his life. Responsibility also involves the fact that the Christian is committed to his task despite all the suffering this involves. Chapter 4 has pointed out the overly optimistic worldview of the *Pastoral Constitution on the Church in the Modern World.*

### Emphasis on the Subject

From a philosophical perspective the importance of responsibility as a normative model for moral theology corresponds to the most significant developments in philosophy—especially the importance of the subject and the insistence on historical consciousness. The turn to the subjective represents a major theme common to many philosophical approaches in the last two centuries which has had repercussions throughout the political, social, cultural, and economic life of man.[36] In ethical terms the freedom and dignity of the individual have become a cornerstone in questions of personal and social ethics. The emphasis on the personal subject and the freedom and dignity of the person could be exaggerated into a liberalistic individualism unless one remembers that the individual person lives in relationship with other persons and communities. Freedom cannot become an absolute, for the individual subject with his freedom and dignity exists in a relationship of responsibility with others and with the whole world.

Emphasis on the human person as a free subject in relation to other subjects and called to act responsibly in his life serves as a basis for the model of responsibility in Christian

---

[36] David Tracy, *The Achievement of Bernard Lonergan* (New York: Herder and Herder, 1970), pp. 1-11.

ethics. The moral theology of Bernard Häring reflects this personalist approach based on the subject in relation to others responding to values rather than being determined in his actions by the nature and finality of his particular organic functions.[37] The documents of Vatican II underline the dignity of the subject as a cornerstone in ethical considerations. In these documents the word responsibility does appear with great frequency although the documents do not systematically develop a model of responsibility for personal ethics or of the responsible society for social ethics; but one could easily show that these documents do contain the approaches out of which one could construct such models. *The Declaration on Religious Freedom* begins by recognizing, "A sense of the dignity of the human person has been impressing itself more and more deeply on the consciousness of contemporary man."[38] The dignity, freedom and importance of the human person constitute a major foundation for the teaching developed in the *Pastoral Constitution on the Church in the Modern World* which frequently employs the terminology of responsibility.

The turn to the subjective has influenced every aspect of moral theology and Christian ethics, but this influence appears most strikingly in the contemporary understanding of sin. Contemporary theologians no longer define sin in terms of an external action which is not in conformity with a particular law or norm, but personalist and relational terms define sin in terms of a fundamental option or core project of his existence in which the person affirms himself in his multiple relations with God, neighbor, self and the world. The

---

[37] Bernard Häring, "The Inseparability of the Unitive-Procreative Functions of the Marital Act," in *Contraception: Authority and Dissent,* ed. Charles E. Curran (New York: Herder and Herder, 1969), pp. 176-192.
[38] *Declaration on Religious Freedom,* n. 1.

individual in the very core of his being accepts responsibility for his life and existence.[39]

Robert Johann has succinctly described the task of philosophy today as pointing out what it means to be a person, for the personal dimension has come to the fore in contemporary philosophy. In the past personhood was seen in terms of nature so that a person made sense of his life by freely assuming his place within the existing patterns and structures of life. Today the person is emerging as an original value transcending the order of the factual and the determinate. Johann, sensitive to the dangers of pure subjectivism or isolated individualism, views the indivdual person in his relation to community and his openness to the Infinite and the Absolute.[40] In philosophical terms the transcendental movement in Roman Catholic thinking exemplified by such important contemporary thinkers as Rahner, Lonergan and Coreth represents the turn to the subjective. Lonergan in *Insight* hopes that the reader himself will appropriate his own rational self-consciousness by understanding what it is to understand.[41] Lonergan views man as called to live up to the transcendental exigencies: Be attentive, be intelligent, be reasonable, be responsible, develop and, if necessary, change.[42]

Christian social ethics has stressed the dignity and freedom of the individual person especially in recent historical and cultural contexts and thus favored the development of the responsibility aspect of Christian ethics. In reaction to

---

[39] Kevin F. O'Shea, "The Reality of Sin: Theological and Pastoral Critique," *Theological Studies,* 29 (1968), 241-259; John W. Glazer, S.J., "Transition Between Grace and Sin," *Theological Studies,* 29 (1968), 260-274.

[40] Robert O. Johann, *Building the Human* (New York: Herder and Herder, 1968), pp. 77-78.

[41] Bernard J. F. Lonergan, S.J., *Insight: A Study of Human Understanding* (New York: Longmans, 1957), p. 28.

[42] Tracy, p. 268.

totalitarian governments, statements of both the Roman Catholic hierarchical magisterium and the World Council of Churches emphasize the fundamental and inalienable dignity of the human person. In the world of technology with its dehumanizing tendencies, there exists a need to explain man's responsibility to direct and guide technology for responsible human needs and not to become enslaved by the creation of his own powers. The term "responsible society" as used in the WCC literature aims at the protection and safeguarding of the dignity and freedom of the individual person. In his famous article, J. H. Oldham emphatically states: "There can be no question in the first place that Christians must stand firmly for the freedom of man to obey God and to act in accordance with their conscience."[43] Man must be free to speak the truth and criticize existing institutions so that creative ideas can advance society. As man, the other person deserves respect, and his personhood ordinarily should not be violated in a violent way. But this free individual subject must acknowledge his responsibility to God, to other persons, and to the whole of society.[44]

The responsible society as a normative model in ecumenical ethics implies demands not only upon the individual, but also upon soceity iself, so that society in no way infringes unduly upon the dignity and freedom of the individual. The institutional power of those who have authority in societies must be limited by a fundamental democratization of the society so that the power of society does not abuse the rights of the individual person.[45]

A study pamphlet issued by the WCC on the responsible society cites the need to encourage the initiative and partici-

[43] Oldham, *The Church and the Disorder of Society,* p. 412.
[44] H. D. Wendland, "The Theology of the Responsible Society," in *Christian Social Ethics in a Changing World,* ed. John C. Bennett (New York: Association Press, 1966), pp. 135-152.
[45] *Ibid.,* pp. 135-136.

pation of the person, of the family, of small groups, and of communities. The twin dangers of totalitarianism and technology constantly menace the freedom and dignity of the individual person.[46] *The Declaration on Religious Freedom* of the Second Vatican Council, although it does not explicitly employ the model of the responsible society, begins by acknowledging the "responsible freedom" of man and the fact that constitutional limits should be placed on the power of governments "in order that there may be no encroachment on the rightful freedom of the person and of associations." Thus *The Declaration on Religious Freedom* argues for the need to limit the powers of institutional government and safeguard the "responsible freedom" of the person in much the same way as the Protestant theologians have applied the normative criterion of the responsible society.

The relationship between the individual, free person "responsible to God and his neighbor" and the state and society is succinctly formulated by the report of Section III of the Amsterdam Assembly of the WCC: "A responsible society is one where freedom is the freedom of men who acknowledge responsibility to justice and public order, and where those who hold political authority or economic power are responsible for its exercise to God and the people whose welfare is affected by it."[47]

## Historical Consciousness

Responsibility as an emerging normative motif in moral theology also corresponds to the philosophical shift from classicism to historical consciousness.[48] Classicism thought

---

[46] *The Responsible Society* (New York: World Council of Churches, 1949).

[47] The full text can be found in *The Church and the Disorder of Society*, pp. 197-205.

[48] Bernard Lonergan, S.J., "The Transition from a Classicist World View to Historical Mindedness," in *Law for Liberty*, ed. James Biechler (Baltimore: Helicon Press, 1967), pp. 126-133.

in terms of the immutable, the eternal and the unchanging; whereas historical consciousness emphasizes evolution, growth, change and historicity. A classicist approach concentrates on order and tries to put things into an order that tends to be conceived in an *a priori* way; whereas historical consciousness reflects the reality of growth, movement and tension that defies complete order and categorization. A classicist view adopts a methodology that operates deductively and in a more *a priori* fashion, but historical mindedness adopts an approach that is more *a posteriori* and inductive.

The newer approaches in moral theology which employ the responsibility motif do so precisely because of the dangers of seeing the moral life of man primarily in terms of conformity to pre-existing norms and structures. Contemporary theology and philosophy highlight the historical and cultural limitations of everything human, thus accentuating the need for growth and change. The progress of modern life and the great strides made in many areas of human existence, as well as even the suddenness and abruptness of catastrophe and tragedy, argue for a world view that gives more importance to evolution, change and growth.

Theological reflection indicates how often the natural law theory in Roman Catholic theology proclaimed as an absolute norm of nature itself what was merely a culturally and historically conditioned reality. In the area of personal morality, the controversy over norm and context in Christian ethics reflects the contemporary philosophical emphasis on subjectivity and historicity so that man does not merely conform in a passive manner to already existing laws and structures without seriously questioning their meaning and existence. All theologians realize the danger of oversimplification which would deny the need for or existence of any law, order or structure in moral theology, but all would agree that too often in the past the model of conformity to existing law and order received undue priority. The controversy over artificial contraception in the Roman Catholic Church also underscores the same philosophical priorities, for those who oppose the hierarchical teaching accuse the older approach of deriving morality from the physical structure of nature and man's faculties rather than appreciating the fact that responsible man can intervene in the order of nature to bring about a more human existence.[49]

In the area of social ethics, the emergence of historical consciousness recalls the limitations in every institution and structure in the political, economic, social and cultural realms. The WCC documents and commentaries consistently underscore the fact that the responsible society cannot be identified with any existing economic system, since the WCC did not want to endorse any existing social structure, especially the American. The very term responsible society is more open to a less structured understanding of reality in that it seems to allow for more dynamism, tension and interplay than the other concepts such as natural law or orders of creation or even divine mandates. Too often in the past a natural law approach in theory has resulted in a social conservatism in practice that tended to identify the status quo as the order determined by God.

The concept of responsible society acknowledges the existence of various forces and groups in society which are in relationship to one another and which cannot be adequately accounted for by a hierarchical structuring of society which assigns each element or class in society to a particular function or role in a well ordered, hierarchical whole. History and even contemporary reflection show that the structure of society existing at any given time tends to promote the interests of the people in power at the expense of those who are at the lowest level of the society. Mere conformity to the existing structures would only perpetuate the existing inequi-

---

[49] *The Birth Control Debate,* ed. Robert G. Hoyt (Kansas City: National Catholic Reporter, 1968), pp. 175-197.

ties and injustices; but the revolutionary needs to remember that some type of structure will always be necessary, and it is irresponsible merely to destroy what is existing without building something else in its place. There will always be differences in society based on a multiplicity of factors, but Wendland argues that a relationship of partnership, while recognizing the differences in the social position of individuals and the resulting social differentiation among them calls for a coresponsibility on the part of all who are involved in the economic enterprise whether it be as owner, manager or laborer.[50]

Catholic social ethics has not formally employed the responsible society as a normative motif, but in contemporary Catholic social ethics there is a distinct movement away from the natural law motif with its emphasis on order and institutions to a stress on responsibility and the dynamic interrelatedness of all in society. The beginnings of this change are clearly evident in the *Pastoral Constitution on the Church in the Modern World,* and Louis Janssens exemplifies the same general tendency. "We are no longer simply parts of a social whole; we are called to take part in the life of society."[51] At times, Janssens gives the impression that man merely accepts the already existing social relationships, but the heart of his theory advocates a greater appreciation of historicity and personal involvement in changing the structures of society, for he develops his entire social ethics in terms of coexistence, cooperation and coparticipation.[52]

The central importance of responsibility as a normative motif in moral theology cannot be dismissed as a passing fad, for it corresponds to the basic theological and philosophical

---

[50] Wendland, *Christian Social Ethics in a Changing World,* p. 140.

[51] Louis Janssens, "The Christian Concern for Society," in *Christian Social Ethics in a Changing World,* p. 166.

[52] Louis Janssens, *Freedom of Conscience and Religious Freedom* (Staten Island: Alba House, 1965), pp. 83-117.

accents in contemporary thought. H. Richard Niebuhr's adoption of the model of man the responder to develop the normative motif of responsibility thus appears to be a more adequate model than the teleological or deontological models of the past. The responsibility motif also coheres better with contemporary theological and philosophical anthropology.

The teleological approach implies that man has knowledge of and control over his end and the means to attain it which, in natural law terms, seems to imply that in the nature of man one can find the blueprint for man's development and growth; but modern man senses that such an anthropological view remains too orderly and too closed. Man today is more aware of change, growth and discontinuity so that he does not conform to a prearranged plan determined by his nature but rather constantly responds to the various situations in which he finds himself, thus discovering and shaping his existence in the midst of these relationships. As we look back over our life the accidental and chance happenings and our responses to them seem to be much more important than any tight plan according to which we determined a particular goal for ourselves and set about obtaining it.

The deontological model also seems too simplistic in an age that knows rapid change, complexity and agonizing ambiguity. Man today questions many of the existing patterns and structures because of his understanding of his own power as well as the incompleteness and sinfulness which affect everything in the light of Christian eschatology. Likewise the emphasis on subjectivity and historicity argues against a model that sees man in terms of obedience to laws and/or existing structures. However, there remain some dangers in the use of the responsibility motif which should be noted. The adoption of such a model does not mean that moral theology no longer considers the good, the right, and the normative; but these must be understood in the context of the model of responsibility.

## III. IMPLICATIONS

The adoption of the responsibility motif as normative in moral theology will have ramifications in the whole field of moral theology. There lurks the danger of a ready acceptance of the concept of responsibility without a realization that its central and normative character will have repercussions in many areas. In a parallel manner the adoption of the concept of coresponsibility in ecclesiology does not mean just the addition of a new term or concept, but would seem to imply a number of very important structural changes. This section of the essay will indicate more precisely what are the further ramifications of the responsibility motif in Christian ethics and on the basis of that suggest what its ramifications should be in ecclesiology. Neither in moral theology nor in ecclesiology can responsibility be adopted as a normative consideration without very extensive changes especially on the level of strategy and institutional structure.

### Personal Ethics

The implications of the responsibility motif in moral theology are apparent in the area of personal ethics in the debate over situation ethics. All would agree that in the past, moral theology overemphasized the law aspect of the moral life, but now in a more positive manner moral theologians must develop the precise place of the various norms in the moral life of the Christian. There seems to be a somewhat widespread opinion that moral theology or Christian ethics will cease to exist within this century if not within the present decade.[53] Such predictions apparently stem from the fact that the moral life no longer relies on absolute norms and that personal responsibility will eliminate the need for the

---

[53] John G. Milhaven, "Exit for Ethicists," *Commonweal,* 91 (October 31, 1969), pp. 135-140.

science of moral theology. This conclusion distorts a proper understanding of responsibility.

The emphasis on responsibility will call for serious and scientific reflection on the way in which people make their moral decisions. Individuals as well as societies and institutions incessantly face the problem of determining proper values and establishing the proper relationship among the various values. An emphasis on the responsible self requires a better understanding of the characteristics, or attitudes, or, in an older terminology, the virtues, which should characterize the self in his multiple relationships. These aspects which have been neglected in the recent past because of a narrow view that considers the moral life only in terms of the existence or non-existence of norms will deserve more study in the future.

Above all, theologians in the future should inquire more into the nature of the moral judgment. How does the Christian person make his moral decisions? Will a concept of judgment as found in the thought of Bernard Lonergan help the moral theologian in describing and understanding the moral judgment? Can the moral judgment be based exclusively on the consequences attendant upon a particular course of action? To what extent is the Christian moral "ought" experientially verifiable? In the past, Christian spirituality developed the famous rules for the discernment of the Spirit which in contemporary form could be of great assistance in developing a critical understanding of the moral judgment and decision.[54] A proper understanding of responsibility as a normative model for moral theology does not eliminate the need for moral theology but raises very important questions about the lesser but precise function of norms, the values to be sought, the dispositions which characterize the responsible

---

[54] Karl Rahner, S.J., *The Dynamic Element in the Church* (New York: Herder and Herder, 1964), pp. 84-170.

self and above all a critical understanding of the moral judgment.

## Social Ethics

The implications of the responsibility motif in social ethics are greater and have not been discussed as much as its implications in personal ethics. Mention has already been made of the fact that the natural law approach tended to absolutize historically and culturally limited situations as in the case of usury, religious liberty and private property. Likewise, the natural law approach of social ethics in the Catholic tradition opened the door to a conservatism in practice by failing to see the imperfections and limited characteristics of all existing structures which can never perfectly mirror the divine order.

Natural law both in its philosophical and theological presuppositions stressed order and rationality. Order very often implied a hierarchical arrangement in which everything had its assigned place and by fitting into the total picture formed a harmonious ordering of all of reality. Chapter 4 has already documented this earlier approach and considered it in a slightly different context. The responsibility motif as normative in Christian ethics must question this fundamental assertion of social ethics in the Catholic tradition with its almost exclusive emphasis on order.

The responsibility motif as normative argues against any seemingly minute plan to be found inscribed in the heart of man. Peace remains the goal and aspiration of men who incessantly strive to achieve it, but peace remains a challenge and a task to which man must commit himself rather than a detailed plan that he can find engraved in his heart. The motif of responsibility with its emphasis on subjectivity and historicity realizes there is in this complex world no detailed plan for finding peace which is imprinted in the heart of man, but man has the vocation to creatively bring about the reality of peace as best he can in a limited and sin-filled world which will never truly know total peace.

Order and reason are not the only elements present in the social situation of man; there also exist disorder and power. Power cannot be construed as something necessarily evil in itself, but rather can be and must be used creatively and responsibly by man to bring about a greater participation in the divine peace. Reason alone is not a sufficient and all-encompassing instrumentality for trying to bring about peace and justice in the world. A mere cursory glance at our society today indicates that order and reason are not the only elements that enter into the picture of man's quest for justice and peace in a limited and sinful world.[55]

The rights of the black man in the United States have been improved in the last few years not primarily because of reason and order, but because of power and force. The structures of universities are being changed today not because of the outcome of rational debate, which universities by definition should foster, but because students are using power to force changes in a lethargic institution which, despite its noble aims, remains only too complacent with the status quo. Today at times the pendulum has swung to the other extreme in a romanticization of power and violence; but the motif of responsibility which calls for man to creatively bring about more just structures and not merely find them already engraved in his heart involves a creative use of man's resources to bring about social change and betterment. Power does not necessarily involve just physical power or even violence.

---

[55] One should indicate the lack of literature on the subject of power in Roman Catholic theology, which corroborates the assertion that Roman Catholic theology has placed too much insistence on order, structure and rationality in the area of strategy and ethical implementation. For one theological study of power, see Karl Rahner, S.J., "The Theology of Power," *Theological Investigations* (Baltimore: Helicon Press, 1966), IV, 391-409.

There are many important forms of moral power and political power which must be developed.

The responsibility motif does not call for an abandonment of reason and an embracing of disorder, but rather such an approach realistically recognizes that there is no order in the sense of a detailed plan already existing, but responsible men must work together to forge ahead in the never-ending struggle for peace and justice. Power without reason and rationality becomes anarchy, but reason also remains inadequate as a total solution for the injustices existing in our society. There certainly does exist in the hearts of men a thirst for justice and peace, but there is no detailed plan, order or structure telling him how to bring this about. Contemporary man despite his limitations and sinfulness understands that he has the task and the vocation to strive to bring about a better order of justice and peace.

Edward LeRoy Long, Jr. divides his comprehensive *A Survey of Christian Ethics* into two major parts — the formulation of the ethical norm and the implementation of the ethical decision.[56] These two major divisions correspond to the twin foci of the ethical enterprise — the elements of standard setting and the ways of implementing decisions. Long divides the implementation of ethical decisions which considers the various strategies involved in practical action into three different approaches — the institutional motif, the operational motif and the intentional motif.[57] Long's distinction between the operational motif and the institutional motif is not precise and sharp, but this overlapping seems to be due to the fact that the two terms describe different emphases rather than totally opposing approaches. The institu-

---

[56] Edward LeRoy Long, Jr., *A Survey of Christian Ethics* (New York: Oxford University Press, 1967).

[57] *Ibid.*, pp. 167-190.

tional motif rests on the primacy of order, insofar as this order is made manifest in structure and institution; whereas
the operational motif, as its name implies, gives greater importance to power. Does office serve as the basis for power
or does power serve as the basis of office? In the institutional
motif power comes from the existing order and institution
which confers power on its office holders; whereas the operational motif sees power and force as the elements which
bring about order and consequently justice and peace. Many
theologians interpret the world around us not as a structure
of 'order' but as a 'sea of influences' or as a conflict of
interests."[58]

A Catholic today must wince when in the contemporary
context he reads the title of Chapter 11 in Long's book,
"Law, Order and the Catholic Tradition," but no one could
take exception to the fact that Long has rightly classified the
approach of the Catholic theological tradition under the institutional motif. Long illustrates the use of this motif from
important figures in the tradition, especially Augustine,
Thomas and, in our own days, the encyclicals of John XXIII.

The adoption of the responsibility motif as normative in
moral theology would temper the institutional motif which
has predominated and in fact been the only motif in the
Catholic tradition. I would not naively abandon the need for
order, institution and structure, but the responsibility motif
has the practical consequence of calling for a greater appreciation of the operational motif in the area of strategy and
concrete action. There is not a detailed order and structure
for society which assigns each person his particular office to
carry out for the good of the whole in accord with some overall plan. The responsibility motif argues against a rigidly
fixed order and structure and calls for a greater flexibility and

---

58 *Ibid.*, p. 216.

interaction among the various elements in the society as they struggle to bring about a more just society.

In this day and age I do not think that one can adopt a purely operational motif or a purely institutional approach; but the primacy of the responsibility motif with its roots in a greater appreciation of the creative vocation of the subject and a greater appreciation of historicity does call for assigning a lesser role to the institutional approach on the level of the implementation of ethical decisions. In this very important area of ethical concern (an area that Long considers equally as important as the theoretical area of setting ethical standards), the adoption of the responsibility motif must call for an important shift of emphasis in Catholic theology and practice.

## Implications for Ecclesiology

Responsibility has emerged as the primary normative motif in moral theology somewhat contemporaneously with the emphasis on coresponsibility in ecclesiology. The responsibility motif in moral theology has had repercussions throughout the discipline; so too one can expect that the coresponsibility theme will have great effect in the area of ecclesiology. Precisely because the centrality of responsibility calls for a change on the level of the institutional motif in the implementation of ethical decisions, one can expect that the coresponsibility theme in ecclesiology will call for the same type of change which in this area will involve changes in the practical structure and life of the Church. From the experience in the area of moral theology, I will tentatively suggest what these changes might be in the area of ecclesiology. (I believe all these changes, even though they would definitely transform the day to day image and working structure of the Church, are compatible with Roman Catholicism's self-understanding of the Church; but I emphasize that my competency only extends to suggestions based on the parallels in moral theology.)

The responsible society with its recognition of the dignity and freedom of the human person saw the necessity of protecting the individual against the abuses of institutional power. One must have some type of check against the power inherent in the institution and its institutional offices. In many ways this calls for a democratization of the society, in this case the Roman Catholic Church; but I do not think that such protections for the individual would destroy the papal and hierarchical functions in the Church if these are properly understood. The opposition of the theologians to the papal teaching on artificial contraception illustrated how power was employed against the possible abuse of power. There was no official structure of theologians or any particular power connected with the office of theologian in the Church, but the theologians in some unity were able to limit effectively what many thought was an abuse of papal power. The establishment of grievance boards in various dioceses now protects the individual in the Church from the abuse of administrative power on the part of office-holders in the Church. These protections and safeguards for the individual must be both of an institutional nature and of a more free type as exemplified in the reaction of the theologians or in the ad hoc opposition of certain groups in the Church to action taken by office holders.

Coresponsibility requires that the Church as institution abandon any hope or plan for organizing and directing all the activities of the members of the society. Law and structure can no longer determine the entire life of the society and the people who make it up, but rather structure and law will have a necessary but not primary role to play in the life of the Church even as an institution. The responsible society relies more on the creativity of its members working together with others and in a sea of influences interacting in the

Church. Canonical reform must be radical in the sense that the new law must reflect the more limited but necessary role of structure and law in the life of the Church.

As a result of the lesser role attached to structure all the power in the Church will not be in the hands of those who hold offices in the structure. There will be many other sources of power in the Church which will constantly be interacting as the Church tries to live up to its mission and calling. For example, I hope the Immaculate Heart Community will discover new ways in which smaller groups within the Church, but not directly and legally tied into the Church structure, will continue to function and operate within the Church and also be an independent source of power within the Church. Religious communities will all be watching this experiment with great interest, and the institutional power structure will definitely be influenced by this movement. In the future, I believe we will have many more groups within the Church which are juridically independent of the institutional structure but will exercise power in trying to bring about change in the institution. There are already such groups in existence in the form of priests' associations, lay associations, and new independent religious communities.

A highly structured institution like the Roman Catholic Church obviously has difficulties in the whole process of incorporating change and development. The institutional motif in contrast to the operational motif views even change in terms of a command or order put into execution by the institution itself. However, in the more operational motif change very often will occur from underneath and sometimes even against the will of some or even many of the office holders. The clash of the two viewpoints is well illustrated by what is happening in many parts of the country today with regard to the sacrament of penance. Priests with solid theological reasoning are employing penance services in which there is no individual confession of sins to the priests. Many priests believe they have a real obligation to celebrate such penance services because of the pastoral needs of the times.

The official teaching of the hierarchical magisterium cannot accept such an approach. While acknowledging the need for a change in the liturgy of the sacraments, especially penance, the *Constitution on the Liturgy* establishes the following general norms: "1) Regulation of the sacred liturgy depends solely on the authority of the Church, that is, on the Apostolic See and, as laws may determine, on the bishop. 2) In virtue of power conceded by the law, the regulation of the liturgy within certain defined limits belongs to various kinds of competent territorial bodies of bishops legitimately established. 3) Therefore, absolutely no other person, not even a priest, may add, remove, or change anything in the liturgy on his own authority" (n. 22). I am not advocating that individuals make whatever changes they want in the liturgy. There is a general need for an overall unity of approach, but this value at times must take second place to more important values which I would see behind the introduction of new penitential rites on the part of the priest.

One cannot really institutionalize the process of change. A changing society is much more inclined to see reality in terms of a sea of influences rather than a structure of orders. Another example of change now being introduced into the Church concerns the pastoral approach to divorced people. More and more priests, on a private basis, are making pastoral provisions for some divorced people to fully participate in the sacramental life of the Church despite the strict canonical prohibition. Likewise some divorced people are rightly being counseled to remarry and still participate in the full life of the Church. Undoubtedly as this becomes a more widespread practice, it will create some tensions and struggles.

The primacy of the responsibility model will bring changes to the life of the Church in the form of a more operational motif in the internal life of the Roman Church. Note that I have gone beyond the call for mere institutional reforms in the sense of making institutional provision through collegiality and other means for bringing more people into the decision making process in the Church. In no sense does the centrality of responsibility and coresponsibility deny the need for decentralization and the application of the principle of subsidiarity throughout the life and structure of the Church, but coresponsibility will call for even more radical changes insofar as it challenges the sole primacy of the institutional motif in the life of the Church.

A more operational motif in the life of the Church will not be a panacea for our contemporary problems. Only a fool would claim that every form of illegal experimentation or every wish of particular groups in the Church would be for the good of the whole Church. There will be constant tension and the danger of using power irresponsibly on the part of all in the Church. Some might retort that the greater importance attached to the operational motif in the life of the Church tends to politicize the Church. This charge is true to the same extent that the undisputed primacy of the institutional motif also constitutes a politicization of the life of the Church but in accord with a political structure that does not reflect the needs of the present time.

A true understanding of coresponsibility in the Church calls for a deemphasis on the institutional and official structure in determining the life of the Church, but there will always be the need for this structure in the Church. In addition there will also be other groups and individuals exercising power within the Church as other waves in the sea of influences. However, the primary source of the life and unity of the Church remains the covenant commitment of the individual believer to the Lord and to his fellow believers in the ecclesial community which celebrates the saving event of the Lord and continues his creative, redemptive and sanctifying work in the world until He comes.

# 6

## Dialogue with the Homophile Movement: The Morality of Homosexuality

The discipline of moral theology or Christian ethics is in a state of transition today. The changing self-understanding of the Roman Catholic Church has affected moral theology. Moral theology also reflects the contemporary emphases in religious and philosophical ethics as well as the changing mores and life styles of our contemporary world.

An area of ethical concern receiving wide attention in the last few years is homosexuality. The militant homophile movement strives to bring the question to the fore and argues for equality for homosexuals in all spheres of life.[1] No longer can society at large or the Christian Church ignore the existence of homosexuality or the homophile community.

---

[1] Richard R. Parlour, *et al.*, "The Homophile Movement: Its Impact and Implications," *Journal of Religion and Health*, VI (1967), 217-234; Foster Gunnison, Jr., "The Homophile Movement in America," in *The Same Sex*, ed. Ralph Weltge (Philadelphia/Boston: Pilgrim Press, 1969), pp. 113-128.

How will the Church, specifically the Roman Catholic Church, respond to these demands? What should be the attitude of the law to homosexuality? The scope of this essay is more narrow: a discussion of the morality of homosexuality and the methodological approaches employed in this consideration. This study should, however, furnish a basis for forming a proper pastoral approach to the homosexual and the homophile community and also indicate an approach to the question of the law and homosexuality. A proper pastoral approach should develop in the light of moral theology, although a Dutch symposium on homosexuality almost ten years ago tried to develop a pastoral approach prescinding from moral theology because they obviously feared the rigidity of moral theology.[2]

A discussion of homosexuality from the viewpoint of moral theology necessarily raises methodological questions for moral theology itself. Christian ethicists have employed different methodological approaches even though they may have arrived at the same conclusion. In considering the morality of homosexual acts this essay will also evaluate the different methodologies employed and also raise specific methodological questions which concern the particular topic of homosexuality as well as the entire gamut of topics considered by moral theology.

Two important methodological questions for the discipline of moral theology come to the fore in the discussion of homosexuality—the use and place of the Scriptures in moral theology and the role of the empirical sciences in the moral judgment. Two earlier chapters have considered these two methodological questions in general, but the present chapter will illuminate these general considerations in the light of the particular question of homosexuality.

---

[2] A Overing, *et al., Homosexualiteit* (Hilversum: Brand, 1961). French translation: *Homosexualité* tr. Y. Huon (Paris: Mame, 1967).

## METHODOLOGY AND BIBLICAL DATA

Christian ethics reflects on human reality within the context of Christian revelation, but there have been differences about the exact role and function of Scripture in the discipline of moral theology. In general, Roman Catholic moral theology has approached concrete ethical questions in the light of a natural law methodology which tended to downplay the role of Scripture. The theological manual written by Noldin-Schmitt, for example, discusses homosexuality very briefly according to the principles of the natural law and merely refers to three Scriptural texts in a footnote.[3] Very often the general approach to Roman Catholic theology included a few proof texts from the Scriptures which were employed to prove the point which had been founded on natural law reasoning.[4]

Protestant theology methodologically gives more importance to the place of the Scriptures in ethical methodology, but a fundamentalistic Protestant approach errs by again using the Scriptures in a proof text fashion without any further consideration. The mainstream of Protestant theology benefiting from the impressive biblical studies begun in the nineteenth century realizes the cultural and historical limitations inherent in the Scriptures themselves.[5] The renewal in Roman Catholic moral theology emphasized the need for a more biblically oriented approach. During and after Vatican II Catholic theology has, at times, gone to the opposite extreme and become almost exclusively biblical to the detri-

---

[3] H. Noldin, S.J., A. Schmitt, S.J., and G. Heinzel, S.J., *Summa Theologiae Moralis: De Castitate* (36th ed.; Innsbruck: Rauch, 1958), p. 39.

[4] Marcellinus Zalba, S. I., *Theologiae Moralis Summa*, Vol. II: *Theologia Moralis Specialis* (Madrid: Biblioteca de Autores Cristianos, 1953), pp. 277 and 378.

[5] James M. Gustafson, "Christian Ethics," in *Religion*, ed. Paul Ramsey (Englewood Cliffs, N. J.: Prentice-Hall, 1965), pp. 309-325.

ment of its historical self-understanding that the Christian shares much ethical wisdom and knowledge with all men.[6]

Chapter 2 has pointed out that today Protestant and Catholic ethicians share a general convergence in their understanding of the place and function of the Scriptures in moral theology. The Scriptures do not have a monopoly on ethical wisdom and thus do not constitute the sole way into the ethical problem for the Christian ethicist.[7] Obviously the Christian ethicist derives his general orientation from a scriptural base and realizes the importance of particular attitudes and ways of life which are contained in the Scriptures. However, in the case of specific conclusions about specific actions Christian theologians realize the impossibility of any methodological approach which would develop its argument only in terms of individual biblical texts taken out of their context.[8]

In the question of homosexuality the biblical data has been interpreted differently, and possibly erroneous interpretations seem to have overemphasized the heinousness of homosexual acts. Although scriptural data forms only one part of theological data, the moral theologian must have an adequate understanding of that data. Christians generally interpret the famous story of the town of Sodom related in Genesis 19: 4-11 as the destruction of the city by God because of its great sinfulness as shown in homosexuality. Recently, D.S. Bailey has revived and revised an interpretation

---

[6] Recall the arguments proposed at the Second Vatican Council to revise the Declaration on Religious Liberty so that the document might have its primary basis in Scripture. See Richard J. Regan, S.J., *Conflict and Consensus: Religious Freedom and the Second Vatican Council* (New York: Macmillan, 1967), pp. 117-129.

[7] John C. Bennett, "Issues for the Ecumenical Dialogue," in *Christian Social Ethics in a Changing World,* ed. John C. Bennett (New York: Association Press, 1966), pp. 371-372.

[8] Josef Blank, "New Testament Morality and Modern Moral Theology," *Concilium,* XXV (May 1967), 9-22.

which maintains that the Sodom story does not refer to homosexuality or homosexual acts.[9] The word "to know" does not
necessarily involve a sexual connotation but rather could be
interpreted as a violation of hospitality. D. S. Bailey points
out that the first explicit references involving the "traditional
opinion" that the Sodomites were annihilated because of their
homosexuality appeared in Palestine only during the second
century B. C. Six Old Testament references (Genesis 13:3;
18:20; Jer. 23:14; Ez. 16:49-50; Wisdom 10:8; 19:8 Ecclus.
16:8) mention the sinfulness of the Sodomites because of
which they were punished, but these texts do not identify the
sin as homosexuality.

Most contemporary exegetes do not agree with Bailey's position that a new and different interpretation identifying the
sin of Sodom as homosexuality only arose in the second century. Perhaps these exegetes are not aware of the in-depth
study made by Bailey. *The Jerome Biblical Commentary,* the
*Jerusalem Bible, Genesis* in the Anchor Bible edition, all indicate that homosexuality is the sin of the people of Sodom
because of which their city was destroyed.[10] Although
Bailey does not find homosexuality in the sin of the people
of Sodom, he still accepts a general condemnation of homosexuality (without the significant heinousness attached to
the Sodom story) in the Old Testament as found in two ref-

---

[9] Derrick Sherwin Bailey, *Homosexuality and the Western Christian Tradition* (London/New York: Longmans, Green and Co., 1955), pp. 1-28. An
earlier denial of the traditional homosexual interpretation of the sin of Sodom
was proposed by George A. Barton, "Sodom," in *Encyclopedia of Religion
and Ethics,* ed. James Hastings, XI (New York: Charles Scribner's Sons,
1921), 672.

[10] Eugene H. Maly, "Genesis," in *The Jerome Biblical Commentary,* eds.
R. E. Brown, S.S., J. A. Fitzmyer, S.J., R. E. Murphy, O. Carm. (Engle-
wood Cliffs, N. J.: Prentice-Hall, 1966), I, 20-21; *La Sainte Bible,* traduite
en francais sous la direction de l'École Biblique de Jérusalem (Paris:
Éditions du Cerf, 1956), p. 25; *The Jerusalem Bible,* ed. Alexander Jones
(Garden City, N. Y.: Doubleday, 1966), p. 35, merely translates the note
from the original French. *Genesis: The Anchor Bible,* ed. E. A. Speiser
(Garden City, N. Y.: Doubleday, 1964), p. 142.

ences in the "Holiness Code" (Leviticus 18:22; 20:13). Homosexual acts between men were considered like many other acts to be major crimes punishable by death.[11]

The New Testament contains three direct references to homosexuality—Romans 1:27; 1 Cor. 6:9-10; 1 Tim. 1:9-10. Paul obviously regards homosexual acts as wrong and a perversion of the meaning of human existence willed by God. Helmut Thielicke, although accepting such a condemnation by Paul, emphasizes that Paul's condemnation of homosexuality does not justify the excessive severity which the Christian tradition has attached to such acts. Thielicke's hermeneutical interpretation points out that Paul's consideration of homosexuality appears only in the context of the more central theological affirmation that disorder in the vertical dimension of man's relationship with God is matched by disorder on the horizontal level. Homosexuality illustrates this disorder on the level of man's relationship with his fellow man. Despite the fact that Paul's understanding of homosexuality would have been colored by its acceptance in the Greek intellectual world, the Apostle considers it not in itself but only as illustrative of the central theological point that man's relation with God affects all his other relationships.[12]

Thus the biblical data indicates that the biblical authors in their cultural and historical circumstances deemed homosexual acts wrong and attached a generic gravity to such acts, but there appears to be no reason for attaching a special heinousness or gravity to these acts.

## METHODOLOGY AND EMPIRICAL DATA

A second important methodological and substantive question concerns the empirical data about homosexuality. The

---

[11] Bailey, *op. cit.*, pp. 57-61.
[12] Helmut Thielicke, *The Ethics of Sex.* tr. John W. Doberstein (New York: Harper and Row, 1964), pp. 277-284.

substantive question seeks to discover the meaning of homosexuality in terms of the behavioral sciences such as psychology, sociology, psychiatry, anthropology, etc. The methodological question for moral theology centers on the way in which such data are incorporated into the moral judgment.

Different Christian ethicists exhibit different methodological approaches to the use of empirical data in determining the morality of homosexual acts. Karl Barth insists that theological and ethical judgments about sexuality, i.e., the command of God in this matter, must constitute a form of knowledge which rests on secure foundations. But these foundations obviously cannot be the empirical sciences.[13] "That man and woman—in the relationship conditioned by this irreversible order—are the human creatures of God and as such the image of God and likeness of the covenant of grace—this is the secure theological knowledge with which we ourselves work and with which we must be content."[14] The command of God thus does not involve any consideration of the data of the empirical sciences.

On the basis of his "secure theological knowledge" without any reference to concrete experience or the data of science, Barth characterizes homosexuality as "the physical, psychological and social sickness, the phenomenon of perversion, decadence and decay, which can emerge when man refuses to admit the validity of the divine command. . . .[15] From the refusal to recognize God, there follows the failure to appreciate man and thus humanity without the fellow-man. And since humanity as fellow-humanity is to be understood in its root as the togetherness of man and woman, as the root of

---

13 Karl Barth, *Church Dogmatic: A Selection,* ed. G. W. Bromiley (New York: Harper Torchbooks, 1962), pp. 194-229. This small volume brings together Barth's considerations of man and woman which appear in three different places in his *Church Dogmatics.*

14 *Ibid.,* p. 200.

15 *Ibid.,* p. 213.

this inhumanity, there follows the ideal of a masculinity free from woman and a femininity free from man."[16]

Barth's position represents a confident and straightforward theological position based on the divine command, although he does remind one counseling homosexuals to be aware of God's command and also his forgiving grace.

John Giles Milhaven has approached the question of homosexuality with a methodology quite different from that of Barth, although they both reach the same ethical conclusion that homosexual acts are wrong.[17] Milhaven explicitly claims to be following the methodology of the new morality. The primary and ultimately the only ethical criterion is love which includes "free determination, commitment, of a man or woman to further the good of a certain person" and can be identified with the promotion of human good.[18] "To understand what is good for a person, he, a man of the twentieth century, relies exclusively on experience."[19] Milhaven's man of the new morality turns to the experience of the community. In this cast those who have the critical experience are "preeminently the psychologists, psychiatrists and analysts."[20] Although there is no unanimity among experts, the most commonly held opinion is that all homosexuals are mentally ill or neurotic. "Thus a Christian moving in the spirit of the new morality condemns homosexual behavior more severely than one using traditional arguments."[21]

The dramatic opposition between the approaches of Barth and Milhaven to the question of homosexuality illustrates the

---

[16] *Ibid.*, p. 214.

[17] John Giles Milhaven, *Towards a New Catholic Morality* (Garden City, N. Y.: Doubleday, 1970), pp. 59-68. This essay originally appeared as "Homosexuality and the Christian," *Homiletic and Pastoral Review*, LXVIII (1968), 663-669.

[18] *Ibid.*, pp. 61-62.

[19] *Ibid.*, p. 62.

[20] *Ibid.*, p. 63.

[21] *Ibid.*, p. 65.

methodological question of the place of the empirical sciences in moral theology. The theological approach of Barth in general does not give enough importance or place to human knowledge in general, let alone the specific empirical sciences of psychology and psychiatry. The Christological monism of Barth prevents any way into the ethical problem from the viewpoint of philosophy and human wisdom, although at times Barth's antiphilosophical rhetoric seems stronger than his actual practice. I would reject any methodological approach which would be so narrowly Christological that it would exclude all human wisdom as helpful for the Christian ethicist.

Milhaven's method of relying exclusively on experience, which in this case is preeminently the findings of psychology and psychiatry, also appears too one-sided. Milhaven himself seems to contradict his exclusive reliance on such experience near the end of his article, for he alludes to "a second and older way a Christian can answer the ethical question of homosexual behavior."[22] This involves the real but limited role of the pastors and teachers of Christ's body. "For many Christians, heeding the words of their pastors and teachers is a wiser, and therefore more loving response to the question of homosexual behavior than reading the evidence of the psychiatrists and psychologists of the secular city."[23] Thus the concluding sentence of the essay appears to stand in contradiction with the approach of one who relies exclusively on experience. Perhaps Milhaven could avoid some of the apparent contradiction by showing that the teaching of the pastors relies on experience, but in the article he does not take this tack. Coming at the end of his article and proposed as a second and older way, this approach seems to stand in opposition to an approach which relies exclusively on experience.

---

[22] *Ibid.*, p. 67.
[23] *Ibid.*, p. 68.

From the viewpoint of theological ethics there are problems with a methodology which relies exclusively on such experience. The Christian realizes that existing man is beset with the limitations of creatureliness and sinfulness. Likewise, resurrection destiny and Christian eschatology introduce a transcendent aspect by which man is always called upon to go beyond the present. What is presently existing can never become totally normative for Christian ethics with its horizon which includes creatureliness and sinfulness as well as the eschatological pull of the future. Chapter 3 illustrated from history the dangers of accepting the present experience as normative.

Perhaps one could counter the above theological criticism by showing that human experience, properly understood, does include all these aspects. I personally would accept an understanding of human experience which can include man's saving relationship to God and all that such a relationship includes. Such experience, however, would have to be related to the full reality of the world around us and could never be reduced to the data of psychiatry, psychology, and analysis. In fairness to Milhaven, the formulation of his method does not call for exclusive reliance on the behavioral sciences themselves but upon human experience. However, in his method in the question of homosexuality, his reliance on these sciences is total to the exclusion of any other considerations of human experience or of historical or scriptural data.

Chapter 3 pointed out that the behavioral sciences themselves only furnish data for the final human judgment which, in a sense, relativizes all the judgments of the particular sciences. Ethics can never make the mistake of absolutizing any one of the empirical sciences, such as psychology or psychiatry. These scientific disciplines have a particular perspective which can never be totally identified with the human perspective.

The question of homosexuality illustrates the hermeneutic

problem within the confines of just one science when the practitioners themselves are divided on a particular point. Thus the individual theologian or person about to make a decision is faced with a dilemma which he is not equipped to solve. If the experts in psychology and psychiatry are divided, how can someone without that particular expertise make a competent judgment? The ethicist cannot merely follow the majority opinion, for history constantly reminds us that majority opinions are not necessarily true.

The fact that the methodology proposed and employed by Milhaven lacks a transcendent or prophetic aspect also stands out in his consideration of love in the context of homosexuality. Milhaven begins with an understanding of love defined in terms of promoting human good and then tries to verify from experience if such love is present. However, one could question this understanding of love within the context of Christian ethics. In discussing the meaning of Christian love, also in the context of homosexuality, Roger Shinn insists on an important distinction between Christian love and some understandings of human love: "But the recognition of a cruciform quality in life, despite its history of distortions, is inherent in Christian ethics. It distinguishes the Christian ethic from the most prevalent alternative in Western culture, the ethic of self-realization that extends from Aristotle to contemporary philosophy."[24]

Self-fulfillment, in my judgment, cannot be excluded from Christian ethics, but must be viewed in the total context of the Paschal Mystery which sees life through death and joy in sorrow. Although I would not accept the complete divorce of self-fulfillment from Christian ethics, I cannot accept the notion of love proposed by Milhaven which does not expressly call attention to the Paschal Mystery. This notion of

---

[24] Roger L. Shinn, "Homosexuality: Christian Conviction and Inquiry," in *The Same Sex*, p. 47.

love appears to be a carryover from the understanding of, and emphasis on, love in Protestant liberal theology which has increasingly appeared in Roman Catholic writings in the last few years. Milhaven himself proposes his ethical methodology in the context of a "secular city approach," but theologians are rightly questioning such an approach because it fails to give due credit to the transcendent aspect of Christianity as well as the understanding of the weakness and failure of man in the present situation. The concept of love proposed by Milhaven appears to reinforce the judgment that his methodological approach with its exclusive emphasis on empirical sciences does not do justice to the fullness of the Christian vision which sees not only the limitations and sinfulness of the present but also the prophetic and transcendent aspect of the eschatological.

Milhaven makes his ultimate moral judgment in the light of the verification of the presence of love through psychology and psychiatry. These are both important aspects which must enter into the moral judgment, but one cannot make a final moral judgment merely in the light of the data from these two sciences. Morality cannot be totally identified with psychology and psychiatry. Some things may be wrong which are not symptoms of neurosis or emotional illness. Likewise, perfectly moral behavior may very well be neurotic. Milhaven in theory relies exclusively on experience, but as a matter of fact in his article he relies on the data of psychology and psychiatry, although he does not appear to consider or mention much of the literature in the fields of psychology and psychiatry on the subject of homosexuality.

What is the psychological and psychiatric data about homosexuality? A first question concerns the etiology of homosexuality. An older, and minority, opinion would make genetic factors the determining element. The more generally accepted theory attributes homosexuality to circumstances in the developing life of the child and person, although there can be a certain conditioning because of genetic factors. Most recently some scientists have revived the theory that attributes homosexuality to hormonal imbalance.[25]

The most important and most debated question is the normalcy of homosexuality and homosexual acts. Is it illness, a totally neutral phenomenon, or something created by the prejudices of society? The data remains somewhat conflicting. Freud interpreted homosexuality as a stunted or truncated stage of human sexuality which naturally tends toward the heterosexual. Until recently, the psychologists and psychiatrists generally judged homosexuality to be a pathological condition or an emotional disorder. This opinion probably remains the majority opinion, although the homophile community generally and some other scientists have questioned this older approach represented by such scholars as Albert Ellis, Daniel Cappon, Edmund Bergler, and Irving Bieber.[26] Recently scholars such as Clara Thompson, Evelyn Hooker, Wardell Pomeroy, and others have proposed a more benign opinion about the nature of homosexuality.[27]

The theologian is not competent to judge between the conflicting opinions of the various scientists within their own disciplines. However, a review of the literature plus personal experience would seem to indicate that homosexuality does not

---

[25] For a summary of these opinions, see John R. Cavanagh, *Counseling the Invert* (Milwaukee: Bruce Publishing Co., 1966).

[26] Christian ethicists such as Milhaven and Robert E. Buxbaum ("Homosexuality and Love," *Journal of Religion and Mental Health*, VI [1967], 17-32) base their negative moral judgment on psychological and psychiatric data proposed by such experts.

[27] This favorable approach to homosexuality is frequently documented in the essays in *The Same Sex* (see Wardell B. Pomery, "Homosexuality," pp. 3-13; Evelyn Hooker, "The Homosexual Community," pp. 25-39). For a summary of the various psychological and psychiatric opinions, see John J. McNeil, S. J., "The Christian Male Homosexual," *Homiletic and Pastoral Review*, LXX (1970), 750-753.

necessarily make every individual a neurotic or emotionally disturbed person. Some homosexuals do seem to live comparatively well-adapted lives in society. The theological ethician must be in constant dialogue with these sciences, but he realizes that even the well-adjusted person can have proclivities and perform acts which are "abnormal" and/or morally wrong. Likewise, the ethician realizes that wrong actions or tendencies do not necessarily point to mental disturbance on the part of the whole personality. The conflicting evidence of these sciences must be viewed in a wider context.

Having considered two of the most important methodological questions in moral theology's discussion of homosexuality, this essay turns to the substantive question itself. Within the pale of Christian ethics there appear to be three generic answers to the question. The more traditional approach sees homosexual acts as immoral. A very few Christian ethicists argue that homosexual acts are in themselves neutral. A more sizeable minority has proposed a mediating position which, while not commending such acts, does not always condemn them. The second part of this study will consider the three generic approaches and then spell out in greater detail the mediating position based on compromise morality which I briefly proposed a few years ago.

## HOMOSEXUAL ACTS ARE WRONG

Different methodological approaches have been employed to arrive at the conclusion that homosexual acts are wrong. Roman Catholic theology in its treatment of theology in general and homosexuality in particular follows the approach and the conclusions of Thomas Aquinas. Right reason is the ultimate moral norm, but right reason builds on the order of nature. In sexual matters, Thomas accepted Ulpian's understanding of the natural as that which is common to man and all the animals. The order of nature which man shares with animal life calls for the depositing of male seed in the vas of the female so that procreation will occur and the species will continue in existence. Thomas and the manuals of moral theology divide the sins against chastity into two categories: the sins against nature (*peccata contra naturam*) and the sins according to nature (*peccata secundum naturam*). The sins against nature are those acts which do not follow the order of nature and thus prevent procreation—pollution, imperfect sodomy, sodomy, and bestiality. Sins according to nature, but against the ordering of reason, include simple fornication, incest, adultery, rape.[28]

Thomas's condemnation of homosexual acts follows from his systematic understanding of human sexuality and its purposes in human life.[29] Since Thomas refers to homosexuality as a sin against nature, one might imagine that he attributes a special heinousness to such acts, but the expression "sin against nature" is a technical term incorporating the understanding of Ulpian. The term "sin against nature" includes sexual acts other than homosexual acts and does not argue for a special heinousness in relation to all other sins, although such sins are more grave than other sins against chastity.[30]

Until recently Catholic theologians have generally repeated and developed the Thomistic consideration of homosexuality. John F. Harvey, who has written more extensively on this subject than any other Catholic theologian, well exemplifies the best of the older Catholic approach. Harvey in his overall consideration of the morality of homosexuality sorts out three aspects of the question: the responsibility of the homosexual for his condition, the objective morality of

---

[28] *Summa Theol.*, II-II, q. 153, aa. 2-3; q. 154, a. 1.

[29] *Ibid.*, q. 154, aa. 11-12.

[30] Bailey's otherwise fine summary of the Scholastic teaching on homosexuality (pp. 110-120) could be improved by a somewhat more nuanced understanding of the sin against nature.

homosexual acts, and the subjective responsibility of homosexuals for their actions.[31]

Harvey maintains that the homosexual is not responsible
for his condition. In an individual case compulsion may di-
minish the subjective responsibility of the homosexual for his
overt homosexual acts, but Harvey believes that the homosexual can and should develop proper self-control. Harvey's
discussion of objective morality begins with the natural law
presupposition that the homosexual act, since by its essence
it excludes the transmission of life, cannot fulfill the procreative purpose of the sexual faculty and thus constitutes a
grave transgression of the divine will. No explicit mention is
made of the love union aspect of sexuality, although a brief
sentence describes the homosexual act as a deviation of the
normal attraction of man for woman.[32]

Recently many criticisms have arisen concerning such an
understanding of sexuality in general and homosexuality in
particular. The older Catholic approach inordinately places
great emphasis on the biological and physical aspect of the
sexual act; the procreative aspect becomes the primary and
sometimes the only purpose of sexuality. Poor medical and
biological knowledge merely heightened the inadequacies
of such an approach. Likewise, an older approach with its
stress on the individual acts did not pay sufficient attention
to the condition of homosexuality. Harvey improved on this
by indicating that the homosexual is not usually responsible
for his particular condition, although he is ordinarily responsible for his wrong homosexual acts. The fact that such an approach based on the natural law either ignored the scriptural
teaching on a particular point or else merely tacked on a few
proof texts has already been mentioned.

---

[31] John F. Harvey O. S. F. S., "Homosexuality," *New Catholic Encyclopedia* (New York: McGraw Hill, 1967), VII, 117-119.

[32] *Ibid.*, pp. 117-118. Note that Thomas Aquinas proposed the same
arguments.

Other approaches have arrived at the same conclusion as the natural law approach followed in Roman Catholic theology; in fact, the vast majority of Christian ethicists have come to this condemnation of homosexual acts. The neo-Orthodox approach of Barth and the new morality approach of Milhaven have already been mentioned as illustrations of different methodologies arriving at the same conclusion, although such approaches as well as the natural law approach of the manuals of moral theology have been criticized.

## HOMOSEXUAL ACTS ARE NEUTRAL

There exists today a comparatively small but significant number of ethicians, including some few Christian ethicists, who would not judge homosexual acts to be wrong. A succinct statement of this position is found in the statement made by the English Quakers:

> One should no more deplore homosexuality than left handedness. . . . Surely it is the nature and quality of a relationship which matters. One must not judge it by its outward appearance, but by its inner worth. Homosexual affections can be as selfless as heterosexual affection, and therefore we cannot see that it is in some way morally worse.[33]

Robert W. Wood in his book *Christ and the Homosexual* was one of the first writers in the area of Christian ethics to adopt such a generic opinion about homosexuality and homosexual acts.[34] *Christ and the Homosexual*, however, is more of a propagandistic polemic against the way Christians have treated the homosexual in the past and consequently betrays many theological shortcomings and inconsistencies, e.g., a

---

[33] *Towards a Quaker View of Sex* (London: The Society of Friends, 1963), p. 26.

[34] Robert W. Wood, *Christ and the Homosexual* (New York/Washington: Vantage Press, 1960).

constant confusion between the morality of homosexual acts and the proper Christian attitude towards the homosexual person, a literalistic interpretation of the words of Jesus not to judge another which would really destroy any attempt at Christian ethics.

Wood proposes as his thesis that homosexual acts are not always and everywhere wrong, but three reasons indicate that homosexual acts for the homosexual are moral. These three reasons are: (1) Homosexuality is a God-created way of protecting the human race on this planet from the suicide of overpopulation; (2) homosexuality makes available opportunities for love for some who are unable to find them in heterosexual relations, a love which truly can be sacramental; (3) homosexuality provides an outlet for the expression of the human personality for those who cannot express themselves fully within heterosexuality.[35]

Neale A. Secor presents a more adequate theological reasoning as outlined in three hypotheses which he proposes in the context of an open-ended approach.[36] (1) All human sexual identifications and behavior patterns, irrespective of desired gender object, are morally neutral, i.e., avoid making prior ethical judgments regarding sexual behavior on the basis of the object of the sexual behavior alone. (2) No matter what the particular sexual behavior (hetero-homo-mono), the test of sin is whether or not the behavior meets presently understood and approved Christian standards (what God wills for man) for all human relational behavior; i.e., avoid making prior ethical judgments regarding sin on the basis of sexual behavior alone. (3) Christian ethical concern for the homosexual exists not because he has a certain sexual proclivity but because he is a person; i.e., avoid mak-

---

[35] *Ibid.,* pp. 151-174.
[36] Neale A. Secor, "A Brief for a New Homosexual Ethic," in *The Same Sex,* pp. 67-79.

ing prior ethical judgments regarding concern for people on the basis of sexual behavior alone.[37]

In a sense, Secor's three points readily are reduced to the fact that sexuality in itself is neutral, and ethical judgments cannot be made on the basis of the object of the sexual behavior alone. Interestingly, Secor implicitly even goes one step further than those who would maintain that the ultimately determining norm is the quality of the relationship. Secor maintains that monosexuality could be moral and thus not against "presently understood and approved Christian standards for all human relational behavior." Can the relationship to self in monosexuality really be expressive of a proper Christian relation? It would be difficult to argue that monosexuality is an expression of Christian love which should require some type of giving to another. Perhaps Secor is guilty of a contradiction by asserting that monosexuality can be in accord with "standards for all human *relational* behavior."

The difference between the two opinions on homosexuality centers on the meaning of human sexuality; i.e., does human sexuality have a meaning in terms of a relationship of male and female in a procreative union of love? Generally speaking, I accept many of the arguments proposed by those who maintain that human sexuality in the Christian perspective has meaning in terms of the relationship between male and female. The scriptural data undoubtedly points in this direction, even to the possible extent that the likeness to God is precisely in terms of the sexuality by which man and woman are able to enter into a covenant of love with one another.

The Christian tradition has constantly accepted the view that homosexuality goes against the Christian understanding of human sexuality and its meaning. I would agree that his-

---

[37] *Ibid.*, pp. 78-79. For a somewhat similar line of argumentation representing the best reasoning I found in the literature from the homophile community itself, see Franklin E. Kameny, "Gay is Good," in *The Same Sex*, pp. 129-145.

torical circumstances could have influenced the condemnation of a particular form of behavior. Likewise, it is possible that the Christian tradition could have been wrong at a particular point. However, there seems to be no sufficient evidence for such a judgment in the case of homosexuality. Despite all the methodological shortcomings and one-sidedness of the natural law approach proposed by Aquinas, it still seems to correspond to a certain human connaturality condemning homosexuality as wrong. Also, the majority of all the data from the human sciences seems to point to the fact that human sexuality has its proper meaning in terms of the love union of male and female.

Interestingly, those who argue that sexuality is neutral and all sexuality should be judged in terms of the quality of the relationship fail to come to grips with the accepted fact that most homosexual liaisons are of a "one night stand" variety. Thus there is not a sexual union as expressive of a loving commitment of one to another. One might argue that the prejudices of society make such sexual behavior almost necessary for the homosexual, since he cannot easily live in a permanent relationship with a person of the same sex. However, at least those who are arguing in favor of such an understanding of homosexual acts should come to grips with what appears to be a generally accepted fact about the nature of homosexual relationships in our society. No one can deny there are many somewhat stable relationships, but these do not clearly constitute the majority of the cases.[38]

There remains another important ethical consideration

---

[38] The various statistics proposed are naturally fragmentary and incomplete. This paragraph is based on: William Simon and John Gagnon, "Homosexuality: The Formation of a Sociological Perspective," *Journal of Health and Social Behavior,* VIII (1967), 177-185. In general, the authors appear to be sympathetic to an acceptance of homosexual behavior, but they conclude from their data: "These data, then, suggest a depersonalized quality, a driven or compulsive quality, to the sexual activity of many homosexuals which cannot be reckoned as anything but extremely costly to them." (p. 181)

which also appears in connection with other problems which are posed today in the area of genetics and the new biology. Does sexuality or the sexual union have any relationship to procreation? The position of the hierarchical magisterium in the Roman Catholic Church would argue that every single act of sexual intercourse must be open to procreation. Obviously such an approach gives one a strong rule and criterion to use in condemning homosexual acts or other seemingly errant forms of sexual behavior. However, even many who would accept the moral use of contraception would not deny all connection between human sexuality and procreation. Paul Ramsey, for example, argues that man cannot put asunder what God has put together in terms of the procreative and love union aspect of human sexuality. Ramsey is well aware that there are marital unions in which the couple either do not intend to have children, or are not physically able to bear children, but these are still accepted as true marital unions. Ramsey argues that these couples still realize that love union and the procreative aspects of marital sexuality belong together, for they admit that, if either had a child, it would be only from their one flesh unity with each other and not apart from this.[39]

Modern developments in genetics raise the possibility that bearing children can and should be separated from the one flesh union of man and wife. In general, I believe that the joining together of the love union and procreative aspects does appear to be the meaning of human sexuality and marriage, but it is evident that neither Scripture nor Christian tradition could respond to the questions raised by the new biology. There does seem to be a strong presumption in favor of such an understanding which cannot be overturned without grave reasons. All too often biologists think that what-

---

[39] Paul Ramsey, "A Christian Approach to Sexual Relations," *The Journal of Religion*, XLV (1965), 101-113.

ever is biologically possible is also humanly possible and desirable. But there are many other important questions from the viewpoint of psychology, sociology, and anthropology which have to be thoroughly investigated before I would be willing to overcome the presumption in favor of the union of the procreative and love union aspects of sexuality.

The fact that human sexuality might be neutral and not structured in accord with the union of male and female seems to be compatible with some new trends in Christian ethics and moral theology. Note how often those who favor the morality of homosexual acts will base their theological arguments on premises proposed in other contexts by such authors as Lehmann and Fletcher. However, there seem to be some unacceptable presuppositions in a theological methodology which would presume that man and human sexuality have no meaning in themselves and in their relationships but are completely neutral. Again, this does not mean that one would be forced to adopt the view that the biological and physical structures of human existence understood in an exclusive sense become morally normative for man—a mistake that Roman Catholic theology has made in the past. But one can, and in my opinion should, maintain that there is a certain structuring or meaning to human existence which contributes to an ethical criterion so that humanity does not appear as something which is morally neutral and capable of doing or becoming anything under certain conditions.

Christian ethics in general and Roman Catholic moral theology in particular have recently emphasized the creative aspect of human existence. Likewise, contemporary theology emphasizes the importance of the self-transcending subject and the meaning which he gives to reality. Too often an older theology merely viewed the subject as one who passively conformed to an already existing order. In the light of these new emphases the model of responsibility seems to be the best model for understanding the moral life of the Christian and overcomes dangers involved in the older teleological and deontological models. Contemporary man realizes that he does have the power and the responsibility to shape his future existence in the world and he cannot merely sit back and wait for things to happen.[40] In this contemporary context Rahner's description of man as a self-creator is pertinent.[41]

The crucial moral question as mentioned in Chapter 3 concerns the limits placed on man as self-creator. In this particular essay perhaps Rahner overemphasizes this aspect of self-creator and does not spell out the limitations of man which he does frequently mention in a generic sense throughout the article. Man cannot be considered as self-creator in the sense that he can make himself into whatever he wants to be. There are definite limitations in human existence which narrow down the possibilities open to man. In our personal existence we realize the built-in limitations in our own personalities and how difficult it remains to change our character and personality. Such changes do not take place overnight but rather proceed very slowly, if at all. There is no doubt than the optimistic exuberance of the 1960's led theology to an overly optimistic and utopian view of the possibilities of human existence. In general, Christian theology constantly reminds us of two very important human limitations: creatureliness and sinfulness.[42] Sober reflection on the last few years reminds us that, especially in the area of social ethics and reform of institutions, there are many built-in limitations and obstacles. Those who were naively optimistic in the early 60's have often become embittered and alienated

---

[40] Albert R. Jonsen, S.J., *Responsibility in Modern Religious Ethics* (Washington/Cleveland: Corpus Books, 1968).

[41] Karl Rahner, S.J., "Experiment: Man," *Theology Digest*, XVI (Sesquicentennial issue 1968), p. 58.

[42] John Macquarrie, *God and Secularity* (Philadelphia: Westminister Press, 1967), pp. 72-85.

precisely because their creative desires for radical change have not come into existence.

Intimately connected with an over-exaggerated understanding of man as self-creator stands an anthropology which defines man primarily in terms of freedom. Freedom is a necessary characteristic of human existence, but man cannot be understood solely in terms of freedom. Pope John XXIII insisted on a fourfold basis for a just social order—truth, justice, charity and freedom.[43] Chapter 4 urged the inclusion of power as another important consideration in social justice.

In the understanding of the state, Catholic theology well illustrates its basic understanding that there is a moral meaning or structure to man. The state is a natural society precisely because man is by nature a social and political animal. Living together with others in the social order does not constitute a limitation or restriction of man's freedom, for man's nature is such that he is called to live in society with his fellows.[44] Thus Catholic theology viewed the state as a natural society which was not an intrusion on the freedom of man. Orthodox Protestant theology in general viewed the state as resulting from the sinfulness of man precisely because the state with its power is necessary to keep sinful men from devouring one another in society.[45] The limitations of the state in Catholic theology do not constitute an infringement of the freedom of the human person because man is by nature a social person destined to live in society with others.

In general, an argument from within the historical context of Roman Catholic theology (I do not mean to imply that

[43] Pope John XXIII, *Pacem in Terris*, n. 35-36. Original text: *Acta Apostolicae Sedis*, LV (1963), 265-266.

[44] Henrich A. Rommen, *The State in Catholic Thought* (St. Louis: B. Herder, 1945); Jacques Maritain, *Man and the State* (Chicago: University of Chicago Press, 1951).

[45] Jacques Ellul, "Rappels et réflexions sur une théologie de l'état," in *Les chrétiens et l'état* (Paris: Mame, 1967), pp. 130-153.

one ceases to be a loyal Roman Catholic if he theologizes in a different manner) places greater emphasis on the structure of love.[46] The structure, corporeality, or visibility of love underscores the Roman Catholic approach to the Incarnation, ecclesiology, and sacramentology. No one can deny that at times Catholic theology has overemphasized the place of structure both in ecclesiology and ethics, but it does not follow that there is no structure whatsoever to love in the Catholic theological tradition today. Thus Catholic theology is quite compatible with an understanding of human sexuality which sees love structured in terms of the bond of love between male and female.

The very fact that Roman Catholic tradition favors the visible and structured aspect of love in many areas does not necessarily make this the correct view. Likewise, one could hold to a concept of visible or structured love and still perhaps argue in favor of the morality of homosexual acts. The argument proposed here is one of "fittingness" rather than proof. The Catholic theological tradition is logically more compatible with an understanding of sexuality structured in terms of the love union of male and female. However, the precise argument for the male-female structure of human sexual love rests on the reasons already advanced.

An unnuanced acceptance of the concept of man as self-creator and a unilateral emphasis on freedom cohere with a totally extrinsic approach to morality. In the past, Catholic morality in the name of an intrinsic morality has tended to canonize physical and biological structures. In the above paragraphs I have refrained from using the word "structure" without any qualification precisely because of the errors of an older Catholic theology. Too often an historically conditioned reality was acknowledged as an essential structure

---

[46] Gérard Gilleman, S.J., *The Primacy of Charity in Moral Theology* (Westminster, Md.: Newman Press, 1959).

of human existence. However, there is still a meaning to man and his relationships which cannot be described as totally neutral. The danger will always exist of absolutizing this meaning when it must be seen in terms of all the elements entering into the human act. However, we do admit there are certain inalienable rights of man which cannot be taken away from him. Certain human relationships, such as slave-master, student-teacher, employee-employer, citizen-government, have a definite moral meaning or structure, so that freedom is not the only aspect involved. Man, human existence, and human relationships can never be merely neutral.

## A THIRD POSITION

A third or mediating position on the morality of homosexual acts has emerged somewhat frequently within Protestant ethics in the last few years and is also now appearing in Catholic ethics. I have briefly proposed such a solution based on a theory of compromise theology, but a consideration and critique of other mediating positions will clarify the theoretical and practical ramifications of this theology of compromise.[47] In general, a mediating approach recognizes that homosexual acts are wrong but also acknowledges that homosexual behavior for some people might not fall under the total condemnation proposed in the first opinion.

The mediating position implied by Helmut Thielicke applies his total ethical vision to the question of homosexuality. Homosexuality in every case is not in accord with the order of creation. Man's homosexual condition, however, deserves no stronger condemnation than the status of existence which we all share as human beings living in a disordered world which is the result of the Fall. The homosexual must try to

---

[47] Charles E. Curran, "Sexuality and Sin: "A Current Appraisal," *Homiletic and Pastoral Review*, LXIX (1968), 31.

change his condition, but Thielicke realizes that such a
change is often not possible. Is homosexual behavior for such
a person acceptable? Thielicke appears to set the theoretical
framework for the acceptance of such behavior in these circumstances, but at the last minute (and somewhat illogi-
cally) he hesitates to grant such acceptance and counsels the
need of sublimation.[48]

H. Kimball Jones has articulated a mediating position
which develops the theoretical framework proposed by
Thielicke and explicitly acknowledges that homosexual behavior in certain circumstances can be morally acceptable,
since there is nothing else the person can do.[49] Jones's approach, however, remains open to the charge of inconsistency—a danger which constantly lurks for any mediating
position. One cannot fault any Christian ethicist for appreciating the pathos of the concrete dilemmas of human existence—in this case the agonizing problems confronting the
homosexual—but such pastoral sympathy and understanding
must find solid and rigorous theological support.

Jones concludes his investigation of Scripture, the theological tradition, and the contemporary psychological data
by asserting "that man is by nature heterosexual in a very
fundamental sense and that his sexual nature can be fulfilled
as intended by God, only within a relationship of love between a man and a woman. This becomes more apparent
when we consider the connection between human sexuality
and procreation."[50]

But Jones then accepts and develops Thielicke's understanding of man existing after the Fall and the consequences
of the disorder wrought by sin. One cannot make a clear dis-

---

[48] Thielicke, *op. cit.*, pp. 281-287.
[49] H. Kimball Jones, *Toward a Christian Understanding of the Homosexual* (New York: Association Press, 1966).
[50] *Ibid.*, p. 95.

tinction between the sinful homosexual and the redeemed heterosexual, for even in marriage the relationship does not escape the disorder of sin. Thus one cannot formulate the problem in terms of sex within a heterosexual relationship versus sex within a homosexual relationship. "The problem is rather sex as a depersonalizing force versus sex as the fulfillment of human relationship."[51]

This argument implies an understanding of sin which I cannot accept and also involves a logical inconsistency with what the same author proposed earlier. Catholic natural law theology has definitely erred by failing to consider the reality of sin in the present world. Nature was considered as existing in itself unaffected by the disordering reality of sin and likewise unaffected intrinsically by the transcendent aspect of the supernatural or grace. In Thielicke and Jones, however, the effect of sin appears to be too total and unnuanced. In the Catholic tradition theology has been more willing to accept degrees of sinfulness and the relative gravity of sins as exemplified in the distinction between mortal and venial sin. Likewise, in the Catholic tradition sin does not totally destroy or totally disfigure the order of creation, to use the phrase more traditionally employed in Protestant theology. The force of sin cannot be such as to entirely change the question so that it is no longer the difference between "sex within a heterosexual relationship versus sex within a homosexual relationship" but rather sex (either hetero or homo—or for Secor even mono) as a depersonalizing force or as the fulfillment of a human relationship.

Jones earlier asserted quite categorically that sex is naturally heterosexual. In my understanding, sin does affect creation, but it does not necessarily abolish the already existing structure of human existence and human sexuality. To use a phrase frequently employed by Thielicke himself, in the

---

51 *Ibid.*, p. 98.

darkness of night not all cats are gray.[52] In other words, sin does not totally destroy the order of creation so that the distinctions between right and wrong based on creation are now totally broken down and these structures no longer point out what is morally good. All must admit that heterosexual relationships can be wrong and sinful. No one doubts that even in marriage sexual relations can be immoral, if one partner merely uses the other partner for a variety of reasons. However, there is a basic meaning of human sexuality in terms of maleness and femaleness which sin neither eradicates, neutralizes nor reduces to the same ethical significance as homosexual relations.

Jones not only accepts a concept of sin which destroys the ethical difference which he admits creation establishes between hetero-and homosexuality, but he also appears to accept a theological methodology in developing his argument which contradicts the methodology employed in his earlier affirmation of the heterosexual nature of human sexuality. In developing "his practical Christian ethics," he rightly rejects the absolute validity of either exhortation or sublimation as the answer to the homosexual's dilemma. Jones accepts, after citing Paul Lehmann, the criterion of a relationship that contributes to the humanization of man. If the homosexual relationship contributes to the humanization of man, then such a relationship, even though it is not the ideal, can be accepted and even encouraged by the Church:

Thus, we suggest, that the Church must be willing to make the difficult, but necessary, step of recognizing the validity of mature homosexual relationships, encouraging the absolute invert to maintain a fidelity to one partner when his only other choice would be to lead a promiscuous life filled with guilt and

---

[52] Helmut Thielicke, *Theological Ethics*, Vol. II: *Politics*, ed. William Lazareth (Philadelphia: Fortress Press, 1969), p. 440.

fear. This would by no means be an endorsement of homosexuality by the Church.[53]

I can agree almost totally with the conclusion proposed by Jones, but he has unfortunately employed a way of argumentation which seems inconsistent with some of his earlier assertions. Granted the existence of the disorder of sin, Jones apparently accepts the quality of the relationship argument which in principle he derives from Paul Lehmann. This type of argumentation is at odds with the earlier reasoning which established the heterosexual nature of human sexuality. Likewise, in words he accepts the pervasive disorder of sin to such an extent that the question can no longer be raised in terms of heterosexual versus homosexual relationships; but he never fully accepts his own statement, for he emphasizes that homosexual behavior will always fall short of the will of God and is doomed to never pass beyond a certain point.

Two other somewhat related mediating positions have also been proposed within the context of Roman Catholic theology. The one solution has been adopted in practice by a team of Dutch Catholics dealing with the practical counselling of homosexuals. In this book first published in 1961 the authors attempt to adopt a "more lenient pastoral approach" which could be explained in terms of the classical distinction between formal and material sin which in certain circumstances can be tolerated as a lesser of two evils.[54]

In a final chapter written for the second edition five years after the original publication H. Ruygers mentions the older classical approach of moral theology to homosexuality but also suggests a new anthropological approach which would not have a biological or physiological concept of nature but rather attempt to develop a more human understanding of

[53] Jones, *op. cit.*, p. 108.
[54] Overing, *et al.*, *Homosexualité*.

man. Ruygers recognizes the danger in such an approach and explicitly affirms that an anthropology which is not based on the biological nature as such but uniquely on the possibility of attributing a free and fully human meaning to that which concerns man does not leave itself without resources for objecting to those who would see no difference between heterosexual and homosexual intimacy. But such a theory is not developed by the author. In general, the theological discussion in this book remains quite sketchy, since the team is more concerned with pastoral counseling.[55] On the level of pastoral counseling they conclude that one cannot a priori exclude the fact that two homosexuals should and could live together.[56]

John J. McNeil, S.J., has recently summarized much of the literature in the field and has tentatively concluded that the suggestion "that a homosexual can in his situation be morally justified in seeking out ethically responsible expressions of his sexuality" could possibly be understood as falling, in traditional terminology, within the principle of choosing the lesser of two evils.[57] McNeil maintains that celibacy does not offer a viable alternative for all; consequently, a relatively ethical and responsible relationship tending to be permanent between two homosexuals would be a lesser evil than promiscuity.[58]

While in general agreement with the practical conclusions proposed by McNeil, I cannot totally agree with his reasoning about the principle of choosing the lesser of two evils. I also believe that one can and should go beyond this principle to propose a somewhat more adequate theoretical solution

---

[55] H. Ruygers, "Regards en arriére," in *Homosexualité*, pp. 175-183.

[56] "La cure spirituelle des homosexuels," in *Homosexualité*, pp. 193-196.

[57] John J. McNeil, S.J., "The Christian Male Homosexual," *Homiletic and Pastoral Review*, LXX (1970), 667-677; 747-758; 828-836.

[58] *Ibid.*, 828-836.

to the dilemma frequently facing the homosexual and his counselor.

McNeil maintains that Catholic theologians in the past have not applied the principle of the lesser of two evils in the case of homosexuality because they considered "any use of sex outside of marriage, or in such a way that renders procreation impossible is always objectively seriously sinful. Where both courses of action represent mortal sin from a theological viewpoint, there can be no 'lesser of two evils' to be chosen among them; the only moral and 'ethically responsible' course of action would be total abstinence."[59]

McNeil then develops several new emphases in moral theology which call into question this judgment about objectively serious sin. The first emphasis is the equal importance given to the love-union aspect of sexuality even in the documents of Vatican II. The second emphasis is the rejection of an act-centered moral theology in favor of a responsible orientation toward growth and reconciliation. From these two emphases he wants to prove that the principle of the lesser of two evils applies in this case, because a more permanent and stable homosexual union would not be always objectively seriously sinful.[60]

McNeil's reasoning appears to be somewhat hazy in this section, for he never explicitly says that he is trying to prove that such actions would not be objectively seriously sinful. I am not too sure that his brief treatment of the question really does furnish conclusive proof. However, a more serious objection questions his understanding of the principle of counseling the lesser of two evils. Catholic theologians have admitted as a probable opinion that, even in the case of two objectively mortal sins, one can counsel the lesser of two

---

[59] *Ibid.*, p. 831.
[60] *Ibid.*, pp. 831-833.

evils.[61] The famous example given by Alphonsus and others refers to counseling a man only to steal from another rather than to kill him.[62] Catholic theology, as alluded to earlier, willingly admits not only a distinction between mortal and venial sins but also a distinction in the gravity of various mortal sins. Thus, even if homosexual behavior were always an objectively grave wrong, one could still apply here the principle of counseling the lesser of two evils.

The principle of counselling the lesser of two evils, like the distinction between formal and material sinfulness which in its more positive formulation today respects the need for moral growth so that one might have to be satisfied at times with what is materially wrong,[63] offers one way of solving the practical dilemma of the homosexual. Such an approach remains within the traditional principles of Catholic thought, but I do not believe it goes quite far enough. In this opinion the act is still objectively wrong, although, for McNeil explicitly, it might not be grave, objective sin.

The theory of compromise tries to add a new dimension to the theoretical solution. Catholic theology has neglected the reality of sin in its moral teaching based on the natural law.[64] Precisely because sin forms a part of objective reality, our moral judgments must give more importance to sin. The presence of sin means that at times one might not be able to do what would be done if there were no sin present. In the theory of compromise, the particular action in one sense is not objectively wrong because in the presence of sin it re-

---

[61] I. Aertnys-C. Damen, C.SS.R., *Theologia Moralis,* ed. J. Visser, C.SS.R. (17th ed.; Rome/Turin: Marietti, 1956), I, 250 and 366.

[62] S. Alphonsus M. De Ligorio, *Theologia Moralis* (Turin: Marietti, 1872), I, lib. 3, n. 565.

[63] Louis Monden, S.J., *Sin, Liberty and Law* (New York: Sheed and Ward, 1965), pp. 133-144.

[64] For a critique of *Pacem in Terris* precisely on this point, see Paul Ramsey, *The Just War* (New York: Charles Scribner's Sons, 1968), pp. 70-72.

mains the only viable alternative for the individual. However, in another sense the action is wrong and manifests the power of sin. If possible, man must try to overcome sin, but the Christian knows that the struggle against sin is never totally successful in this world.[65]

Homosexual behavior well illustrates the theory of compromise. In general, I accept the experiential data proposed by the other mediating positions. The homosexual is generally not responsible for his condition. Heterosexual marital relations remains the ideal. Therapy, as an attempt to make the homosexual into a heterosexual, does not offer great promise for most homosexuals. Celibacy and sublimation are not always possible or even desirable for the homosexual. There are many somewhat stable homosexual unions which afford their partners some human fulfillment and contentment. Obviously such unions are better than homosexual promiscuity.

In many ways homosexuality exists as a result of sin. Those who accept an etiology of homosexuality in terms of relationships and environment can easily see the reality of sin in those poor relationships which contribute to this condition in the individual. In this situation, which reflects the human sinfulness in which all participate in differing ways, the individual homosexual may morally come to the conclusion that a somewhat permanent homosexual union is the best, and sometimes the only, way for him to achieve some humanity. Homosexuality can never become an ideal. Attempts should be made to overcome this condition if possible; however, at times one may reluctantly accept homosexual unions as the only way in which some people can find a satisfying degree of humanity in their lives.

---

[65] For an elaboration of my understanding of the theory of compromise, see *A New Look at Christian Morality* (Notre Dame, Ind.: Fides Publishers, 1968), pp. 169-173 and 232-233.

The principle or theory of compromise differs from the other mediating positions. A position based on the distinction between formal and material sin or even the principle of choosing the lesser of two evils still admits a distinction between the objective and subjective orders. One might interpret such approaches as limiting the influence of sin to the subjective order. The theory of compromise is more radical in the sense that it sees sin as affecting also the "objective" order and thus does not rest on the distinction between the objective and subjective orders.

The theory of compromise differs from the mediating position implied in Thielicke and explained by Kimball Jones, for sin does not totally destroy God's work of creation and redemption. Sin affects this present order but does not do away with all the moral distinctions which are based on both creation and redemption. Thus the argument in the case of homosexuality never does away with the distinction between heterosexuality and homosexuality, even though not all heterosexual relationships are moral and good. The basic meaning or "structure" of human sexuality remains, even though some individuals may not be able to live in accord with it because of the infecting power of sin.

Are there any limits to the principle of compromise? Such a question does not assume great importance in the particular discussion of homosexuality, but the question remains. Theoretically there are limits to the theory of compromise based on the implied understanding of the effect of sin. Sin does not completely destroy moral meaning or do away with moral distinctions. The effect of sin itself is limited. Notice that the same question of the limits also exists for the principle of counseling the lesser of two evils. In general, such limits are the rights of other innocent persons or the rights of society, but even these values may be somewhat infringed upon for the sake of the values preserved through the compromise.

One can object that such a view still relegates the homosexual to second class citizenship.[66] Perhaps many proponents of "Gay Liberation" are making the same mistake today that theologians and churchmen made in the past. Both groups tend to identify the person with his homosexuality, but a sound anthropology argues against any such identification. One can still love and respect the person even though one believes his homosexual behavior falls short of the full meaning of human sexuality. In many other areas of life I can judge a person's behavior as being wrong or less than the ideal and still respect him as a person. The Christian humbly admits that sinfulness also touches him in one way or another and that he can make no claims to being perfectly moral, human, or Christian. Ironically, "The Gay Liberation Movement" seems to be making the same mistake that the Christian Churches made by making homosexuality almost the equivalent of personhood.

---

[66] Franklin E. Kameny, *The Same Sex*, pp. 129-145.

# 7

## Dialogue with
## Bernard Lonergan:
## The Concept of Conversion

Lonergan's recent writing emphasizes the importance of conversion as the transformation of the subject, which thus constitutes the basic horizon of the individual.[1] Horizon is the maximum field of vision from a determined viewpoint and embraces both relative horizon which describes one's field of vision relative to one's development; e.g., psychological, sociological, cultural; and basic horizon which describes the human subject as related to the four basic or transcendental conversions—intellectual, moral, religious and Christian.[2] This essay will attempt to study Lonergan's understanding of Christian conversion and its relationship to the other three transcendental conversions.

---

[1] Bernard Lonergan, S.J., "Theology in Its New Context," in *Theology of Renewal*, ed. L. K. Shook, C.S.B. (New York: Herder and Herder, 1968), I, 44-45.
[2] David W. Tracy, *The Achievement of Bernard Lonergan* (New York: Herder and Herder, 1970), pp. 19-20.

I.

Lonergan asserts that conversion as a theological topic receives very little attention in traditional theology[3]—an assertion which holds quite true in Catholic theology although some Protestant theology has paid more attention to the concept. Leading French theological dictionaries such as *Dictionnaire de Théologie Catholique, Dictionnaire de la Bible*, and *Catholicisme* do not even contain articles on conversion as such. The manuals of Catholic moral theology do not even mention the term in their quite narrow treatment of moral theology. In the past few years, however, Catholic theology has begun to discuss the reality of conversion. Bernard Häring has insisted on the centrality of conversion in the moral life of the Christian.[4] A 1958 article by Yves M.-J. Congar develops the concept of conversion with emphasis on the biblical understanding of conversion and the psychological experience of those who are converted, but the article still to a great extent views conversion in terms of confessional conversion to a particular Christian denomination, specifically conversion to Roman Catholicism.[5]

Why has conversion emerged as an important concern in Roman Catholic theology only in the last few years? Lonergan himself suggests one significant reason: "It is a topic little studied in traditional theology since there remains very little of it when one reaches the universal, the abstract and

---

[3] Lonergan, *Theology of Renewal*, I, 44.

[4] Bernard Häring, C.SS.R., *The Law of Christ* (Westminster, Md.: Newman Press, 1961), I, 385-481; Bernard Häring, C.SS.R., "Conversion," in *Pastoral Treatment of Sin*, ed. Philippe Delhaye (New York: Desclée, 1968), pp. 87-186.

[5] Yves M.-J. Congar, "The Idea of Conversion," *Thought*, 33 (1958), 5-20; a modified and enlarged version appeared in *Parole et Mission*, 11 (1960), 493-523. This later version is reprinted in Congar, *Sacerdoce et Laïcat* (Paris: Éditions du Cerf, 1962), pp. 23-49.

the static."[6] Lonergan thus sees the neglect of conversion in traditional theology as stemming from an approach that has not appreciated the importance of interiority, historicity, and the individual. Conversion tends to be a very existential and individual phenomenon which escapes the categories of what Lonergan has described as the classicist approach to theology.[7]

Lonergan has mentioned an important factor, but there seem to be other factors which also explain the neglect of conversion in Roman Catholic theology in the past. An investigation of these reasons will be useful later in evaluating and criticizing Lonergan's own notion of conversion. Catholic theology, when it did mention conversion in the past, generally limited conversion to the phenomenon of a non-Catholic's joining the Roman Catholic Church. Unlike the *Dictionnaire de Théologie Catholique,* the *Catholic Encyclopedia* published in the United States in 1911 does contain an article on conversion, but the entire article considers conversion only as entry into the Roman Catholic Church.[8]

Dogmatic theology could not avoid a consideration of the reality contained in the concept of conversion, but the discussion generally took place under the heading of grace and justification. Christian conversion became a more important topic in contemporary theology precisely because of the renewed emphasis on biblical theology. The centrality and importance of conversion in the Scriptures and in the life of the early Church insure the fact that a biblically oriented theology must develop such a concept. The terminology of the theology manuals of the past reflected the scholastic philo-

---

[6] Lonergan, *Theology of Renewal,* I, 44.

[7] Bernard Lonergan, S.J., "The Transition from a Classicist World View to Historical Mindedness," in *Law for Liberty,* ed. James E. Biechler (Baltimore: Helicon Press, 1967), pp. 126-133.

[8] B. Guldner, "Conversion," *The Catholic Encyclopedia,* IV, 347-348.

sophical categories and the language of the hierarchical magisterial pronouncements about Christian faith. The current shift to biblical categories and to contemporary philosophical categories, including the existentialist categories, has influenced the greater attention given to conversion in the more recent theological literature. A comparison of the article on conversion in the *New Catholic Encyclopedia* published in 1967 with the article in the 1911 encyclopedia well illustrates the centrality of the biblical foundation in the theological consideration of conversion.[9]

Moral theology in the Roman Catholic tradition has also neglected the concept of conversion. The reasons for such a neglect obviously include some of the factors already mentioned such as the lack of a biblical orientation and the stress on objective universal norms which did not give enough importance to the existential involvement of the subject in freely responding to the loving call of God in Christ. A legalist approach and the separation of moral theology from dogmatic theology favored a view of man's moral actions considered as individual acts in relationship to a norm and not as actions expressing the heart of the person who has received the gift of divine sonship. In fairness to the Roman Catholic tradition in moral theology, the discussion of the virtues, as found, for example, in the approach of Thomas Aquinas, did discuss the moral self and the attitudes that should characterize the Christian self; but the manualist tradition failed to develop or even continue the Thomistic emphasis on the virtues. These manuals likewise failed to develop any other considerations of the person or the moral subject in keeping with more contemporary approaches in

---

[9] *New Catholic Encyclopedia*, IV, 286-294, includes under "Conversion" a four-part article: "Conversion, I (In the Bible)," "Conversion, II (Psychology of)," "Conversion III (Theology of)," "Conversion, IV (Obligation of)." Other entries are: "Conversion to Life of Grace" and "Convert Apostolate."

philosophy which stress the shift to interiority and subjectivity.

There is another important theological reason explaining the failure of Catholic moral theology to develop a consideration of conversion. Conversion presupposes the existence of human sinfulness, for the call to conversion remains an invitation to change one's heart, to be transformed, to pass from death to life, from darkness to light, from sin to love union with God and neighbor. Catholic theology with a poor understanding of the nature-grace relationship did not really appreciate the way in which sin does affect the person. Human nature remains the same in all possible stages of the history of salvation and is apparently not greatly affected by human sinfulness. Moral theology continued to consider sin as an individual action which is not in conformity with an objective law rather than viewing sin as affecting the subject in his intimate relationships with God, neighbor and the world. In general human sinfulness is interpreted as depriving man of sanctifying grace but leaving his human nature intact.

Even the more widely acclaimed statements of Catholic teaching and philosophy seem to me to suffer from a failure to take seriously sin and its effects on human existence. As discussed earlier, the famous encyclical of Pope John on social justice, *Pacem in Terris*, reveals a naive and overly optimistic approach precisely because it fails to give sufficient importance to the reality of human sinfulness as it affects man today. In the concluding paragraph of the introduction of the encyclical Pope John claims that by these laws found in his nature men are taught about their relationships with their fellow citizens and with their states, the relationships that should exist among states and the urgent need to act for a world community of peoples. Unfortunately no discussion of the unconcern, lack of responsibility, selfishness, pride, etc. of men and nations ensues in this encyclical.[10] The overly optimistic tone of the encyclical comes from a rationalism which does not take cognizance of the reality of human sinfulness. Paul Ramsey has pointed out the lack of realism in other aspects of *Pacem in Terris* precisely because the encyclical fails to acknowledge the reality and power of human sinfulness.[11] Elsewhere, I have developed a theology of compromise to deal with difficult human decisions in which the sin of the world is present and forcing one to act in a way that he would not choose if there were no sinfulness present in our world.[12] Chapter 4 has developed in greater detail the critique that Catholic theology has not given enough importance to the reality of sin.

Bernard Häring, who more than any other Catholic theologian has developed the concept of conversion, realized the need to change the concept of sin as it was generally understood in the manuals of moral theology. Sin does not primarily describe an individual, external act but rather an orientation of the person which involves the relationship of an individual with God, neighbor, self and the world.[13] Conversion is the biblical call to a change of heart. Even for the person who has now accepted the loving gift of God in Christ Jesus, Häring emphasizes the need for continual conversion which comes from the fact that man never totally responds to the call of God but always falls short. In his consideration of continual conversion Häring tries to give an acceptable interpretation of the traditional Lutheran formula of man as *simul justus et peccator*. The Christian through the love of

---

[10] *Pacem in Terris*, n. 7.

[11] Paul Ramsey, *"Pacem in Terris,"* in *The Just War* (New York: Charles Scribner's Sons, 1968), pp. 70-90.

[12] Charles E. Curran, *A New Look at Christian Morality* (Notre Dame, Ind.: Fides Publishers, 1968), pp. 170-173; 232-233.

[13] Häring, *The Law of Christ*, I, 339-364.

God dwelling in him by the gift of the Spirit constantly struggles to overcome the sinfulness which still remains a part of his existence. Häring's notion of continual conversion explains in a dynamic way the reality generally referred to as venial sin.[14]

Protestant theology generally has been more open to the concept of conversion or metanoia, for Protestant theology has been more biblical in its orientation, more conscious of the reality of human sinfulness, more aware of the importance of the conscious subject, and more open to expressing the Christian message in the categories of contemporary philosophical understandings of man. Liberal theology in the Protestant tradition tends to downplay the reality of sin and conversion, but the more fundamentalist approaches in Protestantism have emphasized conversion as the central event in religious experience. The famous revivals, which in some form are still with us today, attempt to bring about this conversion in the hearer of good news. The evangelistic movement in Protestantism with its stress on preaching the Word of God aims ultimately at conversion. "Conversion is a revolution of the life of the individual. The old forces of sin, self-centeredness and evil are overthrown from their place of supreme power. Jesus Christ is put on the throne."[15]

The emphasis in evangelical approaches on the individual to the apparent exclusion of the need for the Christian and the Church to become involved in the social issues of the day evoked criticism from other Protestant theologians. Reinhold Niebuhr objected to the approach of Billy Graham for its failure to show the social and cosmic dimensions of Christianity.[16] Somewhat the same criticism together with a more

---

14 Häring, *Pastoral Treatment of Sin*, pp. 91-92.

15 Billy Graham, "Conversion—A Personal Revolution," *The Ecumenical Review*, 19 (1967), 271.

16 Reinhold Niebuhr, *Love and Justice*, ed. D. B. Robertson (Cleveland and New York: Meridian Books, 1967), pp. 154-158.

optimistic view of man underlies Gibson Winter's rejection of confessional proclamation in favor of prophetic proclamation. "By contrast the confessional assembly proclaims a present relationship of forgiveness wrought in the past but effective now and to eternity. The emphasis in the confessional assembly is upon the present acceptance of a relationship to God established in the saving history; the principal moment is the meaning of the present in the light of the past. Hence the crucial work of proclamation is preaching, for the principal issue is to acknowledge this relationship which God has initiated."[17] Recent defenses of the proclamation of conversion have responded to such criticism by emphasizing the social and cosmic dimension of conversion,[18] but the evangelical proclamation of conversion generally tends towards individualism and does not appreciate the vocation of the Christian to cooperate in the work of bringing about the new heaven and the new earth. The place of conversion in theology, the reasons for its meager development in Roman Catholic theology, and the criticisms of conversion theology in Protestantism furnish a helpful perspective in an attempt to analyze the concept of Christian conversion in Bernard Lonergan.

## II.

Lonergan has not developed a systematic explanation of his concept of Christian conversion and its relationship to the other transcendental conversions—intellectual, moral and religious; but he has stressed that theology today needs to de-

---

[17] Gibson Winter, *The New Creation as Metropolis* (New York: Macmillan, 1963), pp. 75-76.

[18] Graham, *The Ecumenical Review,* 19 (1967), 280-284; Emilio Castro, "Conversion and Social Transformation," in *Christian Social Ethics in a Changing World,* ed. John C. Bennett (New York: Association Press, 1966), pp. 348-366.

velop an understanding of conversion as a new type of foundation. "What is normative and foundational for subjects
stating theology is to be found, I have suggested, in reflection
on conversion, where conversion is taken as an ongoing process, concrete and dynamic, personal, communal, and historical."[19] Lonergan points out the philosophical reasons for his
insistence on conversion; but, as is more evident in his treatment in *De Verbo Incarnato,* he is more than familiar with
the scriptural data which stress the reality of sin and consequently also of conversion. Speaking of conversion in general, Lonergan maintains, "It is not really a change or even
a development, rather it is a radical transformation on which
follows, on all levels of living, an interlocked series of
changes and developments. What hitherto was unnoticed
becomes vivid and present. What has been of no concern becomes a matter of high import. So great a change in one's ap-
prehensions and one's values accompanies no less a change
in oneself, in one's relations to other persons and in one's relation to God."[20]

Lonergan specifically considers questions connected with
Christian conversion in two different places, in the last chapter in *Insight* and in the concluding theses of his treatise *De
Verbo Incarnato* in which he develops his theology of redemption.[21]   Both considerations, although developed in
terms of different starting points and perspectives, consider
the question of Christian conversion in connection with the
problem of sin and evil. Lonergan, unlike some in Catholic
theology in the past, does struggle with the problems related
to sin. The development of the theme of redemption in *DVI*

[19] Lonergan, *The Renewal of Theology,* I, 46.
[20] *Ibid.,* p. 44.
[21] Bernard J. Lonergan, S.J., *Insight: A Study of Human Understanding*
(New York: Longmans, 1957), pp. 687-730; B. Lonergan, S.J., *De Verbo Incarnato* (Rome: Pontifical Gregorian University, 1960), pp. 521-734. Hereafter
referred to as *DVI.*

commences by enunciating the fact that redemption means not only the end but the mediation or process to the end; namely, the paying of the price, the vicarious passion and death of Christ the mediator because of sins and for sinners, the sacrifice offered by our high priest in his own blood, meritorious obedience, the power of the resurrected Lord and the intercession of the eternal high priest. The second step explains the scriptural data in terms of the vicarious satisfaction of Jesus, whereas the third thesis (Lonergan was still employing at this time a thesis approach in theology) tries to give intelligibility to these scriptural and theological data in terms of the just and mysterious "law of the cross." The Son of God was made man, suffered, was raised, because divine wisdom ordered and divine goodness willed not to take away the evils of the human race through power but according to the just and mysterious law of the cross to convert (change) the same evils into a certain supreme good."[22]

This thesis does not attempt a demonstration but rather seeks intelligibility. Redemption involves a transformation in which evil is transformed into good, and death is transformed into life. The death of Jesus results from the sin of those who put Him to death which action is the *malum culpae*. Out of loving obedience Jesus accepts this death (*malum poenae*) and thus transforms it into a good because of which the Father raised him from the dead and made him Lord and Messias. In itself death is the penalty of sin, but Jesus transformed death into a means of redemption and life. (Lonergan rightly points out that the death of Jesus does not result from the vindictive justice of the Father who would have to require the death of Jesus to satisfy for the punishment due to sin.)

The principle of transformation or conversion thus be-

---

[22] *DVI*, p. 676. The following paragraphs in the text summarize Lonergan's explanation of the law of the cross.

comes the law of the cross for all those who are united with
Christ Jesus through faith and baptism. Evil in the world results from sin, and man overcomes this evil not by succumb-
ing to the temptation of using evil to overcome evil but by
a daily carrying of his cross with a love that transforms evil
into good. The law of redemption or transformation of evil
into good through love thus becomes the law of life for the
Christian.

At first sight Lonergan's understanding of Christian conversion seems to echo the conversion themes proposed in
some Protestant literature, but a closer examination reveals
significant differences. Take as an example, a comparison of
Lonergan's concept with that proposed by Dietrich Bonhoeffer, who while strongly influenced by Barth and also appreciative of Lutheran emphasis, nevertheless, also argued
for a place for the "natural" in his ethics. Bonhoeffer develops an ethic of formation which describes the way in
which the form of Jesus Christ becomes present in our lives
and in our world. Bonhoeffer's fragmentary *Ethics* begins by
showing the inadequacy and futility of ethical approaches
based on reason, conscience, duty, free responsibility or noble humanity.[23] "It is only as one who is sentenced by God
that man can live before God. Only the crucified man is at
peace with God. It is in the figure of the Crucified that man
recognizes and discovers himself. To be taken up by God, to
be executed on the Cross and reconciled, that is the reality
of manhood."[24]

The transformation or conversion proposed by Lonergan
despite his insistence on its totality in his later, generic considerations of conversion and despite the transformation
motif of the law of the cross, remains much less radical than

---

[23] Dietrich Bonhoeffer, *Ethics*, ed. Eberhard Bethge (New York: Macmillan, 1962), pp. 3-8.
[24] *Ibid.*, p. 24.

the conversion implied in the formation ethics of Bonhoeffer. There are indications of Lonergan's less radical approach to conversion even in his explicit treatment of redemption in *DVI;* whereas *Insight* both in its general heuristic structure and in its specific treatment of sin and the problem of evil emphasizes Christian conversion within a wider context of integration and not radical transformation.

In *DVI* the thesis on satisfaction in the redemption discusses at great length the concept of God's judgment which consists in the fact that the divine will chooses the order of the divine wisdom. There are four possible orderings within the divine justice—good comes forth from good, evil comes forth from evil, evil comes forth from good and good comes forth from evil. All four of these orderings are found in human and Christian life so that the entire Christian life cannot be reduced to any one of these models; thus the law of the cross does not adequately and totally explain the Christian life. God directly wills good; God indirectly wills natural defects and the *malum poenae,* but God only permits and does not will the *malum culpae.*

Redemption involves the reintegration or reparation of the order of divine wisdom which is the eternal law existing in the mind of God. Such an understanding of redemption does not imply the existence of a wiser and more powerful being who corrects the order laid down by God, but rather the present order contains not only the good that God wills but also the *malum culpae* which God in no way wills but only permits and the evil of natural defects and the *malum poenae* which God only indirectly wills. Insofar as evil men sin, their evil violates the order of divine justice; but insofar as all things are subject to divine providence and governance, the violated order is repaired or reintegrated. Thus the mystery of sin and redemption shows forth the multifaceted wisdom and justice of God. The law of the cross based on the ordering by which God brings forth good from evil represents one of the many orderings all of which together comprise the divine justice. The bringing forth of good from evil represents only one aspect or one part of the totality of the divine wisdom and justice so that the law of the cross is not the complete explanation of the justice and ordering of God.[25]

The general structure of *Insight* indicates that sin does not involve a completely radical break and destruction of everything that is human; and thus conversion is not a radical transformation which completely negates the existing human structure. *Insight* employs a moving perspective which develops and builds upon the detached, disinterested, unrestricted desire to know. Sin is viewed as a hindrance to this full development of the self but not as the destruction of this human structure. In fact, Lonergan only explicitly poses the problem of evil and an attempted solution in the last chapter of *Insight*, but the solution remains in total harmony with the basic self-transcendence of man the knower and decider which forms the heuristic structure for the entire argument of *Insight*. In man one can observe openness as a fact—"the pure desire to know." This openness belongs to the very structure of man and continually urges him to expand his basic horizon in terms of what Lonergan later describes as the four transcendent and fundamental conversions.[26]

This primordial fact of openness is "no more than a principle of possible achievement, a definition of the ultimate horizon that is to be reached only through successive enlargements of the actual horizon."[27] Notice that Lonergan here employs the term enlargement, a term which is less radical than conversion. Such successive enlargements in man cannot be achieved precisely because of his sinful state which

---

[25] *DVI*, pp. 622-631.
[26] Bernard Lonergan, "Openness and Religious Experience," *Collection* (New York: Herder and Herder, 1967), pp. 198-201.
[27] *Ibid.*, p. 200.

thus needs to receive openness as a loving gift from the self-communication of God. This gift is not only grace as *sanans* (i.e. healing the basic powers that man has but cannot develop because of the bias, prejudice, etc. which Lonergan describes in *Insight*) but the gift of openness is grace as *elevans* because this ultimate enlargement is beyond the resources of every finite consciousness although it alone approximates to the possibility of openness defined by the pure, disinterested, unrestricted desire to know. The fact that Lonergan introduces his solution to the problem of evil only in the last chapter of *Insight* indicates that evil or sin does not totally destroy the human reality. Lonergan thus philosophizes within the Catholic tradition which has generally upheld the fact that one can go from man to God through his reasoning, whereas elements in the Protestant tradition either because of an insistence on a more total and radical disruptiveness of sin or because of the Neo-Orthodox tenet that one cannot go from man to God see no possibility of such sustained development in our understanding of man and his relationship to God. Lonergan's concept of conversion precisely because of his view of man cannot be as radical as that proposed by some thinkers in the Protestant tradition.

Lonergan's explicit treatment of the problem of evil and sin in *Insight* again does not view sin in as radical a way as in some other theological views. Sin obviously does not destroy everything human for Lonergan. Sin effects man's will, intellect and sense faculties but does not destroy these. The solution to the problem of evil as an harmonious continuation of the subject's self-transcendence calls for the introduction of cognate forms that will allow man to sustain the development that is impeded because of his bias and prejudice. Lonergan stresses that the solution to the problem of evil will always be a harmonious continuation of the order of the universe, and that man will not only acknowledge and accept the solution but also collaborate with it. The problem of evil exists precisely because God takes seriously man's freedom, and thus the solution to the problem of evil must also take seriously the freedom and cooperation of man. Lonergan posits three possible solutions to the problem of evil—natural, relatively supernatural and absolutely supernatural solutions. The solution offered for the Christian is the absolutely supernatural solution whose sole ground and measure is the divine nature itself. Even the absolutely supernatural solution involves higher integration in emergent consciousness, but it heightens the tensions which arise whenever the lower levels are transcended and integrated into a higher level.[28]

The emphasis on conversion in general and Christian conversion in particular seems to vary somewhat in Lonergan's different considerations. His latest article speaks of conversion as a "radical transformation which is neither just a change or development." In the theological consideration of redemption the law of the cross involves a seemingly radical transformation of evil into good or of death into life, but the law of the cross exemplifies only one aspect and not the totality of the divine wisdom and the divine justice. *Insight* with its moving viewpoint and harmonious development based on the pure, detached, disinterested, unrestricted desire to know only introduces a solution to the problem of evil in the last chapter thus indicating that the disruption of sin and evil is far from being total and radical. The absolutely supernatural solution to the problem of evil is still characterized as an integration on a higher level or an enlargement.

The radicality of Christian conversion ultimately depends upon the radicality of sin. Lonergan here follows the Roman Catholic tradition which views sin in a less radical way than approaches in non-liberal Protestant theology. In *Insight* sin does not destroy the development of man but rather constitutes an obstacle that can be overcome in terms of a higher

---

[28] *Insight,* pp. 696-703; 718-730.

integration. In his treatment of sin in *DVI* Lonergan curiously accepts and proposes a very inadequate definition of sin. In both theses in which sin appears as one of the terms sin is defined as a bad human act in which the malice is considered primarily from a theological viewpoint and consists in an offense to God.[29] Even in developing these two theses Lonergan generally ascribes the death of Jesus, at least in the primary place, to the sin of the Jews or of Pilate or of those who actually put Jesus to death. A more appropriate theological understanding of sin would challenge Lonergan's understanding of sin especially as found in *DVI*. Sin describes the multiple relationships of the individual with God, neighbor, self and the world. There also remains a cosmic aspect of sin, somewhat similar to the personified notion of sin found in St. Paul. Sin as this personified force is obviously the primary factor in the death of Jesus; in fact the death of Jesus in one aspect seems to be the hour of the triumph of the power of darkness, but the resurrection marks that transforming victory of Jesus over sin and death.

I would generally agree with the approach that views sin as not destroying the basic structure of man, the self-transcending subject; but Lonergan too often views sin merely as an act or as a reality primarily affecting the subject. The approach to sin in *Insight* in terms of a lack of the cognate forms of faith, hope and charity could be expanded to see sin ultimately in terms of the lack of relationships of love with God, neighbor, self and the world. Sin is not primarily an act but a condition affecting or even severing man's multiple relationships. In this understanding sin, and consequently conversion, would be more radical without denying the continuity between sinful man who remains a self-transcending subject and the man who has experienced a Christian conversion which is an absolutely supernatural solution

---

[29] *DVI*, pp. 526; 578.

to the problem of evil. Lonergan must realize that he has employed different and even conflicting terminology in describing Christian conversion as a radical transformation, conversion, development and enlargement, and integration. Logically, it seems Lonergan should adopt a more radical understanding of sin understood in terms of relationships or of a condition of separation from God, neighbor, self and the world which, however, still sees the sinful man as a self-transcending subject who finds his own fulfillment in the supernatural solution to the problem of evil which is aptly described as Christian conversion.

For most Christians continual conversion remains the most important problem of daily Christian existence, for normally the true Christian should already have overcome the alienation of sin and entered into the basic relationship of love with God, neighbor, self and the world. In this world no one ever completely overcomes the reality of sin, but the law of Christian growth and existence shows forth the rhythm of the paschal mystery in the need to constantly die to ourselves in order to rise in the newness of life. Lonergan mentions this aspect of conversion in both *DVI* and *Insight,* but continual conversion precisely because of its importance and centrality calls for a more extensive development and consideration.

Lonergan's notion of conversion, like that proposed by some in Protestant theology, remains open to the charge of individualism for failure to pay sufficient attention to the social, ecclesial and cosmic aspects of redemption. In *DVI* sin was explained merely in terms of an act and the malice was seen in relationship to God; whereas sin involves man in the core of his being and affects his multiple relationships with God, neighbor and the world. Redemption, at least in *DVI,* emphasized the personal or individual aspect without developing the cosmic and social aspect. One would not expect *DVI* to include a full scale development of the ecclesial understanding of redemption for the Christian but at least some mention of this dimension is necessary. In *Insight* Lonergan does acknowledge a social and cosmic dimension to the reality of sin by showing how bias and prejudice bring about the social surd. This could serve as a basis for developing a social and cosmic understanding of Christian conversion which seems to be implicit in some of Lonergan's thinking, but one would have to conclude that this aspect of conversion needs further development. The complaint among some Protestant scholars that conversion theology has been too individualistic finds somewhat of a parallel in Johannes B. Metz's criticism that the transcendental method employed by Karl Rahner does not give enough importance to the world and history.[30] At the very least, Lonergan needs to develop the social and cosmic aspects of Christian conversion.

## III.

The Lonergan of *Insight,* according to David W. Tracy, sees basic horizon as expanded by the higher viewpoints which involve intellectual, moral, religious and Christian conversion.[31] Having considered the concept of Christian conversion in Lonergan, one must logically consider the relationship which exists among the various conversions. The four conversions do not constitute the central discussion in *Insight.* The major consideration centers on intellectual conversion as the self-transcending subject moves to the higher viewpoints of empirical consciousness, intellectual consciousness, and rational consciousness, which correspond to the actions of experience, understanding and judgment. Chapter 18 treats of moral conversion and ethics in terms of rational

[30] Johannes B. Metz, "Foreword," in Karl Rahner, *Spirit in the World* (New York: Herder and Herder, 1968), p. xviii.
[31] Tracy, p. 19; chap. vii, pp. 163-181.

self-consciousness; Chapter 19 develops religious conversion in terms of general transcendence although most of the chapter explicitates Lonergan's argument for the existence of God. Chapter 20 poses the problem of evil and proposes a possible heuristic solution in terms of special transcendence.

Problems arise from a number of sources. In his later writings, Lonergan stresses that conversion involves a radical transformation which is not merely a change or even a development, but *Insight* speaks of integration, enlargement and development rather than radical transformation or even conversion. Conversion, for Lonergan, cannot be as radical as it might be for others precisely because of Lonergan's understanding of the subject's self-transcendence and the reality of sin. Lonergan himself in his later writings seems to indicate there is little difference between religious and Christian conversion. In an essay entitled "The Future of Christianity" Lonergan develops under the heading of religious conversion many of the same points that he considered earlier in *Insight* and *DVI* in relation to Christian conversion.[32] The problem of evil and the law of the cross seem to be included under religious conversion which calls for renunciation and sacrifice, but Lonergan does not explicitly develop the problem of sin and evil in this very abbreviated context. Obviously Lonergan's understanding of conversion and of the relationship among the various conversions raises a number of perplexing questions. I will venture suggestions which might explain some of the apparent inconsistencies, call for some revisions and raise further questions.

There are definite indications that Lonergan's treatment of the four conversions in *Insight* does not correspond with his later writings on conversion. Although Chapter 19 of

---

[32] Bernard J. Lonergan, S.J., "The Future of Christianity," *The Holy Cross Quarterly* (1969), pp. 5-10; see also a lecture, "Faith and Beliefs," delivered by Lonergan at different places in 1969 and 1970.

*Insight* discusses general transcendence and the existence of God, the discussion remains in the realm of a rational argument for the existence of God. Belief comes into the discussion only in the last chapter when the problem of evil is raised. Lonergan in *Insight* does not really consider religious conversion as involving an orientation to a personal God who is both Other and Redeemer. Although Lonergan mentions the problem of evil at the end of Chapter 18 on Ethics, he does not propose a solution to the problem of evil until he arrives at his consideration of special transcendence which seems to correspond with his understanding of Christian conversion. All would have to agree that the problem of evil and its solution cannot be ignored on the level of moral and religious conversion and just left to the level of Christian conversion.

My proposed solution to the understanding of the relationship among the conversions and of Lonergan's insistence on the somewhat radical and total nature of conversion (realizing that he should temper such language because of his whole understanding of man and of sin) would be to combine the moral, religious and Christian conversions into one generic concept of conversion which retains the somewhat radical character that Lonergan seems to demand of conversion and which calls for a much closer relationship between the moral, religious and Christian aspects of conversion.

A theological perspective would tend to see the moral, religious and Christian conversions as more intimately united and together embracing the total phenomenon of conversion. Lonergan himself in his later writings obviously sees a close similarity between religious and Christian conversion even to such an extent that many people would wonder what is the real difference between them. Catholic theology has insisted upon the universal salvific will of God by which God offers all men the saving gift of his love. The radical conversion of saving belief does not depend upon an explicit acceptance of Jesus as Lord, for all men, whether they have heard of Christ Jesus or not, in the mysterious providence of God receive his loving invitation. Catholic theology has avoided the danger of a narrow Christology which would exclude people from the family of God who did not explicitly acknowledge Jesus as Lord.

On the level of moral conversion, one of the fundamental considerations in the manualistic treatment of grace was the fact that man without the gift of grace could not observe for a long time the substance of the natural law.[33] Christian theology sees the problem of evil existing on the moral level and bringing about a moral impotence even concerning the fundamental substance of the natural law. Thus moral, religious and Christian conversion do not constitute three totally different conversions but rather they are intimately joined in the one total theological conversion. So intimately are they joined that Catholic theology has been willing to admit that where one of these is present the others are present, at least implicitly. One of the three cannot exist in the individual person without at least the implicit existence of the other two. Such a theological understanding corresponds to the biblical notion of conversion as the change of heart which intimately affects man in his relationships with God, neighbor, self and the world.

Does this theological understanding bringing together the moral, religious and Christian aspects of conversion contradict the approach of *Insight* which seems to distinguish four conversions—the intellectual, moral, religious and Christian? Perhaps not. *Insight* with its moving viewpoint considers the self-transcending subject with the exigencies of the pure, detached, disinterested, unrestricted desire to know. Loner-

---

[33] Carolus Boyer, S.I., *Tractatus de Gratia Divina*, ed. tertia (Rome: Pontifical Gregorian University, 1952), pp. 48-63.

gan heuristicly develops his argument in *Insight* in terms of the basic openness of the subject who gradually moves to a higher level of integration. In a later article, Lonergan distinguishes openness as fact or capacity from openness as achievement and openness as gift.[34] Lonergan describes openness as fact as man's capacity for self-transcendence. *Insight* develops precisely in terms of describing the various levels involved in this capacity for openness, but even in *Insight* Lonergan emphasizes that man can never totally achieve this openness, and that total openness is ultimately pure gift on the part of God. The moving viewpoint of *Insight* does not intend to give a total picture, but views man merely in terms of this fact of openness or this capacity for self-transcendence.

In a real, existential order, man can only receive this openness as gift—a gift that far transcends him but still fulfills the capacity for openness which is his. *Insight* purposely abstracts from the fact of openness as gift which in the existential order remains a most important fact, if not the most important fact about man and his relationship to God and others in this existence. A consideration of man merely from the viewpoint of openness as fact or as capacity for self-transcendence can more easily make distinctions between the moral, religious and Christian conversions; but in the existential order the three are more intimately united because the problem raised by each of these conversions remains the same problem of evil and the solution for one is also the solution for the other. In the real order openness as gift brings with it the radical conversion which is at one and the same time moral, religious and Christian even if all these levels are not explicitated in the one reality of this conversion.

This joining together of the three conversions into the one conversion in the existential order does not seem to contra-

---

[34] *Collection*, pp. 198-201.

dict the different viewpoint of *Insight*. Even according to *Insight* these three conversions all occur on the same level of rational self-consciousness or existential consciousness. Here in the existential order these three conversions are better interpreted as three aspects of that profound (but not totally radical) transformation which the Scriptures refer to as the change of heart.

Obviously the question arises about the fidelity of the above explanation to Lonergan's own thought. At the same time such an understanding also raises further questions of its own. What are the exact relationships between and among these three aspects of conversion? Lonergan has been dealing lately, even if only in an indirect manner, with the relationship between the religious and the Christian aspects of conversion. On at least two different occasions Lonergan has cited the work of Friedrich Heiler who lists the characteristics common to all religious belief. These characteristics include some of the items which Lonergan incorporated in his study of Christian redemption and these abbreviated expositions include in an implicit way the factors underlying the law of the cross in the life of the Christian. Lonergan realized the problem and the need to show what is distinctive about Christianity, but he has not managed as yet to develop this aspect.[35]

What is the exact relationship between the moral aspect of conversion and the religious-Christian aspects? Here Lonergan has not given public attention to this relationship although in *Insight* he raises the problem of evil in connection with ethics and moral conversion. The moral impotence of man's effective freedom ultimately raises a problem that man himself cannot overcome. Lonergan in the chapter on ethics merely poses the problem and suggests that "the solution has to be a still higher integration of human living. For

_____

[35] "Future of Christianity," pp. 9-10.

the problem is radical and permanent; it is independent of the underlying physical, chemical, organic, and psychic manifolds; it is not met by revolutionary change, nor by human discovery, nor by the enforced implementation of discovery; it is as large as human living and human history."[36] The higher integration and solution to the problem of moral impotence can only be the conversion on the level of rational self-consciousness which results from the loving gift of God, openness as gift.

What then is the relationship between this moral-religious-Christian conversion and the intellectual conversion which is developed at great length in *Insight?* Intellectual conversion involves the self-structuring process of the human intellect, "the self appropriation of one's rational self-consciousness." Moral conversion in *Insight* involves the movement from the level of judgment to the level of decision. The rational self-consciousness which self-affirmation confirms must expand itself into the domain of doing, acting and making. For this reason there is a closer relationship of intellectual conversion to the moral aspect of existential conversion. Ultimately in the real order the problem of sin enters here, and the ultimate solution requires a solution to the problem of evil. The rationally conscious subject demands that his actions correspond to his knowledge. Decision seen as an individual act certainly follows judgment as a form of higher integration. However, one cannot merely view decision as an individual act, but rather one must consider the rationally self-conscious subject and his moral impotency with regard to effective freedom.

How is intellectual conversion related to the other existential conversion in human existence with its moral, religious and Christian aspects? All would have to agree with the fact that one of these conversions could exist without the other,

---

[36] *Insight*, p. 632.

so that there is no necessary link between them. One could ask Lonergan if his moving viewpoint of *Insight* does correspond with human experience and to what degree the intellectual conversion in the transcendent self does call for a more existential conversion? Lonergan's own willingness to grapple with the problem of evil and sin indicates that the relationship between the two conversions cannot be as continuous as Lonergan would maintain in *Insight*. Sin does bring in the character of discontinuity, although I would agree that this does not destroy all continuity in the development of self-transcendence. But sin and the real order do involve more discontinuity than Lonergan is willing to admit in *Insight*, and for that same reason the solution to the problem of evil in the real order cannot involve a harmonious and continual development from moral conversion to religious conversion to Christian conversion but rather the existing discontinuity does call for a more radical solution which embraces at one and the same time the three aspects of moral, religious and Christian conversion.

If Lonergan continues to emphasize the somewhat radical character of conversion and continues to bring religious and Christian conversion closer together, then it seems he must admit that in the real order there are only two conversions—the intellectual conversion and what we have called the existential conversion with its moral-religious-Christian aspects. Since *Insight* was written merely from the viewpoint of self-transcendence as capacity, the fact there are only these two conversions would not necessarily be contradictory to the development in *Insight*. Perhaps Lonergan can even use *Insight's* development to explain the difference between the moral, religious and Christian aspects of the one reality of existential conversion; but this difference cannot be in terms of the problem of evil, since this problem and its solution are intimately linked with all three aspects of existential conversion.

# 8

# Dialogue with the Future:
# Roman Catholic Theology
# in the United States
# Faces the Seventies

At the beginning of a new decade, it is customary to discuss what the future decade will bring. Anyone familiar with the crystal ball gazing that went on as the 60's came into existence would be greatly chastened in any attempt to prognosticate for the 70's. However, one can try to read the present situation in as accurate a manner as possible so as to look forward to the future.

In general, the American contribution to Roman Catholic theology in the past has been far from outstanding. There have been a few glorious exceptions in the past and in the present; but on the whole, Roman Catholic theology in the United States has lagged behind its development in many European countries. North American scholars have recently made some substantial contributions in the area of biblical studies, although American biblical scholars, in contrast with Protestant scholars in general and European Catholic scholars, tend to be strictly exegetical and lack a certain theological depth and perspective in their work.

There are factors emerging today that will become more prominent in the 70's and should improve the theological tradition in this country. Two specific factors that could have a great bearing on this future development are: (1) the fact that theology will leave the confines of the seminary and be more frequently located on university campuses or in ecumenical clusters with other theological institutions; (2) the fact that until the present theology has generally been the preserve of the cleric and the religious, but in the future there will be an increasingly greater number of non-clerics and religious who will be involved in the theological enterprise and teaching not only in Catholic colleges and universities but also in non-Catholic institutions of higher learning.

The university setting or the ecumenical theological cluster should help overcome the isolation of the Roman Catholic seminary and of its theological curriculum. In such a university set-up the research into theology should be stimulated by the research carried on in university centers in other disciplines, so that theology can rightly take its place along side the other academic disciplines in the university. Likewise, the fact that Roman Catholic theology will be in constant dialogue with Protestant theology will also be a stimulating factor for the growth of the discipline. It is becoming increasingly evident that one cannot do theology today except in an ecumenical perspective. This perspective not only involves the Christian faith commitment, but also a wider ecumenism embracing all mankind.

A number of problems have arisen in the past for Roman Catholic theology precisely because of the seminary confines and clerical domination of the discipline. There has been little or no academic tradition in this country for theological research, precisely because the seminary was not viewed primarily as an academic institution, but rather as a house of formation. Theology tended to be taught more as a task oriented preparation for ministry, rather than as an academic discipline in its own right. For this reason, many aspects of the theological tradition such as patristic and historical theology tended to be touched only superficially.

The history of the Church reminds us that theology as a matter of fact has not flourished in the isolation of the seminary. From the period of Trent onward, Roman Catholic theology has not been in contact and in dialogue with the contemporary sciences of man and society. A cursory reading of the manuals of Roman Catholic theology in use until the last decade reveals these textbooks were not in dialogue with the contemporary thinking of the day. Vital contact with university life helped the German tradition to be more in touch with the academic thought of the day, although the negative Roman reaction in the 19th century merely caused the seminary walls in most countries to rise higher and higher until the time of Vatican II. However, I am not proposing the German model as totally acceptable, because even in that situation, academic traditions still separate Roman Catholic theology from Protestant theology.

The lack of a clerical monopoly in the field of theology and theology's increasing participation in the college and university will force the theologian to be primarily an academic person. Too often the theologian teaching in the seminary is saddled with other functions and responsibilities that take up a great quantity of his time, perhaps even the majority of his time. A perennial problem for the seminary professor will always remain the dual role of his academic and pastoral responsibilities. These two roles are not incompatible, but the theological role was too often downplayed in the past. The non-clerical theology professor will tend to be primarily an academic person and thus should help to make all the members of the profession aware of their academic responsibilities.

The dual pastoral and theological role of the cleric or religious theologian also heightens another tension which can be viewed in terms of the difference between scientific theology and popularization. In general in the United States during the last decade the same people have very often fulfilled both the role of the professional theologian and the role of the popularizer. I am sure that many Roman Catholic theologians experience this tension—and not only the cleric with a pastoral function, for in a sense any Christian who is interested in the mission and function of the Church shares the desire to bring the theological renewal to more people in the Church and especially to priests working in the pastoral ministry in daily contact with the people of God. The professional theologian cannot devote the majority of his time to this important mission without allowing his theological expertise to suffer.

Another related factor has also contributed to developing the dispersion of activities and energies on the part of the few people on the American scene who have shown any kind of theologial expertise. The needs of religious education and theology have been so intertwined that the same people have been involved in both enterprises—a fact that again brings about a weakening of concentration in the theological endeavor as such. Again this phenomenon is explicable in terms of the few theologians doing research and publication in this country and the great potential and need for bringing the understanding of theology today to the vast numbers of the Christian people. American religious education and catechetics, like theology itself, have really not been able to develop a strong body of experts in the field. As a result, the people who are involved in the theological renewal are also very frequently involved in the renewal on the level of religious education.

The theological enterprise in the Roman Catholic Church in this country has also been hampered by the fact that Vatican II has brought with it an entirely new understanding of

Dialogue with the Future 249

the science of theology and its methods. It is an unfortunate fact that in the Roman Catholic Church in the United States, there are very few contributing theologians who have been teaching theology for more than ten or fifteen years. As a result, it has been necessary for many younger people in the field to assume leadership positions and deprive themselves of the time and conditions necessary to pursue their theological development at this important stage.

Another related factor that has affected the situation has been the cult of the theologian in this country. The theologian has been esteemed as a hero by many segments of the Catholic community precisely because of different stands that he may have taken in the last few years. The "jet setting celebrity role" does not augur well for the sustained development of the theological enterprise, but there are signs that the theologian in the next decade will be able to eschew such a role so that he can concentrate more on his own theological endeavors.

The fact that Roman Catholic theology will be less seminary-centered and less clerically-dominated in the future should also free Roman Catholic theology from an undue hierarchical interference and control. There can be no doubt about the fact that such control has added to the plight of Roman Catholic theology in our country at the present time. Again it is necessary to emphasize that this does not deny the office and function of the hierarchy in the Church, but rather underscores the integrity of the theological discipline. Theology thus best serves the Church when it is allowed to develop as an academic discipline with its own academic integrity and freedom.[1] Although hierarchical interference has stifled the theological enterprise in this country, theologians

---

[1] For a development of this particular understanding of the academic freedom of Roman Catholic theology and for a review of recent literature on the subject, see John F. Hunt, Terrence R. Connelly, *et al., The Responsibility of Dissent: The Church and Academic Freedom* (New York: Sheed and Ward, 1969), pp. 113-128.

also share some blame. Unfortunately, in the past, theologians of a particular outlook—be they of a more liberal or of a more conservative variety—have been unwilling to disagree with those among whom they find a generally likeminded approach. There will be a much greater need for theologians in the future to criticize one another's work with the realization that in this way the discipline of theology will grow and develop.

Circumstances surrounding the way in which theology is done and will be done in this country also dovetail with methodological approaches in theology itself. The shift in recent years has been to a more historically minded and consequently inductive methodology.[2] Theology as a more inductive discipline must always be in contact with all the other disciplines studying man and society. Obviously, such contact and dialogue is essential for moral theology or Christian ethics which deals both with methodological and substantive questions about the living of the Christian life, but even the more theoretical questions of systematic theology require a constant dialogue with contemporary philosophy as well as with the other contemporary sciences that treat of man and society. For example, ecclesiology especially as applied to questions of church structure must consider not only the biblical models and images of the Church but also contemporary sociological models of community and worship which may develop in the experience of groups in our contemporary society. The very fact that Roman Catholic theology in this country is heavily dependent on European theology shows that our own theology has not been in contact with the best of American thought. In a true sense, we have the challenge to develop an American theology which

---

[2] There exists a growing body of literature on this subject. For an explanation of historical consciousness in general and in the thought of Bernard Lonergan, see David Tracy, *The Achievement of Bernard Lonergan* (New York: Herder & Herder, 1970), pp. 193 ff.

must, therefore, be in closer dialogue with the contemporary American academic scene.

However, one should not conclude that the new environment, in which Roman Catholic theology will exist, will of necessity bring with it only unmixed blessings. As is true in all human situations this side of the eschaton, the potential for growth and development also harbors some negative aspects which could definitely impede theological growth. A sober reflection on the theological scene in contemporary Protestantism in the United States does not augur for any utopia on the way.

There are a number of possible pitfalls for Roman Catholic theology in the '70's. The danger of activism on the part of students studying theology, especially as a preparation for ministry, will continue to threaten the theological enterprise. I do not intend to criticize active involvement in the needs of the contemporary world on the part of the Church or the theologian or candidates for ministry in the Church. Likewise, as pointed out above, a more inductive theology can not merely exist in the context of the library and the research tools of the Wissenschaft school, but an unreflective trend to activism coupled with the lack of academic tradition in theology in our own country remains a genuine threat to the development of the discipline.

Theology students, especially those preparing for a pastoral ministry, seek a relevant theology which is in dialogue with modern man and modern science; but such students easily forget the long and difficult process of understanding the science of theology itself and its relationship to other disciplines. The danger of those who want immediate results from their study lies in the fact that these students will often gain a superficial knowledge or smattering of many things but will never really have an adequate theological understanding.

Undoubtedly, a poor understanding of the discipline of

theology has contributed to a sterile intellectualism which in turn creates an atmosphere conducive to the reaction of anti-intellectualism. Speculative or scientific theology cannot be divorced from practice. Theological speculation which does not come to grips with the practical reality of man's historical self-understanding cannot be good speculation. "Theory and practice cannot really be separated from each other. The practical application is a structuring element of truth itself (H. G. Gadamer); truth is meant not only to interpret the world but also to change it (K. Marx). Theology does not become more scientific by haughtily avoiding all concrete, practical questions."[3]

Ideally, the shift to a university setting or to a setting in a theologically ecumenical enterprise should provide Roman Catholic theology with a locus in which it can be in dialogue on a scholarly level with other academic disciplines, but reality does not always live up to expectation in this regard. In all disciplines today the research explosion and the extensive publication of articles and books makes it almost impossible for any individual to keep up in his own chosen field of research and to continue his teaching in his particular field.[4] The necessary and seemingly interminable meetings and committees which are so absolutely necessary for the restructuring of the contemporary college and university merely heighten the problem of finding the opportunity for dialogue between theology and the other disciplines represented in the university or college. Perhaps a first step can be made in terms of curriculum reform which would bring various disciplines together to study a particular problem

---

[3] Walter Kasper, *The Methods of Dogmatic Theology* (Glen Rock, New Jersey: Paulist Press, 1969), p. 51.

[4] This assertion applies to other academic disciplines the crisis of culture which Bernard Lonergan has described as affecting Catholic philosophy and theology. See *Collection: Papers by Bernard Lonergan,* ed. F. E. Crowe, S.J. (New York: Herder & Herder, 1967), pp. 252-267.

from their respective viewpoints. In this way both students and faculty could participate in an interdisciplinary dialogue that would bring together the different disciplines as they react to specific problems. "Think tanks" or dialogue groups among faculty members with different academic specialities would also greatly contribute to the dialogue that theology needs.

Another factor that will complicate the life of Roman Catholic theology in the future comes from the threat of theological fads. Protestant theology has known a number of theological fads in the past decade. The very fact that there was a somewhat tight hierarchical control and surveillance obviously helped Roman Catholic theology from developing similar fads, but the possibility of such fads will be one of the dangers arising from a greater theological freedom in the future. Such freedom will call upon the theologian to respond in a responsible manner and to object to whatever fads might appear on the theological scene. It will be impossible in the future to avoid all such fads, but this does not call for stricter hierarchical control which would stifle theological investigation and which would no longer be even possible in the contemporary and future settings of Roman Catholic theology.

An understanding of the different setting in which Roman Catholic theology will find itself in the future thus indicates some of the perspectives, prospects and possible pitfalls for the discipline in the coming decade and the future.

# 9

## Epilogue:
## The Present State
## of Catholic Moral Theology

The essays in this book have shown some of the interests, approaches and concerns of moral theology. Reflecting on these essays in particular and also on the general developments in the area of Catholic moral theology in the last few years, this concluding chapter will try to sketch and assess the present state of Catholic moral theology.

First, it is no longer possible to speak of Catholic moral theology as if it were a monolithic theology. In the past Catholic moral theology with its general acceptance of the same type of natural law methodology and its role as an interpreter of the teachings of the hierarchical magisterium tended to give the impression of being one theology in methodology and content. Today there exists a plurality of methodologies which are employed by Catholic moral theologians, so that it is much more accurate to admit the existence of Catholic moral theologies when speaking in a strict sense about the methodological approaches to questions of moral theology or Christian ethics. The generic term moral theology refers more to the area of concerns of the discipline rather than to the specific description of the methodology employed.

In the midst of this plurality of approaches within the pale of moral theology, it is important to note that the question should no longer be seen primarily as a difference between the old and the new moral theology or the conservative and the liberal moral theology. Obviously these classifications do have some generic meaning, but they do not adequately describe the present state of affairs. A more penetrating analysis reveals that within the new approaches to moral theology there are actually many differences of opinion concerning both methodological and substantive questions. Dialogue, discussion and differences among the proponents of newer approaches in moral theology are healthy and indicate that moral theology has significantly advanced beyond the stage where a group of newer theologians called into question the older methodology and teachings. Obviously the struggle between the older approach and newer approaches is continuing and in the popular mind still probably represents the state of moral theology today. In the future the plurality of methodological approaches and moral theologies within the Roman Catholic Church will continue to grow. Some of the preceding discussions indicate that such a development is already on its way.

Pluralism and diversity do not exist only on the level of methodology. There is also pluralism and diversity with regard to particular moral questions. In the future it will become increasingly difficult to speak about *the* Roman Catholic solution to a specific, complex moral question. The reaction of the Roman Catholic theological community to Pope Paul's encyclical condemning artificial contraception, which was issued in July 1968, has brought to the fore the possibility of dissent from such authoritative papal teaching.

The fact that there has never been an infallible teaching on a specific moral issue, together with the now recognized right to dissent from authoritative, non-infallible teaching, argues for the realization that there will be in the future even greater diversity within Roman Catholic theology on specific, complex moral questions. Thus it will be increasingly difficult in the future to speak. of *the* Roman Catholic teaching on such a specific point. Obviously in more general matters there can and should be a great amount of agreement and certitude, but on specific questions the complexity of the question itself calls for diversity and a possible pluralism of answers. The essay on homosexuality in this volume introduces and explains a newer methodology which comes to a different conclusion on the morality of homosexuality for a particular person because of the theological recognition of the presence of sin. Among Catholics there has even been some questioning of the traditional teaching on premarital sexuality.[1]

The question of abortion serves as a good illustration. Catholic moral theology like all Christian and truly human ethics must have a great respect for the value of life. The ultimate reason for the reverence for life resides in the fact that the Christian sees life as God's gift to man. Life is valued not primarily because of what it makes or accomplishes or contributes to society, but rather life has value because of the gift of God. Christians thus are called upon to promote human life precisely because life is the gift of God. There is agreement on the need for respect for life; there may be

---

[1] David Darst and Joseph Forgue, "Sexuality on the Island Earth," *The Ecumenist*, VII (1969), 81-87; Gregory Baum, "A Catholic Response," *The Ecumenist*, VII (1969), 90-92. For a recent ecumenical symposium discussing sexuality from various perspectives, see *Sexual Ethics and Christian Responsibility: Some Divergent Views*, ed. John Charles Wynn (New York: Association Press, 1971).

different reasons proposed for this respect so that a diversity can even enter in at this level.[2]

On the particular moral question of abortion there is now and will be increasingly in the future a diversity of opinion even within Roman Catholicism precisely because the abortion issue involves two very important questions on which there is even now disagreement and diversity. The first question concerns the time when life begins, while the second question considers the way in which conflict situations are solved in those cases where there is a conflict between the fetus and other values or persons.

There is diversity among Roman Catholics today on the question of when human life begins. Joseph Mangan, for example, argues that it is "at least solidly probably true" there is a human person from the moment of conception, and no one can directly attack this fetus.[3] Dr. Denis Cavanagh, a gynecologist, doubts that there is a separate human being from the first moment of fertilization; but certainly from the time of implantation after which twining or recombination is impossible, the fetus imbedded in the uterine wall deserves respect as a human life.[4] A. Plé, arguing from the limited theological perspective of avoiding the dangers of traducianism, believes in a delayed animation theory, but he recognizes that such a theory is only probable. Plé still maintains that every abortion, even if the fetus has not yet received

---

[2] Daniel Callahan, "The Sanctity of Life," in *Updating Life and Death,* ed. Donald R. Cutler (Boston: Beacon Press, 1969), pp. 181-222.

[3] Joseph T. Mangan, S.J., "The Wonder of Myself: Ethical-Theological Aspects of Direct Abortion," *Theological Studies,* XXXI (1970), 133. This entire issue of *Theological Studies* is devoted to abortion and well illustrates the diversity existing among Catholics on this subject.

[4] Denis Cavanaugh, M.D., "Reforming the Abortion Laws: A Doctor Looks at the Case," *America,* CXXII (1970), 406-411. Such an opinion could have interesting practical consequences in such areas as the use of the I.U.D. or the prevention of conception after rape.

from God a human soul, is a grave crime against human life.[5] Joseph Donceel also accepts the developmental theory for the beginning of human life in the fetus.[6] John Giles Milhaven apparently favors such an understanding and likewise accepts the morality of abortion for certain reasons.[7]

It is not exact to say that in the past Catholic theology condemned all abortion. Catholic theology realized the possibility of some conflict situations and tried to solve these conflict situations by the application of the principle of the direct and indirect effects. Catholic theology traditionally condemned direct abortion, but permitted indirect abortion when there was a sufficient reason. Abortion in the case of a cancerous uterus serves as the primary example.[8] Several Catholic theologians today are questioning and denying the validity of such an approach to conflict situations because too often the direct effect is determined solely by the physical structure of the act itself. With different theoretical approaches these theologians would see the possibility of more conflict situations in which the life of the fetus could be taken.[9] This differs from the narrower conclusions based on

---

[5] A. Plé, O.P., "Alerte au traducianisme. A propos de l'avortement," *Le Supplément*, XXIV (1971), 70.

[6] Joseph F. Donceel, S.J., "Abortion: Mediate or Immediate Animation," *Continuum*, V (1967), 167-171; Donceel, "A Liberal Catholic View," in *Abortion in a Changing World*, ed. Robert E. Hall, M.D. (New York: Columbia University Press, 1970), I, 39-45; Donceel, "Immediate Animation and Delayed Hominization," *Theological Studies*, XXXI (1970), 76-105.

[7] John G. Milhaven, "The Abortion Debate: An Epistemological Interpretation," *Theological Studies*, XXXI (1970), 106-124.

[8] Gerald Kelly, S.J., *Medico-Moral Problems* (St. Louis: Catholic Hospital Association, 1958), pp. 68-83.

[9] Cornelius J. van der Poel, "The Principle of Double Effect," in *Absolutes in Moral Theology?* ed. Charles E. Curran (Washington/Cleveland: Corpus Books, 1968), pp. 186-210; P. Knauer, S.J. "La détermination du bien et du mal moral par le principe du double effet," *Nouvelle Revue Théologique*, LXXXVII (1965), 356-376; P. Knauer, S.J., "The Hermeneutic Function of the Principle of Double Effect," *Natural Law Forum*, XII (1967), 132-162.

the difference between the direct and the indirect effect.

Interestingly, there appears to be on the level of social morality an almost contradictory thrust which insists on certain things as the only possible Catholic or Christian approach. I believe there are some theologians today who claim too much in speaking about *the* Christian position on complex social issues such as war, nuclear deterrence and selective conscientious objection. On all these questions there seems to be a legitimate room for differences within the Catholic community. Yet obviously there are other areas such as prejudice, suppression of basic human rights, cruel and unnecessary punishment in which one can more easily speak about the Catholic opinion or the Christian opinion.

To clarify the question as much as possible, I see a growing pluralism even within Roman Catholicism on specific, complex moral questions. This opinion with its obvious philosophical presuppositions maintains that agreement and certitude decrease the more complex and specific a question becomes.[10] The abortion question with its two basic but complex questions does admit of a number of different solutions. In less complex and specific issues, and especially on the more general level of principles, there can be such a thing as the Catholic or Christian teaching.

A very interesting characteristic of the essays in this book is the lack of any specific essay on "Dialogue with Protestant Ethics." At first the absence appears to be a serious lacuna, but in reality it indicates a great step forward in the whole field of Catholic moral theology. There is no specific essay dealing with Protestant ethics because no one can be a Catholic moral theologian today without reading and studying

---

[10] This approach seems to be in keeping with the theory proposed by Thomas Aquinas that as one descends to specifics and particulars there is some possibility of exceptions in general moral principles, *Ia, IIae,* q. 94, a. 4 and 5.

Protestant thought on every question. Notice how often Protestant authors are cited in this book. There is no doubt that there should be an ongoing dialogue of Protestant and Catholic theologians on ethical matters. These pages also show that occasionally there is as much or even more agreement between myself and some Protestants than there is between myself and some other Roman Catholics.

There are two important reasons for this increased practical cooperation and working together between Protestant and Catholic ethicists which stem from the ecumenical developments of the last few years. On the one hand Catholics and Protestants share the same Scriptural source of their theology and claim a somewhat common history. In addition both are addressing from similar perspectives the same problems that are facing our contemporary world. It is only natural that Protestant and Catholic ethicicans must be in contact with one another's work and research.

This closer relationship in practice brings up the more interesting theoretical question of the exact relationship between Protestant and Catholic ethics. Difficulties in making such a comparison arise from the fact that just as there is no one, Roman Catholic moral theology but rather a number of different theologies or methodologies within Catholic moral theology, so in Protestant ethics there has been an even greater diversity and pluralism. In the past the methodological differences loomed quite large. Within Protestantism there was the emphasis on faith rather than works, whereas Catholic theology emphasized works. Protestant theology emphasized Scripture and sometimes Scripture alone, whereas Catholic theology stressed Scripture and tradition or Scripture and reason. Protestant theology tended to stress freedom, whereas Catholic theology was based on order. Protestant theology generally paid much more attention to sin, whereas Catholic theology did not give enough importance to the reality of sin.

In the United States today as illustrated in the preceding pages there seems to be a growing convergence between Catholic and Protestant theological ethicists so that these differences no longer completely separate Protestant and Catholic ethics. In the process of dialogue and discussion many of these traditional points of differences are being superseded. It can truly be said that quite frequently there is methodological agreement between Catholics and Protestants. Even now and increasingly in the future the split will not always be between Catholics and Protestants, but some Catholics will find themselves in agreement with some Protestants and in disagreement with some Catholics. Contemporary issues such as war, nuclear deterrence and selective conscientious objection show this methodological and content agreement that already does exist across denominational lines. On these and many larger issues facing society in the future there will be an increasing tendency away from differences of opinion on denominational lines. Take for example the important questions concerning genetic and biological possibilities in the future. The differences in this area now are not based on something peculiarly Catholic or Protestant, but on one's assessment of the relationship between the possibilities of any one science and the human or the Christian perspective.

The growing lack of differences based on denominational lines seems even more prevalent and true in the moral theology being done in the United States. Again this does not mean that every Protestant doing ethics proposes things which are in keeping with the Catholic self-understanding at the present moment, but at times one cannot discern any real differences between one ethicist who is Protestant and another who is Catholic. Yet there often do remain characteristic difference based on different Protestant or Catholic presuppositions such as the role of reason in ethics or the relationship between the divine and the human. It seems

262 Catholic Moral Theology in Dialogue

that moral theology on the European continent has not developed as far along these lines as has Catholic moral theology in the United States. If Roger Mehl's recent work can
be taken as representative of European thought about the
differences between Catholic and Protestant ethics, the rigid
differences proposed by Mehl no longer seem so inflexible in
this country.[11] Perhaps the difference lies in the fact that
many European Protestant theologians are working out of
a more strict Lutheran or Neo-Orthodox background. In this
country there are fewer theologians working from such
bases, but it is precisely such backgrounds that would highlight differences with Catholic ethical methodology.

There are certainly different theological presuppositions
in the ethical approaches of Protestants and Catholics. One
obvious difference is the understanding of ecclesiology and
of teaching authority in the Church. There might also be
different understandings of the reality of justification, although here too there may be more room for agreement
than was realized in the past.[12] Catholic moral theology generally has worked out of a metaphysical and ontological
framework, but some contemporary Catholics seem to be
working out of more sociologically and psychologically
oriented frameworks. Catholic moral theology has insisted
on the fact that reason is a source of ethical wisdom for the
Christian, but many Protestants today also accept this.

---

[11] Roger Mehl, *Catholic Ethics and Protestant Ethics* (Philadelphia:
Westminster Press, 1971). For a somewhat older view of the differences
between Protestant and Catholic ethics from the Catholic viewpoint originally presented in 1963, see Franz Böckle, *Law and Conscience* (New York:
Sheed and Ward, 1966).

[12] For an attempt to show basic agreement between Catholic and Barthian
views on justification, see Hans Küng, *Justification: The Doctrine of Karl
Barth and a Catholic Reflection* (New York: Thomas Nelson & Sons, 1964).
For a very sympathetic critique of Küng's basic thesis, see Karl Rahner,
S.J., "Questions of Controversial Theology on Justification," *Theological
Investigations* (Baltimore: Helicon, 1966), IV, 189-218.

Recent Catholic endeavors have criticized the monolithic natural law approach of the past and proposed different alternatives which give a much greater flexibility to their ethics. The inflexibility of older Catholic teaching was a constant source of negative criticism among Protestantism. Likewise some aspects of Catholic theology seem to be more aware of the reality of sin and its effects. Both Protestants and Catholics can and do employ the Scriptures in a similar way in their theological ethics. Today there does seem to be a growing recognition of the fact that differences between Protestant and Catholic do not necessarily bring about different ethical methodologies or conclusions. In the future it seems it will be more obvious that Catholic and Protestant differences do not necessarily effect ethical methodology or conclusions.

Another characteristic of Catholic moral theology today is its interest in the wider problems facing man and society. In the 1960's it was only natural that the first areas of concern would be the renewal within moral theology itself. In general this consisted in a new spirit and emphasis on the fact that all Christians were called to perfection and to living out the gospel in their daily lives. A second emphasis was a calling into question of some of the accepted teachings of the Catholic Church. The birth control debate went on throughout the greater part of the 1960's.[13]

As renewal in the Catholic Church gave greater importance to man's life in the world it was only natural that greater attention should be given to the complicated problems facing modern man and his society. Questions of war, civil disobedience, poverty and the biological revolution have all come to the fore as important areas of concern for moral theology. The consideration of such topics requires a

---

[13] William H. Shannon, *The Lively Debate* (New York: Sheed and Ward, 1970).

competency and knowledge that most Catholic moralists have not possessed in the past. One way of coming to grips with these questions is through an interdisciplinary approach so that all the competencies can be brought to bear on the particular question under discussion. This type of dialogue is being facilitated today by independent institutes, colloquia and interdisciplinary seminars.

In a sense moral theology today is experiencing an identity crisis. Perhaps it is trite to speak of such a crisis, since so much in our society is undergoing the same type of crisis. However, there are phenomena both in our culture and in our contemporary understanding of the Christian faith which contribute to this crisis. In many ways the crisis of culture consists in the fact that contemporary man is overwhelmed with data and facts, but beset with the problem of meaning and intelligibility. The increase of data only complicates the basic problem of meaning. In the midst of such complexity the search for meaning is even more difficult.[14]

The renewal in Catholic life and theology occasioned by Vatican II is contributing in its own way to the identity crisis. An older Catholic approach emphasized the differences and the uniqueness of the Catholic faith. Now the emphasis is on the need for dialogue with other Christians, non-Christians and the world. Previously in moral theology there was a tight, somewhat authoritatively proposed methodology which obviously had its own distinctive characteristics. Today there is the realization that there can be many possible methodologies, and theologians are searching for more adequate ethical methodologies. But the very bewildering complexities of the times make the search all the more difficult.

---

[14] Bernard Lonergan, S.J., *Collection*, ed. F. E. Crowe, S.J. (New York: Herder and Herder, 1967), pp. 252-267.

These methodological questions involved in the search of moral theology for its own identity will continue to be of paramount importance in the immediate future. Moral theologians must reflect on the way in which they use the Scriptures and the sciences in arriving at their moral judgments, to mention two questions already considered in this book. In addition there will be attempts to develop methodologies in keeping with a variety of different philosophical approaches which are currently of great interest. People will also continue to push the question of the exact relationship between Christian ethics and human ethics. Since this is a most important contemporary concern and corresponds with the frequently asked question, "Why be a Christian?", this question will receive even more attention in the future. The first essay in this volume has attempted to give the outlines of a possible solution to the problem. Again it is interesting that the primary question is no longer the relationship between Protestant and Catholic ethics but the relationship between Christian and other religious and philosophical ethics.

This is a rather sketchy picture of the present state of moral theology. Looking back over the developments in moral theology in the 1960's one is astounded at the great changes which have occurred. One can only speculate on the developments that lie ahead in the 1970's.

# Index